Recreational

Leadership

Recreational
Leadership

Group Dynamics and Interpersonal Behavior

Jay S. Shivers
University of Connecticut

PRINCETON BOOK COMPANY, *Publishers*
PRINCETON NEW JERSEY

Library of Congress Catalog Card Number 79-92381
ISBN 0-916622-17-7
Printed in the United States of America

This book is dedicated to
JED MARK SHIVERS
with love and great respect
Sapere aude

Acknowledgments

It is with a sense of satisfaction and gratitude that I acknowledge the debt which I owe to those who have provided me with both material and moral assistance in the development and completion of this manuscript.

I am particularly pleased to recognize the efforts of Dean Emeritus Dr. Allen V. Sapora, an acknowledged leader in the field of recreational service education, for his well-thought-out and tempered statement which makes up the Foreword to this book.

I express my love and esteem to my wife Rhoda for her unflagging support and direct contribution to both my professional and personal growth and development. Finally, I thank my son Jed who has given me moral comfort and persistent affection, thereby helping me to complete this work — and to whom I dedicated this book. *Omnia Vincit Amore.*

J. S. S.

Foreword

L eadership is a complex phenomenon in every phase of modern society. In this book the author develops a comprehensive analysis of the scientific literature related to the field and delineates this information as a significant variable among individuals and groups. He accomplishes this by presenting leadership theory and explaining it as a process. Generalizations are minimized; specific factors about the subject are conceptualized and made clear to aspiring leaders.

To function effectively, those who assume responsibility as leaders must understand basic leadership principles. It is especially important that recreationists (leaders), who are in positions to influence people to express themselves through leisure pursuits, exercise these skills with care.

Recreational activities are tremendously important to the quality of life. This book examines human behavior dynamics at different age levels; it clearly points out the role of the recreationist as an innovator of positive behavior, an analyst of group needs, and a leader who acts rather than reacts.

The author deals with the functional aspects of leadership by providing numerous examples of how theory has been and should be applied in practical situations. The origin, misconception, risks, techniques, and other characteristics of recreational leadership are dealt with in a manner that will inspire both students and professionals in various disciplines.

Recreational Leadership: Group Dynamics and Interpersonal Behavior moves forward with new concepts, bringing together the most recent scientific research and relating to the dynamic changes taking place in the field of recreational services and leisure studies.

> *Allen V. Sapora*
> *Dean Emeritus*
> *University of Illinois, Urbana-Champaign*

Preface

This text began as a simple revision of the author's original work, *Leadership in Recreational Service,* published in 1963. It has emerged as a completely new statement. While the book is still organized into four basic parts, the contents are wholly new — recast in light of the latest scientific advances dealing with the phenomenon of leadership and the related subjects of group dynamics and interpersonal behavior. So many new studies have been developed and recorded that there is now more data and a greater base for inclusive perspectives.

What this book provides is a detailed explanation of the processes and techniques of leadership in relation to the field of recreational service. Although it is written fundamentally for students in colleges and universities who are preparing to enter that field, it also should be of considerable value to recreational practitioners, laymen who volunteer for community service with recreational agencies, educators and government officials who are concerned with the professional competencies demanded for employment in recreational service, and administrators in related fields (i.e., group work, social work, psychology, and counseling).

Three concepts motivated the writing of this book. First, very few of the thousands of articles, pamphlets, theses, and books that have been written about leaders and leadership have been oriented toward the field of recreational service and its personnel. There are, perhaps, only two or three books that cover the subject, but these have either dealt with personnel administration, program direction, and activity instruction, or offered only superficial observations. It still appeared that there was a definite need for an objective critical analysis of the entire phenomenon of leadership as it concerns the field of recreational service — what it is, what it does, its source or sources, and who is involved in its process. The discussion of leadership is not delimited to agency, time, or place, but includes many types of situations in whch the direction and development of individuals, groups, and their objectives are purposefully influenced and guided.

A considerable body of information is now available on outcomes of leadership in group situations, motivational aspects of human behavior, and interpersonal relationships, much of which has been condensed and simplified in this volume for better understanding by students and practitioners. Because of the vast repertoire of literature, it has been necessary to be selective: to group similar writings, and to choose from several excellent presentations the one which best summarizes them and provides additional data.

Some of the basic questions which this book attempts to answer are whether or not the recreationist is to lead or merely mirror the wishes of most of his constituents. Is he to develop each of his followers' talents or is he merely to organize the prevailing current opinion? Is he to be an independent thinker or is he to conform? Indeed, who is a leader? What does the leader do? Does leadership rely on personality only? Many of the answers to these questions may be found in this text. Additionally, the book indicates how one may become a leader and what methods certain individuals have used to reach leadership status. There are no facile rules or principles that gain a leader's place, but rather a fortuitous set of circumstances coupled with an individual's personality that answers a particular need of a group of people at a particular time or place.

Finally, it is the author's intent to explain the characteristics of the leader and describe the situations which call him into being, and to define leadership and its essential components for practical use and study. The translation of theory, as recorded by researchers, into correct practice by those who have a need to know such information, is the most important contribution which this work can make to the field of recreational service.

Jay S. Shivers
Storrs, Connecticut
February, 1980

Table of Contents

PART I

Leadership and Interpersonal Behavior

CHAPTER ONE

Leadership Concepts and Contemporary Research

Leadership is a well-known and universal phenomenon. Wherever a human social order exists, the basis for leadership also exists. But who is selected and by what procedures is still not entirely understood.

LEADERSHIP THEORIES

Theories about leadership abound, and some realistic models have been formulated to assist in the study of this significant aspect of social interaction. Nevertheless, a precise understanding of the intricacies and variables that promote or deny leadership to a particular person continues to elude behavioral scientists investigating this phenomenon. Situations that arise as a result of social change, interpersonal conflict, and dynamic social interaction all produce manifestations which may evoke leadership. Why certain conditions foster the emergence of leadership and why an individual strives for, or is propelled to, a position of leadership have become the essence of experimental studies conducted by social psychologists and other professionals interested in interpersonal behavior within groups. In this chapter we will attempt to epitomize what is already known about leadership so that students can appreciate the problems involved in arriving at a working definition of the concept.

The Theory of Group Function

Because it is impossible to classify leaders according to universal personality characteristics, a new approach to studying leadership evolved. According to this theory, leadership is not a property of persons but of groups; it is viewed as a series of acts directly constrained by group structure. Although group theorists vary somewhat in outlook, their general idea is the same: leadership is understood as a collection of functions concerned with goal achievement and group maintenance, the particular functions defined by the internal and external properties of the group. Leadership is seen as actions undertaken by various members of a group to achieve goals or objectives for which they have joined the group.[1]

---

1. D. Cartwright and A. Zander, eds., *Group Dynamics, Research and Theory* (Evanston, Ill.: Row, Peterson & Company, 1953), p. 538.

Thus group maintenance, goal identification, goal achievement, and membership satisfaction are aspects of leadership. A person is permitted by the group to wield influence and does so only so long as the leadership task he is engaged in meets the needs of the group. Leadership is passed from one member to another as the variables confronting the group change and as capable potential leaders are made manifest to group perception.

In addition to these fundamental premises, the group theory of leadership asserts that the traits of a leader necessary for the successful functioning of a group will vary, determined by external and internal group influences. Different groups, or even the same group, under different kinds of conditions will probably need different kinds of leaders and leadership activity. Further, to the extent that any individual within the group contributes to the satisfaction of goal achievement or group maintenance, he will be performing a leadership role. Finally, the group approach suggests the separation of formal from informal leadership. When leadership is seen as a set of functions, the personal characteristics of a particular leader are not emphasized.

Although the functional approach to leadership marks the thinking of many involved in research, they plainly diverge in what they stress as singular leadership functions. Perhaps R. B. Cattell takes the broadest approach, stating that any behavior which moves a group closer to its goals can be termed a leadership function.[2] Thus, all members of the group are potential leaders. D. Kretch, R. S. Crutchfield, and E. L. Ballachey however, specify fourteen functions that, depending upon the nature of the group and its situation, may delineate the leader's role. Which functions will be emphasized, as well as the manner in which they will be performed, depend upon the internal and external qualities of the group.[3] F. Redl, using a psychoanalytic approach, introduces a central figure (the leader) and differentiates ten kinds of emotional relationships, perceived to be leadership functions, between the central figure and other group members.[4]

Theoretical as well as empirical studies emphasize the significance of two fundamental types of leadership: goal achievement and group maintenance. It is apparent that any number of different behaviors can serve both these paramount functions. Moreover, any member of the group can behave in ways that will assist the group in accomplishing its goals and/or sustaining itself. It should be recognized, however, that these leadership functions tend to be centralized in the hands of a few people, especially in groups that exist for a length of time.

---

2. R.B. Cattell, "New Concepts for Measuring Leadership in Terms of Group Syntality," *Human Relations,* Vol. 7 (1951), pp. 167-184.

3. D. Kretch, R. S. Crutchfield, and E. L. Ballachey, *Individual in Society* (New York: McGraw-Hill Book Company, 1962).

4. F. Redl, "Group Emotion and Leadership," *Psychiatrist,* Vol. 5 (1942), pp. 573-596.

Studies of formal groups have revealed these functions in the behavior of leaders. A. W. Halpin and B. J. Winer concluded that consideration of others and initiating and directing behaviors were of considerable importance in establishing leadership.[5] It is necessary to remember, however, that the nature of the group, its maturity, and its immediate situation will determine the transcendent functions, its articulation, and its implementor. Under circumstances in which divisiveness within a group threatens the group with imminent dissolution, there is every reason to expect that group maintenance will characterize the behavior of its leaders as well as its members. It is possible, too, that such stressful conditions will cause new leaders to emerge to handle the crisis.

In his investigation of small informal discussion groups, R. F. Bales learned that eventually the members raise to a position of leadership either a task specialist or a socio-emotional specialist.[6] The former moves the group toward its objective in an authoritative manner and is typically disliked; the latter is concerned with the harmony of the group, reduces member conflict, and is usually well liked.

The development of leadership in informal groups was also investigated by H. H. Jennings, who employed a sociometric technique.[7] She made two important discoveries: (1) sociometric choices indicate varied styles of leadership, which suggests that leaders modify their behavior according to the needs and interests of those who are their potential followers; (2) in the personality descriptions of the chosen leaders, behaviors or skills were listed that represent goal achievement and group maintenance functions. Group leaders influence the behavior of group members, but are, in turn, expected to fulfill the demands of the leadership role as it is perceived by the members.

It is worthy of notice that in informal groups there are many other factors that decide whether an individual will or will not engage in leadership behavior or become a leader. Even if the person is suited to lead the group, he may have no desire to do so.[8] It has also been shown that individuals are more likely to assume leadership roles when designated

---

5. A. W. Halpin and B. J. Winer, "A Factorial Study of the Leader Behavior Descriptions," in R. M. Stogdill and A. E. Coons, eds., *Leader Behavior: Its Description and Measurement* (Columbus, Ohio: Bureau of Business Research, Ohio State University, 1957), monograph 88.
6. R. F. Bales, "The Equilibrium Problem in Small Groups," in T. Parsons, R. F. Bales, and E. A. Shils, *Working Papers in the Theory of Action* (New York: The Free Press of Glencoe, 1953).
7. H. H. Jennings, *Leadership and Isolation,* 2d ed. (New York: David McKay and Company, 1950).
8. J. Weroff, "Development and Validation of a Projective Measure of Power Motivation," *Journal of Abnormal and Social Psychology,* Vol. 54 (1957), pp. 1-8.

leaders prove inadequate.[9] Another factor might be a person's status within the group. Those who are relatively well placed in the group hierarchy may decide to engage in leaderlike behavior, whereas those who are less well placed may feel slighted and refuse to become involved.

There has been serious debate over having leadership responsibility concentrated in the hands of one or a few persons or widely distributed throughout the group. Some have stated that centralized leadership is required in order to carry out objectives and prevent disruption. Others take the stand that authoritarian behavior lowers group morale and promotes conflict. Studies by Leavitt, Bavelas, and others indicate that both points are valid: the centralization of leadership results in better group performance on tasks but lowers group morale.[10] White and Lippitt suggest that had such groups been established for a longer time period, there would have been a consequent deterioration of group effectiveness due to lowered group morale.[11]

The question, should leadership be democratic or autocratic, has also been raised. In the case of an authoritarian leader, all significant group functions which affect group behavior are in the leader's hands, and he alone dominates the group. The democratic leader exercises his influence by sharing responsibility and decision-making with other members. There is evidence to show that both kinds of leadership may draw favorable response. Some followers can respond only to authority because of previous conditioning experiences or their own need to be controlled. Moreover, under highly stressful conditions of personal danger or fear, individuals may be strongly attracted to authoritarian leadership.[12] Others, having been nurtured within a democratic structure, react favorably to democratic leadership.

In either case, the fundamental belief of the functional approach to leadership holds — the relative effectiveness of authoritarian and democratic styles will rely upon the internal and external properties of the group. Research by F.E. Fiedler offers extensive support for this conviction.[13] Using selected measures, Fiedler identified leaders on a

---

9. R. L. Kahn and D. Katz, "Leadership Practices in Relation to Productivity and Morale," in D. Cartwright and A. Zander, eds., *Group Dynamics,* 2d ed. (New York: Harper and Row, 1960), pp. 554-570.

10. H. J. Leavitt, "Some Effects of Certain Communication Patterns on Group Performance," *Journal of Abnormal and Social Psychology,* Vol. 46 (1951), pp. 38-50.

11. R. White and R. Lippitt, "Leader Behavior and Member Reaction in the Social Climate," in D. Cartwright and A. Zander, eds., *Group Dynamics,* 3d ed. (New York: Harper & Row, 1968), pp. 327-330.

12. J. T. Lanzetta, "Group Behavior Under Stress," *Human Relations,* Vol. 8 (1955), pp. 29-52.

13. F. E. Fiedler, "The Contingency Model: A Theory of Leadership Effectiveness," in H. Proshansky and B. Seidenberg, eds., *Basic Studies in Social Psychology* (New York: Holt, Rinehart and Winston, 1965), pp. 538-550.

continuum ranging from high socio-emotional involvement to high task involvement. In correlating these sources with group success in many different groups, Fiedler found no agreement in the obtained relationships. Under some group circumstances, the socio-emotional leader was effective; in others, a task leader produced more effective group action.

To accommodate these findings, Fiedler provided a theoretical analysis of variance concerning group exigencies in terms of their "task-structure," "leader-member relations," and "position power" properties. Applying these factors, he characterized some groups by a structured task, favorable leader-member relations, and a leadership position that carried authority; others lacked in all of these aspects; and others fell between these two poles. By recasting his previous findings and by using new research, Fiedler was able to demonstrate that groups which are either very high or very low in all three dimensions produce more effectively with a task-oriented leader than with a supportive socio-emotionally-oriented leader. The latter has greater success with groups which contain moderate attributable forms.

It is apparent that in spite of the leadership function's dependence upon the group, the latter must still rely upon some worthy individual. The group theory of leadership does not discard the individual in favor of "a group mind." It recognizes that there is a distinct need for individual performance and even for individual willingness to perform. The theory stresses the concept that individuals are the foundational elements of any group and become the limiting factors on any leadership structure.

If leadership were interpreted only as a function of the group, there could be no question of individual qualities that emerge as a result of group need. Everything would be done by group consensus. This is patently not true, because group structure also works within constraints, the more so as unabated internal and external pressures force the group to change. As the group confronts conditions that may require the technical expertise and intelligence of now this one and now that one, individual personality patterns are injected into the process. What the individual is, what he brings to the group in a particular situation, how membership perception permits him to gain influence, these suggest that leadership as a function of the group does not exclude the idea of individual leadership. Regardless of where leadership resides, within an individual or within a group structure, the element of situation or problem still remains to be explained. Changing situations may force a change in leadership. It is this line of reasoning which led directly to the situational approach to leadership study.

The Situational Theory of Leadership

Leadership as a function of situation arises from the need of a group to perpetuate its members' initial satisfaction. Whenever the group faces a problematical situation, either internal or external, it must rely for leadership upon an individual who has demonstrated capacities for solving the problem. As the situation changes, a new leader may take over. As Gibb indicates:

> Since individual personality characteristics are, by contrast, very stable, it is to be expected that group leadership, if unrestricted by the conscious hierarchical structuration of the group, will be fluid and will pass from one member to another along the line of those particular personality traits which, by virture of the situation and its demands, become, for the time being, traits of leadership. This is why the leader in one situation is not necessarily the leader, even of the same group, in another different situation.[14]

Among the scholars who have aided in unraveling the complexities of leader-member relationships and demonstrated the vital role of motivation in determining the behavior of leaders is Fred Fiedler. Fiedler and his colleagues developed the LPC (least preferred co-worker) scale to measure leadership styles and movement toward the satisfaction of group goals.[15] The scale presents a series of adjectives for personality traits to a respondent who is asked to choose the adjectives that best describe the person with whom he worked the least well, i.e., the least preferred co-worker.[16] The least preferred co-worker is rated on such personality traits as pleasantness, efficiency, and cooperativeness.

The scale measures how positively or how negatively a person feels toward his least preferred co-worker. The person who manifests negative feelings says, in effect, that an individual's poor work performance is clearly associated with undesirable personality characteristics. Such a rater is highly task-oriented. The person who gives a positive rating is stating that he can distinguish between personality and work performance; he is concerned with establishing good interpersonal relations. Furthermore, Fiedler states that low LPC people in leadership positions feel much more positively about a group and about themselves when the group has achieved its goal. High LPC people in analogous positions do not show this difference. Fiedler also reports that when a group is confronted with a stressful situation that threatens goal achievement, leaders are likely to react in accordance with their LPC ratings. Thus, Fiedler interprets LPC ratings in this manner:"We visualize the high-LPC individual as a person who derives his major satisfaction from successful interpersonal relationships, while the low-LPC person derives his major satisfactions from task

14. C. Gibb,"Leadership," in G. Lindzey and E. Aronson, eds., *Handbook of Social Psychology,* 2d ed., Vol. 4 (New York: Addison-Wesley, 1969), p. 248.
15. F. E. Fiedler, *A Theory of Leadership Effectiveness* (New York: McGraw-Hill Book Company, 1967).
16. *Ibid.,* pp. 40-41.

performance."[17]

Fiedler cites other data which suggest that groups confronted by stressful situations are more likely to achieve their objectives when the leader is a low LPC type. If Fiedler's findings are confirmed by further study, leaders in groups that are deteriorating will tend to be LPC negative, the high LPC leaders having been rejected as ineffective. The success of low LPC leaders would tend to maintain group membership, and as a result the group might become more efficient in achieving its goals, without any referral to the leader's LPC score. Whether the task-centered leader is more effective than the person-centered leader is thought by Fiedler to be dependent upon the situation. The LPC test was created to determine leadership effectiveness by evaluating the leader's style. Test results did not show that either style was superior in every leadership situation. Hence, Fiedler hypothesized that only differences in situation could determine the relative effectiveness of the two leadership orientations.

The most apparent difference among situations is the degree to which conditions are favorable to the leader. Fiedler stated three factors in a group situation that indicate the degree of favorableness to the leader: 1) the leader's personal relationships with group members — how much the leader is liked and admired; 2) the organizational structure of the group — the specific way duties and responsibilities for each member of the group are assigned; and 3) the leader's actual power or authority — his actual control over rewards and punishments that can be meted out to the group membership.

Fiedler theorized that under highly favorable conditions (the leader has the support of the group, the goal is clearly identified, and the leader's power is real) the task-centered leader would be more effective than the person-centered leader. Similarly, in situations which are very unfavorable for leadership (the leader has poor relations with group members, the task is dimly perceived, and the leader has little actual power) the task-centered leader would again be more effective. Under adverse conditions the leader would be expected to focus on the task to be accomplished in order to achieve group goals.

Whenever the situation is moderately favorable, however, the person-centered leader appears to be more effective than the task-centered leader, because group members require support of a personal nature to assist them in carrying out their assignments in order to accomplish their goals. The person-centered leader ordinarily focuses his attention on building individual morale and maintaining good personal relations as a motivation and instigation for group members to complete their tasks successfully.

Both kinds of leaders can be effective under the right conditions.

---

17. *Ibid.,* p. 45.

Nevertheless, there are some important questions that can be raised about Fiedler's assumptions and model. Does the leader have to function primarily as a task-oriented or person-oriented individual? Fiedler has very carefully stated that the LPC score indicates which orientation is more significant to the leader. It is possible that concentration on both people and tasks is the most highly productive leadership style.

Much can be said for a situational approach to leadership theory, but there is too little information currently available to allow a pronouncement that the leadership function depends exclusively on conditions which the group encounters.

The Necessity for Leadership

Leadership is not something that can be forcibly imposed upon a group. It is a phenomenon that emerges in reaction to at least four discernible forces. These forces — the individual with leadership potential, the follower who will be a member of the leader's group, the group, and the situation which provides the confrontation — come together to create the leader. Leadership is a function of any one of these forces.

Until recently, research and theory concerning leadership seem to have favored the situational approach. Now, however, the stage is set for a new round of definitive experiments which should shed further light on the human predilection for leadership. Situationists themselves are beginning to detect in individual leaders attributes which are of sufficient power to have a marked effect on leadership behavior. Each concept of leadership that we have touched upon briefly has support. Yet, no single theory offers entirely satisfactory answers, or even provides the kind of verifiable information that should underlie an adequate theory of leadership. We must seek further.

The Theory of Group Facilitation

Current research demonstrates the need for more carefully controlled experimental conditions under which answers of greater validity and precision can be obtained.* One concept of leadership suggests that leaderlike behavior is behavior that facilitates group goals. As groups participate in their different activities, the various members make certain contributions toward the objectives of the group. These contributions differ in kind and degree. To the extent that any member's contributions are particularly valuable, they are looked upon as leaderlike; as any member is recognized by others as a reliable generator of such contributions, he is leaderlike. To be thus recognized is to have a role relationship to other members. If leadership is viewed as a facilitative role

---

* For full description of current research, see the works by Fiedler (1973, 1976, 1977), Lassen, and Rosen listed in the Selected References at the end of this chapter.

relationship, it follows that particular behaviors on the part of the leaderlike person are not what make his contributions valuable, but rather his relationship to others in the group.

This interpretation of leadership suggests that a group designates individuals as facilitators on the basis of at least two generalized classes of behavior. Bales and others offered experimental data which indicate that many groups recognize special facilitators as those who promote task achievement, on the one hand, and those who promote personal satisfaction among group members, on the other.[18] Leaderlike behavior is therefore generated by several individuals within a group. Group members whose contributions are not recognized by others do not thereby cease to contribute toward group goals. Nevertheless, it is more correct to state that their activities are more leaderlike than they are themselves. Any discussion of role relationship admits the fact that where there is no recognition, there can be no interaction. The interactional aspects of leadership require, in the same way as do other role relationships, the sharing of attitudes and expectations by role participants.

Bales designates the task specialist and the socio-emotional specialist as the individuals whose unique contributions are necessary for the achievement of group goals leading to task satisfaction and individual member satisfaction. Prerequisites for the task specialist are the capacity to plan and solve problems and the ability to persevere until the desired accomplishment is achieved. In groups that experience coordinated action toward a goal, it is likely that the group recognizes one or more of its members because these members have knowledge pertinent to the task, have ingenuity, are practical, are persuasive, are capable of identifying problems, are skilled in planning and coordination, and are dependable.

The socio-emotional specialist, on the other hand, maintains good interpersonal relations. Although some groups exist presumably for the purpose of achieving specific objectives, such accomplishment may be assisted or retarded by membership interpersonal satisfactions or dissatisfactions.[19] Other groups appear to have few objectives other than the pleasure that members find in interacting with one another. Most groups have both kinds of interest. Whatever the group's primary goal, its achievement can be smoothed by any member who serves as a source of satisfying intermember relationships. In his leaderlike behavior, the socio-emotional specialist is highly supportive, extroverted, tension resolving, encouraging, equanimous, and impartial.

A socio-emotional leader is confronted with a contradiction: how can he

---

18. R. F. Bales, "Task Roles and Social Roles in Problem Solving Groups," in E. Maccomby, T. M. Newcomb, and E. L. Hartley, eds., *Readings in Social Psychology,* 3d ed. (New York: Holt, Rinehart & Winston, 1958), p. 441.

19. Kahn and Katz, "Leadership Practices," pp. 557-558.

offer support and warmth to all group members and, at the same time, offer positive and negative criticism to individuals? According to Fiedler, accepted leaders tend to depersonalize their relationship to group members. They become task-oriented rather than person-oriented. When task objectives are shared, the supportive behaviors can be subordinated to goal achievement, and in these circumstances discrimination between effective and ineffective individuals becomes objective.

Whatever the leaderlike activities that serve to promote satisfying interpersonal relationships, they will be most effective if (as in the case of goal accomplishment) they permit a group member to increase his own utility through others. Satisfying interpersonal relations, like task completion, is the result of personal interaction within the group as a whole. How certain members behave to promote effectiveness, thereby gaining recognition and leadership status, must still be explained. What the leader is as a person, what the leader must do to gain acceptance, and how the leader employs his capacities to perpetuate influential interaction remain for consideration.

Central Figure Theory

In the search to determine where and why leadership occurs, a pattern recurs in which recognition is conferred upon a central figure. In almost every culture, most groups have a central figure. This individual may be indigenous, he may have been appointed, or he may have imposed himself upon the group. In each case, he is looked upon as a leader. Why should this be so? Is it in fact so? Zoological resources cannot be overlooked in attempting an explanation.

One basis for such distinction may lie in man's evolutionary process. Desmond Morris writes that the ancestral forebears of man probably lived in much the same manner as the primate species, apes and monkeys. These social animals are dominated by a single male. The entire life-style of the group revolves around this one central figure. The dominant male is the most powerful, usually the largest of the animals. Consequently, every member of the group seeks to appease him rather than face bodily harm. The dominant male is at once the group protector and arbiter. He prevents outside forces from overcoming the group, and he assumes control of intragroup quarrels that might threaten safety or unity. He makes the decisions and reaps all benefits first. His authority is absolute and godlike:

> Turning now to our immediate ancestors, it is clear that, with the growth of the co-operative spirit so vital for successful group hunting, the application of the dominant individual's authority had to be severely limited if he was to retain the active, as opposed to passive, loyalty of the other group members. They had to want to help him instead of simply fear him. He had to become more "one of them." The old-style monkey

tyrant had to go, and in his place there arose a more tolerant, more cooperative naked ape leader. This step was essential for the new type of "mutual-aid" organization that was evolving, but it gave rise to a problem. The total dominance of the Number 1 member of the group having been replaced by a qualified dominance, he could no longer command unquestioning allegiance. This change in the order of things, vital as it was to the new social system, nevertheless left a gap. From our ancient background there remained a need for an all-powerful figure who could keep the group under control....[20]

It is not surprising, then, that one aspect of leadership should focus on the concept of central-figure domination based upon a biologically transmitted heritage. If, as Morris suggests, man retains the primitive impulse to be subordinate to an all-powerful figure, then it is inevitable that man should accede to this impulse in spite of any more recently learned cooperative social techniques.

Writing in 1957, Ross and Hendry discussed the concept of the central figure within groups. They noted that even though a group recognizes a certain person as the central figure, he need not be the most competent, influential, liked, or helpful person in directing the group toward its goal. Most groups do have a central figure who is the leader, however:

This leads one to suspect that groups and organizations "need" such a central figure who is called the "leader." In a significant sense this person *is* the leader because he is perceived by the members of the group to be the leader. This is not simply a matter of semantics; for the person so designated is actually given influence, authority, and status which he would not have as a "member" of the group.[21]

Why do groups desire a central figure for leadership? The answers suggested by social expectations, appearance, ideas, talent, empathy, or practical payoff are not adequate. More puzzling still, if the central figure is not the most competent, influential, liked, and helpful member of the group, why is he then accorded a status which tends to reinforce his leadership position? The answer might be that there is a biological impulse which continues to operate as stimulus to behavior. To satisfy a felt inadequacy, the group is compelled to raise one person above all others. Only in this way can the age-old desire for protection against hostile elements be satisfied.

Not only does the group instinctively choose a central figure to take on

---

20. D. Morris, *The Naked Ape* (New York: Dell Publishing Co., Inc., 1967), p. 147. Reprinted by permission.
21. M. Ross and C. Hendry, *New Understandings of Leadership* (New York: Association Press, 1957), p. 34.

the leadership role; it also attributes specific abilities to him, accepts activities which he performs to be those of leadership, and even defines leadership as those functions which are exercised by the person holding a central position. Such a biologically based theory does not imply that others within the group may not also be responsible for satisfying goals or supporting interpersonal relations. On the contrary, it recognizes that other group members may be great facilitators, energizers, and task achievers without being recognized as the group's central figure. When all is said and done, the central figure carries each individual's perception of leadership for that particular group.

Centrality and Leadership

When a special place in the group is designated for one member, a complicated mass of variables begins to operate. Whether group expectations will be fulfilled by the leader depends upon a range of elements all converging simultaneously. Among these factors will be anticipations of those who rely upon him, the emotions and attitudes of group members at any given time, the job to be done, the character of the organization, the current atmosphere in which the group abides, external forces for cohesion or disintegration, internal forces for subversion or disaffection, and, most specifically, the leader's own experiences, intelligence, understanding of how he should perform, and his capacity to do so. Until the group decides to follow someone else, the designated person remains the leader. That any individual is so elevated implies that he has something that makes him expedient for this role. Thus the creation of the central-figure role is yet another facet of leadership not previously resolved by contemporary theories of leadership.

One other possibility emerges as a motive for leadership assumption, and that is the insatiable desire to lead. There are individuals whose craving for power is so compelling that they must seek out leadership roles by placing themselves in situations which favor the emergence of a leader. They are neither turned aside nor frustrated by rejection of their leadership attempts. Their stimulation comes from a personality drive that can only be satisfied when leadership is attained. A hunger for power can be the major motivating force to lead.[22] C. Gibb reinforces this concept when, in his review of the relationship between personality and leadership, he concludes that leaders are generally inclined to score higher than others on measures of dominance.[23] If it can be supposed that such measures actually mirror a desire on the part of a person to be in dominant positions, then the contention of the need to lead may be evidenced.

---

22. D. Cartwright and A. Zander, eds., *Group Dynamics,* 3d ed. (New York: Harper and Row, 1968), p. 311.
23. Gibb, "Leadership," pp. 218-221.

The Confidence Factor

Undoubtedly leaders believe in themselves. Individuals who are motivated to lead do so because they are confident that their leadership attempts will be appreciated, that they will gain the influence they require, and that the leadership role will be accorded to them. Such individuals may have the ability to solve problems or accomplish tasks that are beyond the capabilities of other group members and potential followers, but not necessarily. Leaders seem to be convinced of their probable effectiveness in whatever situation they find themselves. If an individual did not believe that his appraisal of a situation was accurate and more to the point, effective in achieving a stated goal, he would be less likely to make leadership attempts. One of the more consistent findings in the literature dealing with leadership research is the fact that leaders have higher self-esteem than do nonleaders.

Another probable reason for the relationship between self-esteem and leadership may be traced to the leader's ability to communicate his confidence insofar as the group's potential accomplishment is concerned. This kind of communication is particularly important in those situations where group members have only a vague perception of goals or the methods for reaching such goals. Under these circumstances the group members will use the leader's confidence as a gauge to determine their capacity to perform tasks designed to lead to goal achievement and their subsequent progress. The leader must never permit his group to lose confidence in him. High self-esteem evokes equally high self-confidence. The leader must transmit this to the group for the sake of group cohesiveness and its ability to act as a unit.

Communication plays an essential part in the determination of leadership. Implicit in any understanding of leadership is the idea that leaders and followers must be able to communicate with one another. Without communication there can be no leadership. More to the point, however, is the fact that effective communication tends to promote leadership behavior. The person who communicates effectively is in a more advantageous position to acquire information about alternatives, to gain cooperation, develop coordination, and organize the group membership so that task accomplishment is facilitated. Research indicates that individuals who communicate best with others in a group tend to be selected for leadership roles or are, in fact, looked upon as leaders by group members.[24]

A network of communication is highly important. The person who can coordinate the various pieces of information fed to him in consequence of his position within the communication network will enhance his leadership

24. M. E. Shaw, "Group Structure and the Behavior of Individuals in Small Groups," *Journal of Psychology,* Vol. 38 (1954), pp. 138-149.

role by combining, swiftly and efficiently, relevant items. More subtle communication components will also be at work in consolidating group acceptance of a leader. One such component may be the extent to which members of a group share certain ideas. P. J. Runkel, for example, determined that commonly held ideas dramatically increase effective communicability between people in whom there is a shared value system.[25]

This requirement of commonly held conceptual dimensions among people may be an extenuating ingredient which supports the finding that the I.Q. of leaders is apt to be somewhat higher than that of other group members.[26] If there were a great discrepancy between the leader's I.Q. and that of other group members, it is possible that the leader's inability to translate his ideas into simpler language would block communication. Of course, highly intelligent individuals who want to be leaders might find ways to circumvent this difficulty, but it does seem that they would rather interact with those for whom they have a closer affinity.

Any comprehensive attempt to clarify leadership theory must deal with role relationships, group structure, personality characteristics associated with leadership, emotional needs and attitudes of group members at any time, the climate or environment in which the group exists, and those circumstances which give rise to problems or situations requiring resolution. The probability exists that leadership is input, process, and product related to the synergistic development of all these interacting variables. The outcome of such interchange doubtless creates a condition for the preferment of a given leader. Such designation cannot in any way alter membership contributions toward effective group life.

The Theory of Social Influence

Of the many factors affecting the phenomenon of leadership, perhaps the most important is social influence — how an individual's behavior is affected by others. To gain a quantitative measure of this effect, investigators have formulated any number of psychological tests and measures: discrepancy hypotheses, theories of cognitive dissonance, theories of interpersonal perception, and assessments of social desirability, dogmatism, and conformity. All point to one overriding factor: within various groups, there is a form of implicit interpersonal determination, an ability of the group to evaluate its needs, which is manifested on several levels including perceptions of competence insofar as progress toward group goals is concerned, group standards or norms in the sense of values, and specific traits which the group desires.

One way in which a leader can exercise influence is to modify group

---

25. P. J. Runkel, "Cognitive Similarity in Facilitating Communication," *Sociometry,* Vol. 19 (1956), pp. 179-191.
26. Gibb, "Leadership," pp. 217-218.

norms. How does the leader prevail as an agent of a change when conformity to group values or standards is one of the perceived assessments made in the selection of this leader? Is it possible that as a person's status level is raised within the limits of group life, certain tolerance ranges are simultaneously opened? This might explain how leaders can redirect a group's effort or even change its value system without losing the support of the membership. Tolerance of innovative methods or acceptance of nonconforming conduct might presage the arrival of an individual as a leader.

It can also be assumed that nonconforming behavior in one member might be looked upon as conforming behavior in another. An expedient method for expressing these relationships is to look upon status from the point of view of the perceiver. How the individual perceives another may well incorporate all of the sources of input necessary to create a leader as well as the working qualities of this position. Thus, emergent leadership requires one individual's recognition of another's behavior and personal qualities. It affords expanding assurance of one's influence. It so modifies social presumptions as to permit behavior deviant from the group norm without costing that individual either his acceptance or status with those who perceive him as a member of the group. As an individual gains status within the group, he may act more autonomously insofar as the exercise of influence is concerned. Whether the individual chooses to do so or not will depend upon his own inclinations, social and emotional needs, personal perceptions, and motivations.

Relationships such as these require careful investigation because they are directly concerned with the development of leadership. Not only is there a symbiotic relationship between the concepts of influence and leadership, but there are also important mechanisms, personal and extrapersonal, generating and controlling their development. The consequence of conforming behavior at one time may be in direct relation to another's anticipation of, or indulgence toward, nonconforming behavior at some other time. Credibility, visibility, and comprehension, revealed in the light of previous experience, are means to attitudinal change. Research in this area basically reflects the idea that leadership is a relationship between an individual exercising influence and those who are influenced. This social process is most advantageously observed within the framework of group life:

> As a current focal point for studying influence effects from social interaction, leadership has ramifications to many other concerns relevant to group process, including conformity, morale, and social change. The study of leadership must accordingly contribute to knowledge about the dynamics of influence processes because, in a strict sense, leadership is neither a unique personal attribute, nor is it

separable from social influence more generally.[27]

The leader's successful rise is associated with the existing environment, both as group members know it from current communications and as they retain associations of persons or points of view, past and present. An alteration of the influence framework must inevitably reduce the opposition which these elements impose and promote. The leader's influence depends not so much on the individual or the situation as it does on the way in which the individual is thought of, what he projects himself to be, and what he reflects insofar as the current problem is concerned. Nevertheless, after the leader attains his position through influence, what he does may not fulfill previous expectations. In order to preserve his position, he is under constraint to satisfy new expectations which develop as the situation changes.

There are several theorists who contend that influence is not a reasonable basis for leadership. T. Newcomb and others reject the idea that the person with the most influence is a leader. Newcomb defines leadership as a "facilitative role relationship" and not the exertion of influence. He states:

> It is often the case that actual influence, in the sense of affecting the course of events, may be exercised in ways that are hardly recognized at all by other group members. Tremendous influence may stem from a person who works behind the scenes. . . .[28]

Whether or not leadership is viewed as a facilitative role, relationship influence is a major factor in determining leadership. Newcomb's concept of group achievement through facilitative behaviors occurs only if individual contributions are not recognized as such by other group members who may be helped by such contributions. However, those who actually facilitate group goals probably will be recognized as having done so, and through this recognition they will gain influence with others in the group.

It must be remembered that the overt exercise of influence is not required for one to have leadership status or to perform the leadership role. Individuals who work behind the scenes, powers behind the throne, may be willing to submerge their ego needs in order to fulfill their desire to exert influence. Such individuals may have to operate by indirection, perhaps within the confines of a leader's entourage. Despite his apparent lack of leadership role, he gains his ends by controlling others; whether his influence is direct or indirect, he still leads if his ideas are acted upon. Such

27. E. P. Hollander, *Leaders, Groups, and Influence* (New York: Oxford University Press, 1964), p. 3.
28. T. M. Newcomb, R. H. Turner, P. E. Converse, *Social Psychology: The Study of Human Interaction* (New York: Holt, Rinehart and Winston, Inc., 1965), pp. 474-475.

persons will have influence with the overt leader and may be looked upon as assuming leadership functions. It does not matter that the group or collection of followers accords the central figure the position of leadership. What is significant is that the influence of the leader is brought to bear on the group and they act in ways which he desires. This is real leadership. The degree to which one person influences another is the leadership impact which results from the ability to motivate individuals to act in a certain direction.[29]

Types of Influence

Leadership is really the relationship developed between people as one individual attempts to gain influence with another. Where influence is consensual, leadership emerges. Where influence is imposed, there can be no leadership, only acquiesence to authority. Contemporary social psychology has long accepted K. Lewin, R. Lippitt, and R. White's classification of leadership styles into autocratic, democratic, and laissez-faire.[30] A real, as well as a semantic problem, arises when the term leadership is used, however. Can any but a democratic context exist for leadership? Can anarchy contribute to leadership? Doesn't the imposition of authority automatically prohibit leadership from occurring? These questions must be examined before any definitive explanation of leadership can be made.

Lewin and his associates describe the effects of the three leadership styles on groups of three different environments. Under *autocratic* leadership, policy is determined and tasks are dictated without reference to group desires. The leader is personal in his praise and criticism, but he remains aloof from the group. In a *democratic* setting, all policies are a matter for group consideration with leader participation. The leader is objective in praise or criticism and freely participates in group activities. Under *laissez-faire*, there is complete freedom of group or individual decision without leader participation. The leader serves as a resource and contributes only when requested. There is no attempt on the leader's part to interfere with or take part in the activities.

The laissez-faire concept, as defined by Lewin and his associates, is not characteristic of a political system in the way that democracy and autocracy are. A more fitting term would have been *anarchy,* which specifically refers to a political system and therefore shares a common frame of reference with democracy and autocracy. As used by Lewin and his associates, the term laissez-faire seems to describe the characteristics of

29. M. Kalb and B. Kalb, *Kissinger* (Boston: Little, Brown and Company, 1974), p. 98.
30. K. Lewin, R. Lippitt, and R. White, "Patterns of Aggressive Behavior in Experimentally Created 'Social Climates,'" *Journal of Abnormal and Social Psychology, Society for the Psychological Study of Social Issues Bulletin,* X (1939), pp. 271-299.

anarchy rather than those usually attributed to laissez-faire. Anarchy denotes the absence of social or government control over individuals. The individual perceives himself as completely free of all restraint and acts in ways calculated to bring satisfaction to himself. However, if each person simply goes his own way, the likelihood of accomplishing necessary tasks, even those needed for survival, is questionable. When people do not share common goals and are not willing to work for a broader social unit, the basis for leadership is lacking, and the society must decline as a result.

Nor can autocracy be considered as a basis for leadership. It is a political form in which one person has supreme or dictatorial power. Leadership cannot be equated with any aspect of coercion; coercion is precisely what autocracy is founded upon. Any form of physical threat — death, torture, or imprisonment — may afford the leader a reluctant although active following, but it is a following based upon fear and not upon volition. When those led do not follow willingly, there is no leadership; there is only dictatorship.

Headship versus Leadership

An attempt should be made to distinguish between influence exercised as part of an organizational system and that which emerges spontaneously from human relations. The acceptance of influence, which is conditional upon the consent of potential followers, is leadership. To distinguish this from domination, or headship, C. Gibb offers the following definition:

The principal differentia are these: i) Domination of headship is maintained through an organized system and not by the spontaneous recognition, by fellow group members, of the individual's contribution to group goals. ii) The group goal is chosen by the head man in line with his interests and is not internally determined by the group itself. iii) In the domination or headship relation there is little or no sense of shared feeling or joint action in the pursuit of a given goal. iv) There is in the dominance relation a wide social gap between the group members and the head, who strives to maintain social distance as an aid to his coercion of the group. v) Most basically, these two forms of influence differ with respect to the source of the authority which is exercised. The leader's authority is spontaneously accorded him by his fellow group members, the followers. The authority of the head derives from some extra-group power which he has over the members of the group, who cannot meaningfully be called his followers. They accept his domination, on pain of punishment, rather than follow. The business executive is an excellent example of a head exercising authority derived from his position in an organization through membership in which the worker, his subordinates, satisfy many strong needs. They obey his commands and accept his domination because this is part of their duty as organization members and to reject him would be to discontinue membership, with all the punishments that would involve.[31]

This does not mean that individuals who hold positions of *authority*, or at least give the appearance of leadership, cannot also be leaders. Leadership and headship can reside in the same person. It is apparent that much of the so-called leadership of the world is of the headship variety. It follows, then, that most people tend to think of leadership in terms of organizational structure and title. Despite the obvious identity between leadership and position attainment, a certain amount of confusion has been noted. There still remains a tendency to designate as leadership those dominance characteristics and functions which clearly belong to the concept of headship.

It is erroneous to consider as "leaders" those who have rigidly restricted, programmed functions within an organizational hierarchy. The organizational position of headship requires tightly made choices, regulated by controlling policies. The interpersonal qualities usually conceived to be a part of the leader-follower relation are conspicuously lacking. Bavelas asserts that the functions of those in headship positions may be definably different from personal attributes or characteristics.[32] He suggests that on the whole such "leaders" are those who carry out certain tasks rather than share idealized personality traits. Bavelas indicates his orientation by asking not who the leader is, but what functions are to be satisfied by his leadership position.

Interaction and Influence

Leadership in an important social phenomenon that occurs wherever individuals interact and form groups. Although there are a number of possible definitions, leadership is most often defined as the exertion of influence *with* others. Whoever is conceded to be most influential in the interaction between people is the leader at that particular time. Intelligible leadership structure is much more prevalent when the group is large, deliberating time is short, the objective is difficult, and the consequences are either extremely significant or a matter of complete indifference.

In all the catalogued research from the fields of social psychology, group dynamics, and human interaction, some controversy remains over who is most apt to become a leader, or why one individual is recognized as a leader while others — who may be just as competent — are either overlooked or rejected. Current views of leadership occurrence may be termed "*inter-*

---

31. Gibb, "Leadership," p. 213.
32. A. Bavelas, "Leadership: Man and Function," *Administration Science Quarterly*, Vol. IV (1960), pp. 491-498.

actional." Accordingly, any attempt to predict the leadership role in any group situation must consider all of the interacting variables that produce the desired central figure. These variables include personality makeup of group members, group syntality, problems which the group confronts, the kinds of activities which the group must perform to achieve its goal, and the personal attributes which may promote the emergence of one person as a leader.

The individual or individuals who are most conspicuous and are perceived by themselves and other group members as most likely to contribute to group goal achievement and group maintenance will assume leadership. The interactional viewpoint, that as the situation changes, the person who is recognized as the leader in the group will also change, is open to question. When the condition affecting the group stabilizes, leaders tend to share common traits. Achievement-oriented individuals who have good interpersonal skills, resistence to frustration, empathy, and good intellectual ability are much more likely to have leadership potential.

In other than leadership situations, there are individuals whose exploitative need dominates any sense of ethics, driving them to any lengths to gain influence over others. Investigations carried out to determine the propensity of individuals to employ such Machiavellian tactics show that people who scored high on the Mach scale [see Glossary] were more likely than those concerned with good human relations to use manipulative and coldly calculated acts designed to obtain whatever ends they desired. It was also shown that the manipulator does not always succeed. Only in situations of insufficient information precluding a decision, of extremely volatile emotions, or of close personal confrontations do Machiavellian types gain influence. But such personalilties and the exploitative means they use to gain ends should not be considered within the leadership context. On the contrary, it is probably more appropriate to classify such behavior with demagoguery, headship and dictatorship.

Another contemporary approach defines leadership in terms of a group's situation and the variables that influence the emergence of leadership. Proponents of this view claim that a high incidence of leadership acceptance can be traced to extragroup leadership recognition and appointment. The cultural environment is an influence in determining who will finally enjoy leadership. The structural mold of the group may also have important effects. Certain group members may be perceived as having the kind of personality or technical competence which the group needs and values. Some individuals may emerge as leaders because their social and emotional constitution supports group members. Others, who are formally hailed as leaders, are chosen because of the ultimate reward or satisfaction they can obtain for the membership. Potential leaders cannot vary too much from the expectations of the group nor from the values which group members hold. Furthermore, the abililty of the membership to achieve success is associated with their own capacities to perform well and will therefore have some effect on leadership development.

One of the most important influences on leadership is communication. It can be illustrated that leaders dominate the communications network within the group. Although greater contributions to the communications process do not necessarily ensure the emergence of leadership, the likelihood is strong that they will. The entire process of communication is directly related to the degree of influence any person will obtain, the individual's visibility within the group or organizational context, and the extent to which original ideas, suggestions, or plans will be implemented.

Leadership does not rely upon status quo to maintain itself. Once the leader is determined, he must continually provide the action, climate, and goal identification to sustain what the group initially perceived in him. There are any number of tactics which leaders employ to remain in the leadership position. This, again, is not to be confused with any manifestation of behavior commonly used to advance in corporate, bureaucratic, or organizational models where headship is the determining factor. Leaders face a marked ambiguity in themselves. Leaders wish to remain leaders, but realize that they must simultaneously develop potential successors. How they resolve this dilemma will be discussed at some length in Chapter 14.

Leadership is characterized by different behaviors which vary with the leadership situation. A number of studies showed the most prominent leadership behaviors to be of two basic types: socio-emotional, wherein the leader concentrates on group maintenance, and task-oriented, wherein the leader concentrates on group goals. On occasion, the two behaviors coalesce in one person. The group's situation determines which behavior its leader must demonstrate. Where supportive leadership is required, the warm and personable leader will emerge. Where anxiety and stress characterize the group, the task-oriented leader may better serve its needs. It seems safe to say, at this time, that there are several behaviors which leaders may use as conditions change and pressures are exerted upon them to act or react in certain ways. What has worked well in previous situations may not work in current ones. In this respect, then, situations play a determining role in the emergence of leadership and how the leader will perform.

It is obvious from much of the foregoing discussion that the kind of person the leader will be is contingent upon any number of variables: the personality of the individual chosen to lead; the group or agency in need of leadership; the situation in which the group finds itself at any given moment; the purposes or aims of the group or organization; the temperament of the individuals who are members of the group and the dynamics of their interpersonal relations; the group's self-image; the hierarchy of the group (if any); and the impinging pressures from the society, culture, or subculture of which it is a part and from which its members come. These and countless other collisions, both major and minor, will be directly reflected in the kind of leader the group will choose and the manner in which the leader will perform.

Leadership is an extremely intricate and enigmatic social phenomenon. Many are called but few are chosen. Why this should be so, how this phenomenon comes about, and how leadership is maintained tantalize social scientists and laymen alike. Discussions, investigations, and leadership theory reveal several concepts that seem worthy of note and further exploration. Using these basic concepts, we intend this text as a guide for the study of leadership as it applies to the field of recreational service.

SELECTED REFERENCES

Argyris, C., *Increasing Leadership Effectiveness* (New York: John Wiley & Sons, Inc., 1976).

Bass, B. M., *Leadership, Psychology and Organizational Behavior* (Westport, Conn.: Greenwood Press, Inc., 1973).

Berkowitz, L., ed., *Advances in Experimental Social Psychology*, Vol. 5 (New York: Academic Press, 1970).

Blumenson, M. and J. L. Stokesburg, *Masters of the Art of Command* (Boston: Houghton Mifflin Co., 1975).

Cassel, R. N. and R. L. Heichberger, eds., *Leadership Development: Theory and Practice* (North Quincy, Mass.: Christopher Publishing House, 1975).

Dale, E., *The Humane Leader* (Bloomington, Ind.: Phi Delta Kappa, 1974).

Fiedler, F. E., "Predicting the Effects of Leadership Training and Experience from the Contingency Model: A Clarification," *Journal of Applied Psychology,* Vol. 57 (1973), pp. 110-113.

Fiedler, F. E. and M. M. Chamers, *Leadership and Effective Management* (Glenview, Ill.: Scott, Foresman & Co., 1974).

Fiedler, F. E. and others, *Improving Leadership Effectiveness: The Leader Match Concept* (New York: John Wiley & Sons, Inc., 1976).

Fiedler, F. E. and others, *Leadership* (American Management, 1977).

Lassen, W. R. and R. R. Fernandez, *Leadership and Social Change* (La Jolla, Cal.: University Associates, 1976).

McCroskey, J., D. Larson, and M. Knapp, *An Introduction to Interpersonal Communication* (Englewood Cliffs, N. J.: Prentice-Hall, 1971).

Rosen, N. A., *Leadership Change and Work — Group Dynamics: An Experiment* (Ithaca, N.Y.: Cornell University Press, 1969).

Schachter, S., *The Psychology of Affiliation* (Stanford, Cal.: Stanford University Press, 1959).

Shaw, M., *Group Dynamics: The Psychology of Small Group Behavior* (New York: McGraw-Hill Book Company, 1971).

Stogdill, R. M., *Handbook of Leadership* (New York: The Free Press, 1974).

Triandis, H., *Attitude and Attitude Change* (New York: John Wiley & Sons, Inc., 1971).

Vroom, V. H. and P. W. Yetton, *Leadership and Decision-Making* (Pittsburgh: University of Pittsburgh Press, 1974).

CHAPTER TWO

Leadership in Recreational Service

"Take me to your leader" is not merely a humorous punch line, it is a universal acknowledgement of the need for leadership, and a plea. In a world increasingly full of human organizations, success or failure rests on leadership. Never have there been so many organizations which encroach upon the daily lives of most people in the world. Whether the organization represents a multi-national corporation or a smaller enterprise, it is obvious that all organizations require leadership. They need leaders whose primary concern is the development of human relations necessary to engender loyalty, productivity, and a desire to support the organization and its goals. People, not things, determine the effectiveness of any organization and ultimately sustain its existence.

Influence for Organizational Leadership

The field of recreational service, and those organizations which comprise its functional structure, deal with people. People are involved in carrying out the duties and responsibilities of any given recreational service agency, and it is to the people who make up the constituency of the agency that the service is dedicated. Without their enthusiasm, the agency cannot provide the kind of comprehensive recreational service (program, places, direction) which professional personnel are mandated to give. Employees affect the ability of a recreational service agency to function effectively. Unless there is an atmosphere of cooperation and willingness to work toward achieving specific goals, the value of the agency will be minimal.

External Forces

Because the constituency of an agency cannot be forced to accept that agency or to participate in or otherwise support agency activities and enterprises, because an agency cannot impose its concepts of what is enjoyable or valuable upon its constituency, a recreational service agency must depend upon the good will and voluntary interest of those whom it is attempting to serve. It should guide the public by applying sound techniques and strategies to which most people can respond.

Advocacy and greater political awareness have replaced, to a certain extent, previous public apathy. There is a growing restlessness among people to expect public agencies to meet their needs which frequently manifests itself in confrontations during direct personal interviews, in mass meetings, at public hearings, or through an agency's own fact-gathering procedures. The public is beginning to recognize its own power to control public sector organizations and most likely will continue to assert itself in the future to attain its goals. To meet this situation, public functionaries must overcome the bureaucratic tendency to live behind the anonymity of governmental structure.

The day of the domineering clerk is over. The realization that government exists for the people, not the reverse, has finally come into its own. People are starting to demand a voice in the development of plans, programs, and operations of agencies. They want more of a say in how their money shall be spent, by whom, for what purposes, and then they want an accounting of the effectiveness of the expenditures.

If this is true for public sector organizations, it is no less true of the private and quasi-public sector organizations. Private corporations which offer services to people are just as vulnerable to disaffection and contempt as are public agencies. A disenchanted public applies pressures to which agencies succumb unless they are willing or able to devote considerable time and effort to using leaders effectively. Leadership is the single most important ingredient that any organization must have if it is to maintain itself and reverse a hostile environment brought about by rising discontent.

Both public and private agencies are now aware that the public is tired of incompetence, arrogance, and indifference. Many organizations, in every sector of society, must undergo an agonizing reappraisal of personnel behavior, program offering, facililty development, and communication policy if they are ever to gain the support of their constituency. Leadership is the key to achieving success in these areas.

Leadership and Interaction

Man's ability to interact in a meaningful way with others is at the root of all human society. How the individual is enabled to act to create trust and confidence is the foundation of leadership. Leadership is one of the ethical methods by which others can be persuaded to lend themselves to those enterprises which have as their goal the enhancement of human life. The fundamental element of the individual's social environment is the presence and existence of other people. The human relationships which are determined by and determine the interaction process are profoundly influenced by leadership. If individuals are led there is the greatest likelihood that the product of such interaction will result in personal satisfaction, enjoyment, and goal achievement.

It is obvious that the careful cultivation of public support requires leadership. Bureaucratic fiat and regulation of public behavior through prohibitive directives, without justification of the rules, must be eradicated. Just as citizens have begun to learn to command their employees in government, so must public agencies learn the techniques, properties, and qualities of leadership in order to function for the good of the public. An agency should employ persons who have the technical competence and skill to help people fully realize the greatest satisfaction and personal growth. To ensure that employee skill is focused primarily on this ideal and not wasted on defending the agency against attack, the organization must perform those leadership tasks which will evoke mutual trust, confidence, and support.

Internal Forces

The internal structure of any agency can be positively maintained by a democratic climate. Management-employee relationships have only recently become humanized; formerly, organizational relationships were strictly of the superior-subordinate kind. Position was all. Supervision meant transmitting orders without discussion. Relations developing out of an imposed authority rarely produce the whole-hearted support of the individual in the inferior position. Most individuals of intelligence resent directives not open to discussion or to an understanding of why certain concepts or functions must be done in certain ways.

Authority handed down without channels for communication or recommendations of alternatives will always create dissatisfaction and eventual disinterest on the part of the subordinate. There are, of course, individuals in subordinate positions who enjoy an authoritarian relationship and would find themselves incapable of performing without it, but this is not the norm. Almost all organizations operate under conditions which suggest that only superior-subordinate relationships are tolerated within the structure and any questioning of the hierarchy will be met with disciplinary action.[1]

Leadership and Democracy

Leadership permeates any organization's structure and may create a climate in which democratic interdependency can develop; it is the philosophy of the administrator which sets the tone. If the chief executive believes in democratic leadership practices, it is probable that everyone connected with the organization will benefit from such belief. When the opportunity to be a part of the decision-making process is offered, a failure to do so may be due to unwillingness or inability. Good leadership practices prevent mere lip service to a given concept.

---

1. S.J. Unger, "The FBI File: Men and Machinations in the Court of J. Edgar Hoover," *Atlantic Monthly,* Vol. 235, No. 4 (April 1975), pp. 37-52.

Leadership is democratic. It invites open discussion of any practice. Each person's suggestion is given the same degree of respectful hearing. The Orwellian, "All animals are equal but some animals are more equal than others," [2] does not apply. When individuals feel that they have a part in effecting policy which guides the agency, or that their suggestions for activities, plans, or programs of the agency are recognized as contributory, they will be much more likely to devote greater effort toward the agency's success. When they become so involved with an organization that they begin to identify with it, they want the programs and other themes which are synonymous with the agency to be effective. In this manner, as the agency achieves its objectives, the workers in it obtain satisfaction.

Leadership must be based on the democratic principles of providing factual information and open communication. The ability to make judgments, freely arrived at without fear of retaliation, coercion, or manipulation, affords the greatest possibility for acting intelligently and responsibly, and exerting a positive influence. The essence of democracy is that it permits participation in the decision-making process by those who will be directly and indirectly affected by any decisions made. Democracy is concerned with people as individuals. It is not just a passive system of values, but an active process. Democratic practice ensures that when liberty is available people are capable of determining their own destinies and may freely associate with others, the more readily to achieve their common goals.

Leadership is a democratic relationship of mutual dependence and shared developmental responsibilities. Each person is encouraged to participate insofar as his abilities, intelligence, and needs permit. The leader offers whatever counseling he can. He moves to assist others as help is required. By empathizing, rapport may be established between him and his constituents. By encouraging self-discipline, he enables each person to make his own decisions. In some instances, mutual trust and respect develop the confidence of participants so that they can deputize others to represent and act for them.

Democratically operated organizations are not anarchical. People have certain duties and responsibilities to fulfill. They also have an opportunity to express themselves on issues which may influence agency officials' decisions. Democracy is viewed as a system or process which induces participation by group members and permits ready access to the decision-making process. As John Dewey declared in his democratic ideal:

> A democracy is more than a form of government; it is primarily a mode of associated living, of conjoint communicated experience. The extension in space of a number of individuals who participate in an

---

2. G. Orwell, *Animal Farm* (New York: Signet Classics, 1945), p. 123.

interest so that each has to refer his own action to that of others, and to consider the action of others to give point and direction to his own, is equivalent to the breaking down of those barriers of class, race, and national territory which kept men from perceiving the full import of their activity. These more numerous and more varied points of contact denote a greater diversity of stimuli to which an individual has to respond; they consequently put a premium on variation in his action. They secure a liberation of powers which remain suppressed as long as the incitation to action is partial, as it must be in a group which in its exclusiveness shuts out many interests.[3]

Organizational Objectives and Leadership

Working for money alone will not elicit from professionals the loyalty, devotion, and assumption of responsibility necessary to do more than that which is merely required. The individual who is bound to the agency through identification with it will perform in ways that money can never buy. All of the detailed work which is lovingly undertaken for the good of the agency and, incidentally, for the worker's own satisfaction is due to the inspiration of morale. No organization can purchase morale. It is an intangible factor that develops with harmonious and sound peer relationships. Like the development of rapport, morale originates in a climate of personal interaction and group identification. Organizations can hire technical proficiency, but they cannot pay for individual dedication. The agency must offer the kind of warm interpersonal relationships which emerge from an administrative structure based upon leadership rather than headship.

It is possible to recruit well-qualified workers, only to lose them through the insufferable imposition of petty tyrannies, mind destroying conformity to stale ideas, and rigid adherence to behavioral patterns that may no longer be necessary or even worthwhile. Many will not agree with democratically run organizations because of the apparent time-consuming aspect of democratic practices in decision-making. However, employee morale will soar, each person will have a chance to contribute, and each will have made an extra effort reflected in an attitude of belonging which may not have existed previously. More importantly, lines of communication will be opened between superiors and subordinates. Suggestions can be made without the threat of retaliation that so often stands between employees and employers. When workers feel that they make an important contribution to the success of the agency and are rewarded monetarily and with recognition, greater cohesiveness within the organization is likely. This willingness to remain with the agency, despite outside blandishments,

---

3. J. Dewey, *Democracy and Education* (New York: The Macmillan Company, 1966), p. 87.

may also effect worker productivity, creativity, and responsiveness to agency needs.

Organizational objectives can be reached when professionally educated, enthusiastic, reliable, and intelligent people are employed to carry out the functions for which recreational service departments are operated. But even the most aggresive of these individuals can be thwarted and eventually demoralized if there is no outlet for their talents, ideas, and abilities. Most debilitating of all is the continual negating of supportive human relationships as a result of line and staff inflexibility. When professionals are given free reign to put their ingenuity to positive use in the development of creative and satisfying programs, the foundations for better human relations are also laid. Leadership can foster rapport and encourage the kinds of personnel relationships that function and grow in an environment designed to promote association, communication, and a desire to perform at top capacity.

Leadership and Interpersonal Relations

The capacity to be effective in interpersonal relations has become a paramount objective of organizational leaders. By interpersonal relations is meant the entire spectrum of behavior between persons acting reciprocally in situations of informing, working together, modifying attitudes, problem-solving, and persuasion. This involvement with interpersonal relations in various organizations comes at a changing point in social history.

The transitions which social agencies are experiencing have the impact of crisis about them. Their problems are typically derived from the frustrations and fears which are manifested when an individual concludes that he is just an insignificant cog in an impersonal machine. Competent employees may simply quit in resentment against oppressiveness. Of course there is always the possibility of conforming to the demands of those in authority, but automatic conformity, regardless of degree, diminishes the person's faculty to answer as an individual. Whatever his potential may have been, whatever original ideas could have flourished, whatever his selflessness, all is reduced to the extent that hostility exists toward the encouragement of free and useful relationships with others.

In spite of current interest in human interpersonal relations, bureaucratic inertia has interfered with the promotion of free and constructive relationships. Authoritarian or headship relations continue because those in administrative positions are unwilling or unable to dissociate themselves from those values in which they have faith. Administrators' behavior and attitudes tend to reflect the system under which they have been prepared and are, therefore, not in tune with current events. Only if they are able to recognize out-of-date attitudes and conduct can there be any hope for an alteration of conditions.

Individuals may no longer be thought of as instruments of organization. Rather, the organization must be conceived as an instrument for the betterment of society. To serve the needs of people best, the quality of interpersonal relations within the organization must be improved. To this end, each member must develop self-awareness, sensitivity to others and to human conditions, and skill in communication. The initiation of change calls for both empathy and personal commitment.

Communication, Coordination and Modification

Among the interpersonal processes vital to any understanding of the leadership phenomenon are communication, coordination, and modification. Of these, the essential function is communication. All leadership is based upon an idea which one individual attempts to transmit to others. It is the process of transmission — as well as reception — of verbal and symbolic thought, the nuances generated by tone, gesture, stance, and visual impact, which dominates leadership attempts. The unspoken language of manner, emotion, and expression may do much to clarify intent or may completely disrupt the interchange of ideas.

Associated with and contingent upon communication is the union of individuals into a cohesive force. The ability of individuals to pool their resources, subordinate personal goals for group goals, and work together for the common good is the process of coordination. At a time when specialization and division of labor often block integration, there remains the need for widespread sharing of functions if tasks are to be accomplished in the most efficient and effective way. Underlying this need is the human process of interpersonal relationships. The unity of purpose gained through voluntary association can only be developed when each individual clearly understands the benefit to be derived from interdependent activity.

Closely related to and similarly dependent upon the processes of communication and coordination is modification. Modification is understood as the transformation of personal values, outlook, or biases in one or more individuals involved in a relationship. Achieving coordination may require the element of compromise, where each party accepts a modified attitude toward a given person, place, or object. To the extent that emotions lie at the core of most interpersonal relationships, modification will depend upon the degree of involvement and the strength of accord that can be attained. Intensive involvement may demand radical modification. In such an environment significant learning is promoted because antagonistic reactions are reduced, thus enhancing interpersonal insight and emotional support.

Each of the three processes described above has a bearing upon the others. Directed communication is impossible when those to whom the communication is aimed will not make the effort to understand, to combine complementary abilities and information toward a common cause. Unless there is some basis for modification, there cannot be mutually determined understanding. When individuals are unable to set aside hostile points of view or compromise to achieve a desired end, there is no foundation for coordination. Simultaneously, comprehension of the process of communication can eliminate much distortion of meaning and open up avenues of information so that antagonism is minimized and empathy is maximized. Communication may do much to effect cooperative endeavors for combined action; modification can be both outcome and causative agent in the encouragement of communication and coordination.

The Recreationist's Role

The recreationist, who is a professional careerist in the practice of recreational service, is in a field dedicated to the idea that people's lives can be enhanced through provision of and participation in recreational activities. To this end, the recreationist is called upon to give guidance, instruction, direction, and leadership to those individuals and groups which make up the actual and potential clientele which his agency serves. The recreationist may be requested to offer advice on behavioral problems which have no connection with recreational service. He may be asked to give counsel to people who have come to rely upon his professional expertise or problem-solving ability. This is so because he represents an agency which is viewed as part of the governmental establishment. Whether the recreationist participates in the organization and development of recreational service programs for a community or a particular group, or is solicited to act as a mediator between antagonistic groups, he finds many leadership opportunities to be explored: intradepartmental as well as extradepartmental problems; problems in daily living that his community may face.

The Enabling Service

Each person must learn to adjust to his environment from the day of birth; equally he must learn to interact with other people as he grows in his role as student, citizen, and worker. Ways must be found to resolve problems that continually arise in satisfying personal needs and contributing to the social heritage. For some, life will be a rich mosaic of fascinating experiences with needs satisfied, problems solved, and social expectations fulfilled. Others will never achieve the depth of satisfaction nor the peaks of success that might have been theirs, but will learn to cope and find the means for enjoying a relatively balanced life. Many will work out a social equation that meets the requirements which society imposes, but at great personal cost. Those who are unable to meet the minimum expectancies of the social order and cannot fend for themselves endure a pitiful existence and may be potentially dangerous.

Nothing is more terrible than a human life which is wasted. When individuals do not have the ability or the means to achieve the potentialities residing within them, society is the loser as well as the individuals. This tremendous loss of capacity forms one of the contemporary crises that harass society. The thwarted individual, denied once too often, then attempts to strike back at an apparently indifferent society. Combs and others have provided the essential facts for assisting those who need help:

> Even if practical reasons for being concerned about fulfillment of human potential were not valid, we should still be concerned about helping people on purely humanitarian grounds. Frustration and unhappiness is not just a matter of economics. It is a human tragedy and that, in itself, would be reason enough to warrant concern. As a nation we have accepted the "pursuit of happiness" as an important value for our society. Even if we "never made a nickle" from achieving this goal, it would still be worth striving for, both for ourselves, and for our fellow men, simply because life is better that way.[4]

The recreationist is a member of one field concerned about the pursuit of happiness and the welfare of others. The recreationist believes that people have the innate right to choose among many possibilities in fulfilling their potential for the good life. These choices require a sufficient breadth of information to ensure satisfaction. The recreationist offers the kinds of information that will enable people to make intelligent, responsible, and autonomous selections among many tempting, but seldom appropriate, alternatives. It is the primary function of the recreationist to produce an effective climate in which people may enhance their life through recreational participation.

Recreational Service As a Public Function

Recreational experience is universally recognized as one of the basic needs of human living. When such a need has been deemed important to society, government frequently takes steps to see that it is met for the common benefit and welfare of the people. This by no means implies that all recreational activities are governmentally controlled or supervised. It does mean that some organized and informal experiences are carried on under direct supervision, that self-directed activities are also available, and that participation is voluntary.

Public recreational service agencies provide space, facilities, and

---

4. A. W. Combs, D. L. Avila, and W. W. Purkey, *Helping Relationships: Basic Concepts for the Helping Professions* (Boston: Allyn and Bacon, Inc., 1971), p. 2.

professional leadership to organize and administer recreational programs. In this society few people really attain recreation, i.e., a state of effortless, fulfilling experience. A handful realize recreation through their vocation, religion, education, or avocations. Most people are mainly concerned with diverting themselves and escaping from the complex activities of "serious" living.

Recreational Service and the Consistency of Change

A renaissance is needed. The public must be educated to the countless avenues open to them in attaining recreation. Recreational service in these changing times can enhance the learning process by which individuals realize the powerful potential they have for leading more effective recreational lives.

Public recreational activity should supplement and complement individual direction and initiative. The public recreational service should serve in a consulting capacity, exploring new areas and activities which its clientele can utilize in the search for recreation. The future should bring a swing away from continued public supervision toward private or individual exploration of the possible courses open to those seeking recreational experience. Perhaps, in the distant future, all that the public agency will have to offer is the facility and equipment, with a resource person on hand when needed.

Originally, people found whatever recreational experience they desired by private means. Leisure was generally circumscribed and not universal. Later, private philanthropy contributed to some operation of recreational service. During the earliest phase of the recreational service movement, activities for children were emphasized; now all ages can be accommodated within the varied forms of government-sponsored services of this type. Instead of an individual basis of support there now exists complex and organized administrative service on the three levels of government. Cultural factors which have fostered this change include the shift from an agrarian economy of isolated rural families to a technological, industrialized economic base set in an urbanized structure, and the great leaps taken by the physical, biological, and the applied social sciences. All of these have combined to affect the outcome of any recreational experience in which individuals engage.

PREPARATION FOR LEADERSHIP

The effectiveness of the professional recreationist as an enabling agent is based upon an education which is systematic, directed, and appropriate for resolving the problems which the social environment develops. The intellectual application required to achieve certain tasks begins with a professional preparation. But there is more to professional practice than intellectual content and discipline. Professionalism demands sound judgment, personal commitment to the field, and a standard of behavior based upon integrity, ethics, and a sincere concern for people. These are the bases for professional conduct, but they do not reflect the basis for leadership. Leadership is a complex of intellectualization, personality need, and practice. One can *learn* about the phenomenon of leadership; one must *practice* to be a leader.

Leadership can begin with the intellectual content and personal dedication found within the rigorous education of the profession, but leadership is action-oriented and requires fulfillment in doing. Knowledge without practice is futile. Obviously, knowing how something should be done and actually doing it are two different things. We must start with the concept of knowing and thereby produce an individual who has the background for leadership. Whether the individual will become a leader depends upon how he views himself and other factors which tend to elicit a leadership response. Among these factors are personal satisfaction, desire for recognition, an intrinsic need to project oneself, fulfillment from entering into supportive relationships, and a sense of achievement as a problem-solver. Additionally, the times, place, potential followers, or favorable conditions could trigger a leadership response.

The potential recreationist must be exposed to the conceptualizations of his future field and the values and ethics which support it. Without these frames of reference, the service will be less than professional and possibilities of applying leadership theory will be nullified. The education of a future recreationist is developed in terms of knowledge about the field in all of its ramifications, the behaviors of people, problem-solving approaches, decision-making, and the aims of those to whom and for whom he has responsibility. A brief examination of professionalism may be of assistance at this point.

Public Recreational Service and Professionalism

When recreational experience is described in terms of professionalism, the meaning becomes very different from the definition of the nature of recreation. Professionalism in recreational service connotes highly specialized preparation, organization, humanitarian appeal, certification, and general acceptance by society and other professions as a recognized field.

Professional Learning Experiences

Because recreation is a part of human behavior, the recreationist must be steeped in educational functions which enable him to supply positive action in any situation. He should have basic courses in psychology and, when this is mastered, progress to advanced courses in social and educational psychology. Since the basis of all leadership is psychological understanding, the pre-professional must have this knowledge in order to perform his work most effectively.

A basic education in communication is also of prime importance. Such preparation would include course work in self-comprehension, understanding the feelings and needs of others, practical knowledge of the social group situation, public speaking, sources and types of influence within some organizational framework, and sensitivity to others or empathy. There must be some kind of integrated learning process to pull together elements of social psychology, group work, motivational theory, and communicative behavior. Such information provides the student with references as to why, where, and how effective communication can be made operational. Typically, such a course also deals with the methods by which the leader in the field of recreational service employs communication to attain, stabilize, and retain influence with others as he or she practices.

The graduate of a college- or university-level recreational service educational program should have a thorough knowledge of recreational philosophy in concert with modern educational philosophies; what it is, what it means, and a definitive frame of reference for its use. His studies should include a wide association with the liberal arts and humanities, which broaden learning and sensitivity to knowledge. There should be major studies in recreational service as it relates to other organizations of the social order.

Such course content would produce keener insight into the learning processes and develop technical and specialized skills in the transmission of ideas. At its most effective, the program would provide a logical progression of intellectual activities culminating in the practical application of theory to actual field conditions.

THE NEED FOR LEADERSHIP IN RECREATIONAL SERVICE

Everyone who is professionally employed within the field of recreational service must provide some leadership to others, regardless of the capacity in which the individual is employed. Whether it is on the administrative, supervisory, or policy level, the need to work effectively with others while gaining their willing cooperation requires leadership. The development of employee dedication and desire to work in a professional capacity comes in consequence of the openness and faith which characterizes the reciprocity between leader and led. Perhaps Charles K. Brightbill was most acute in his observations when he stated:

Because leisure will impose challenges heretofore unknown to free men, because its impact upon the democratic social fabric can be either a generating influence or a devastating force, and because recreative living requires human perceptions different from the traditional, the finest kind of leadership needed.[5]

The cutting edge of recreational service comes at the program level. Here the client-centered relationships are developed as recreationists attempt to provide guidance, direction, and advice to individuals and groups wishing to participate in recreational offerings. Leadership at the program level has commonly been thought to be the only form of leadership available. That this is patently wrong is illustrated by the complex interrelationships which occur within and outside of a department. Influence is felt whenever there are collections of people who appear to have some common interests and desire to work together for some perceived goal, but it is also concerned with individuals and groups who have a dimly perceived goal, unsatisfied needs, and an inability either to articulate their feelings or contrive some vehicle through which they may attain partial or complete satisfaction.

Leadership may therefore be observed as a vital function at all levels of work within the field: specific recreational concerns that deal with any of the program categories; the gathering of individuals who have no aims and simply want the security of a group; employee dissatisfaction at the conformity imposed by bureaucratic measures; frustration with *status quo;* or the purposive involvement of a professional who is trying to resolve certain problems occurring among his peers. However it is manifested, leadership is a primary requisite of recreationists.

The development of the recreationist (leader) is a matter of self-discovery. Learning to use one's resources cannot be gained from books, rather it is a question of personal insight and perception. There is something of an existential aspect to the development of the leader because it is a process of becoming. While this is not the *only* orientation from which leadership can develop, it does provide a conceptual basis for understanding the process of leadership. The philosophical origin of the phenomenological view of man is expressly demonstrated in contemporary existentialism.[6]

The existentialist looks upon man as responsible for his existence and development. As he is and how he realizes his potential is placed upon the person's own shoulders. This view sets man and his environment together and examines what the individual can do to gain relevancy in his life. It asks what reality is and what the individual can do, for himself, in effecting a

---

5. C. K. Brightbill, *Man and Leisure* (Englewood Cliffs, N. J.: Prentice-Hall, Inc., 1961), p. 281.
6. R. May, "Existential Psychology," in T. Millon, ed., *Theories of Psychopathology and Personality,* 2d ed. (Philadelphia: W. B. Saunders Company, 1973), pp. 200-201.

more significant and enjoyable experience. To this positive search for meaning, what is is not judged *a priori,* but realistically by timely criteria that are required to *be* and to *become* in an accountable and need-fulfilling manner. Because man is capable of seeing himself as an indivisible and particular part of his experience, he has the ability to make choices, i.e., decision-making and taking action. The given situation may restrict his choices, but environment cannot explain behavior. As a goal-striving personality, an individual will always make choices designed to offer self-actualization or otherwise contribute to the enrichment of his potentialities.

The *becoming* quality of life is based upon the potential leader's own system of beliefs and personal meaning. Some of the beliefs that combine to fashion a recreationist are so personal that information from sources other than the self would be puerile. Other beliefs necessitate interaction and confrontation with ideas of an extra-personal nature.

Approaches to the Task of Professionalizing Recreational Leadership

Potential recreationists must be selected on the basis of outgoing personality and concern for others. The recreationist must view his role as one of enabling others to achieve. Commitment to the idea that interaction is the raw stuff of self-actualizing is fundamental, as is the lack of ulterior motives and a humanitarian approach.

A new conception of recreational service as a field of activity and as a possible profession has appeared. It is apparent that recreational service requires persons of superior quality, tact, and preparation. There is also an immediate need for an organization which could stand as a "watchdog" agency for employment practices. Such an organization would be in a position to make sure that all positions calling for recreationists are filled with professionals.

Recreational service, like education, is too important an area of public concern to be in the hands of those who mean well but who cannot perform well. Care must taken that the field is not inundated by mediocrities. If an organization existed which could systematize field problems, ethical standards and codes, professional qualifications, research and technical studies, there is a chance that the field of recreational service would attain professional status, a goal not yet achieved although practitioners aspire to professionalism.

Several things must be acquired if the field is to become a fully qualifed profession in the eyes of society and the other accepted professions:

1. There must be a powerful professional organization which will control applications into the field by the initiation of high standards for entrance and practice, and which will perform other functions to maintain the public's awareness of the field.

2. Recreational service, as a field, needs to attain an economic and community standing of such quality that it will attract people of ability.

3. There must be a specialized education based on foundations of western philosophy and the social, natural, and physical sciences for better understanding of human abilities and learning.

4. A system of valid testing will have to be constructed to appraise the ethical behavior of potential candidates for admission into the field at any time they enter upon their professional learning experience.

5. There must be limited accessibility into the field through a system of board examinations given by recreationists to applicants after they have graduated from accredited institutions. The entire aspect of state reciprocity and national recognition must be worked out in great detail before the machinery called for can be set in motion.

6. There will have to be established an ethical-practices code to which all practitioners must adhere.

7. There must be some centralized governmental authority, preferably on the state level, to certify and license recreationists and to enact legislation that will help the field carry out its functions economically, effectively, efficiently, and in accord with well-conceived ethical-practice codes.

The Leadership Impact

What is the effect of leadership upon the individual in the organization? Leadership actually defines individual growth and development of followers and often is the unique factor which determines whether or not a worker will be retained by the department rather than deciding to seek employment elsewhere. In any group or organizational situation there is a tendency for some hierarchy to be initiated. In every organizational milieu there is a constant process of appraisal by which the individual's ability — functional performance and social interaction — is gauged. Within the hierarchy, the leader is recognized as an eligible guide and initiator to the group or organizational member. Hence, the leader becomes one more connection in a line of authority figures on which almost all individuals depend throughout their lives. Many authority figures constrain individual choice by exercising their influence through the position they hold; others narrow possible alternatives through the imposition of wealth or shrewd maneuvers. Leaders open up choices while focusing efforts on specific goals. In this they succeed either by their superior intellect, ability to meet situational exigencies, personal insight, and empathy, or in consequence of group processes.

The adroit leader represents to followers a quality of consistency and consideration. His values are mirrored in ethical behavior and he projects a charisma which implants an unshakable faith in his inevitable success.

More important is the followers' perception that their interest lies with the leader's interest. The leader is the personification of the group aggregate. The leader, therefore, determines the direction for the organization to follow and his conduct will become the standard emulated by others. It is in this way that the leader's values become the values of the group.

CHAPTER THREE

The Interpersonal Life

In almost all group situations, individuals consume much time determining what others are really like. Most people want to know the motivations which influence behavior and how accurately they judge them in others. Nearly everybody is content to reveal snatches of themselves to a select few, but most are wary of exposing their innermost feelings except to a cherished confidant. Since we exist within a social context which requires submersion of the subjective aspect of human relations, our understanding of self is played down. However, it is recognized that whatever motivates human behavior is important because it provides the knowledge necessary to anticipate human responses to environmental stimuli.

Some persons, particularly those who have executive positions within organizations, hold the belief that human motives are unintelligible and that individual behavior can best be analyzed and directed by externalities, i.e., tangible rewards and observable reactions. They think of people as objects, magnifying conformity and having little regard for individual constancy and uniformity in personality under changing conditions. They believe in directing the personal and societal behavior of those they can influence, and thus, in conditioning these individuals' responses to biological urges or to such extra-personal impositions as customs, codes, domination, and regulations. Conversely, there are those who think of people as deterministic, i.e., motivated chiefly through the comprehensions, analyses, and drives derived from intellect. They are occupied with the consistencies in a person's behavior and understand its regulation as a responsibility of individual will and personal ethics.

Probably, the truth lies somewhere in between. If people only respond to externalities, there is no logical explanation for individual uniqueness and imaginative contributions. If, however, man is thought of as arbiter, there is no explanation for his gregarious nature, which requires the cooperation of others. In order to understand human nature, one must think of individuals in terms of such environmental influences as the culturally specified roles that one plays, or the hidden factors of mind and personality — how the individual sees, idealizes, and understands himself — which also supply regulatory influences on behavior. In determining behavior, all of the forces which impinge upon it must be revealed: environmental situations; subjective motivations; and, particularly, interpersonal relationships.

LEADERSHIP AND HUMAN BEHAVIOR

In order to examine leadership, it is important to appreciate the complexity of the human personality and to understand something of the process governing each individual's subjective responses to others, both individually and in groups. How much of a person's "inner self" is exposed to others varies markedly from person to person; some people seem to share their emotional responses easily while others are virtually incapable of expressing their deepest feelings. Yet each person's "hidden" or subjective self exerts an enormous influence on his behavior with regard to other people. A leader must appreciate the role of the subjective self as it motivates behavior and influences the individual's interpersonal life.

The Self-Concept

The emergence of self which profoundly affects behavior develops as a result of interpersonal interaction. The self-concept, or the image the individual holds of himself, is based upon continuous interaction with others. Throughout life, most normal people are concerned with what others think about them and actively seek approval from others. During the process of growth from childhood to adulthood, the individual constructs an image or perception of conduct that calls forth approval and affection. This image exerts a regulatory influence on the person as he develops his own distinctive identity and the system of values and convictions by which he assesses himself as well as others.

Once developed, a person's self-concept is the unifying factor in his personality, bringing together his inner self — the self known only to him — and his external self that he shows to others. As the individual moves through life, he adopts those values, ideologies, and experiences which appear relevant to his self-concept and either repudiates or modifies those that do not. Occasionally, however, a situation arises which threatens the individual's self-esteem. The resulting anxiety causes him to protect his inner self; he may adopt any one of a number of defensive positions which will affect his behavior accordingly.

In certain instances we may believe that we are not able to control particular impulses, the performance of which lead only to pain, punishment, or rejection. Or we may undergo dissonant experiences that fill us with mental dread.[1] Examine the following statement, as an example:

---

1. G. A. Vlett, *A Synopsis of Contemporary Psychiatry,* 5th ed. (St. Louis, Mo.: The C. V. Mosby Company, 1972), pp. 71-74.

I am at odds with certain thoughts that I have about my appraisal of certain others. I am incapable of accepting and supporting feelings as I experience them. They make me apprehensive, and if I cannot contend with them insofar as their actual nature is concerned I will be unable to control myself. Unaware of this, I look for a scapegoat. Rather than face the torment of guilt feelings, I seek a safe object for blame. It is possible that my feelings are so intense that I simply withdraw, disengaging myself from reality by fantasizing, regressing, or other acts of defense.

In this way we can hide behind a barrier of our own making where we neither reveal ourselves nor allow others to appreciate our real selves. Nevertheless, there is a part of us which always knows who we are, what we are, and has a realistic appreciation of us. This contrasting behavior is self-defensive; it assists in banishing painful experiences to the subconscious while we luxuriate in and reflect relative security in the conscious state.

While the defense mechanism helps to make life satisfactory and offers a form of constancy in our relationship with others, it may also encourage a tendency toward closed-off thinking by narrowing possible choices which might produce greater insight and comprehension for our own benefit. When we hide behind a facade of our own making, we are erecting protective devices that are also barriers to self-understanding. It is unlikely that we will recognize personal deficiencies and be able to alter them. From our defensive posture we display differential behavior — adjusted to the event and reaping commendation — as we confront other individuals in the social milieu. The problem is that the two facets of our selves have different dimensions and, yet, overlap.

Actually, we are many things because of our attempts to modify our behavior as we deal with others in the various social settings we encounter. We become the expression of many subjective and objective selves. With each transference, patterns of behavior and alterations in our image are induced. At any moment these various selves provide us with those qualities that give us identity.

The Inner Self

Our subjective self is what we think we are and hope to be. It includes all the desires, hopes, and idealistic dreams that we want for ourselves. It is the self that we know best, and which we protect most of all. Some psychologists assert that the one basic need of man is to preserve this self-image, and that all behavior may be explained and even predicted in the light of the individual's desire to maintain it. The one basic human need is the urge for self-esteem. All other so-called needs or drives are in reality subservient to this one:

From birth to death the defense of the phenomenal self is the most pressing, most crucial, if not the only task of existence. Moreover, since human beings are conscious of the future, their needs extend into the future as well, and they strive to preserve not only the self as it exists but to build it up and strengthen it against the future of which they are aware. We might combine these two aspects in a formal definition of the basic human need as: the preservation and enhancement of the phenomenal self.[2]

Thus, a person's interpersonal behavior may reflect his struggle to protect his inner self. It is through conformity that we tend to find security and sustain our balance. We are what we are because we are afraid to be what we would like to be. We have, therefore, come to employ defense mechanisms. The problem is that although these exercises do guard us from emotional failure, we can never really comprehend who or what we are if we cannot free ourselves from these maneuvers. At the worst, they can eventuate in the ultimate destruction of the self. Some (though not all) of these mechanisms, which are important and identifiable behavioral forms, are withdrawal, sublimation, direct aggression, indirect aggression, suppression, repression, fantasy, and rationalization.

Withdrawal. Withdrawal is the immediate method by which the individual seeks to remove himself from stress or difficulty. It is probably the least painful procedure for the ego. All that is required is cessation of whatever activity is being undertaken. Of course, withdrawing from any situation where mastery is impossible is the sensible thing to do. However, simple frustration should not lead to withdrawal if there is the probability or possibility that the individual may succeed. Withdrawal leaves one with a sense of inadequacy and defeat.[3]

An example of this behavior may be seen in the failure of an elementary-school-age child to perform some physical feat requiring muscular strength and coordination beyond his years. The individual, lacking readiness to function in a specific act, should withdraw, not irrevocably from all physical activity, but into some other activity where his physiological development is consistent with the required action.

Sublimation. Sublimation is a directing of hostile or aggressive impulses into acceptable lines of behavior, as in the case of a musician who works out his anger by playing rather than striking out at someone. Sublimation may also be a realization of socially acceptable desires by indirect means, as in the case of a childless woman who takes up teaching. As Mikesell has

---

2. D. Snygg and A. W. Combs, *Individual Behavior* (New York: Harper, 1949), p. 58.
3. E. Rosen, R. E. Fox, and I. Gregory, *Abnormal Psychology,* 2d ed. (Philadelphia: W. B. Saunders Company, 1972), pp. 60-61.

stated:

> The individual with a love of art need not fold his hands in abject worry when he sees that the lack of means might not enable him to educate himself in the skill of an artist. He should plan to sublimate in case of actual disappointment in art training by forming study clubs of art, becoming an art critic, or having a splendid library of art books. With an insight into sublimation, a man who sees that his wishes for a college education might not be realized could eventually plan to give vent to his ambition by becoming an expert in some particular line of thought.[4]

Direct Aggression. Direct aggression or discharge is an outburst of hostile behavior which completely disrupts a preconceived action from reaching an objective. It is generally called "loss of temper" and may be seen in such loss of control as inability to speak or function coherently. In children, or those who are considered emotionally immature, the tantrum is a way for the individual to relieve himself of frustrating conditions. The playground is a good place for viewing direct aggression. The child who does not get his own way in game activities or who picks up his ball and quits the field when a decision goes against him, thereby spoiling the game for everyone else, shows temper and direct aggression.

Direct aggression as a method of retaliation after frustration may be seen in this example from the record of the Tenth Street Dragons, a preadolescent boys' club operating within a fictitious recreational center in New York City:

> Tommy was the acknowledged leader of the group. To this worker, Tommy was an indigenous leader of an autocratic type. Perhaps he came to power because of his pugnacity and physical ability. There were nine boys in the original club. Harrry was an original member of the club, but he also had leadership aspirations. He was successful in alienating three members from Tommy's sphere. In any team game Harry always chose his three cohorts first. Finally he was successful in bringing two other boys into the club as members of his clique. There was continual disagreement betwen the two boys.
>
> During a game in which the contestants hop toward each other in an attempt to bump the opponent off balance, Tommy simply charged into Harry and knocked him sprawling. Harry wasn't able to get up for a while, and, when he did, he left the center. A few days later he came to the worker to say that he was leaving the club. Tommy's attack had embarrassed him to the extent that he was not able to face the group.

4.W. H. Mikesell, *Mental Hygiene* (New York: Prentice-Hall, 1939), p. 328. Reprinted by permission.

In this instance it is easy to understand Tommy's behavior. He was not able to cope with a situation where he would lose his leadership status, and he thus took the most direct steps to eliminate his opposition. His open hostility and physical attack overwhelmed and cowed his antagonist to the point of withdrawal.[5]

Indirect Aggression. Indirect aggression is a well-understood form of action. Whenever the individual may not be able to "blow off steam" from pent-up emotional stress for fear of retaliation, he must discover safe objects or persons against whom he can express his aggressiveness, although they will have had nothing to do with his frustration or state of stress.[6] Thus, in the child's pecking order, it is usually someone weaker who is attacked in order that the attacker's frustration or annoyance be compensated.

It is considered a criminal offense for adults to assault anyone, regardless of wrongs, particularly of a verbal nature, which have been inflicted. At the very least, physical violence is boorish vengeance for an insult or for loss of face or property. The adult, therefore, has conceived of the indirect assault which compensates for feelings of frustration and hostility which may not be discharged directly.

Satire, sarcasm, innuendo, or aspersion, or the questioning of customs, codes, or authority are the usual forms of indirect aggression. Well-known phrases, used to describe an antagonist or indict a society, have been created because of the frustrations and tensions to which the author was subjected. Zola's courageous "J'accuse" condemned a bigoted France; FDR's use of an oath from Romeo and Juliet, "A plague on both your houses," found outlet against warring union factions; Bevin's "that desiccated calculating machine" ridiculed Hugh Gaitskell. All of these epithets can be assumed to have been derived as compensations for their author's inability or disinclination to use direct physical force as the method to relieve his hostility.

The recreationist must be able to understand individual use of behaviors which are manifested in overt or indirect aggression. He must realize when such behaviors represent rational and irrational resolution. The individual who adjusts to group living, and its attendant frustrations, with conduct disproportionate to any thwarting he has suffered, indicates this indirectness. Indirect aggression satisfies a peculiar need in the individual who utilizes it. The recreationist, understanding why the individual acts the way he does, is better able to counsel, condone, or negate such activity.

---

5. T. Millon, *Modern Psychopathology* (Philadelphia: W. B. Saunders Company, 1969), pp. 273-274.
6. J. Dollard, "Hospitality and Fear in Social Life," *Social Forces,* Vol. 17 (1938), pp. 15-25.

Suppression. Suppression may be defined simply as hidden feelings. When the individual has experienced some highly emotional provocation but cannot, because of social convention, conveniently discharge or express himself, he suppresses that emotion.[7] Many individuals cannot express themselves because they are fearful of convention, painfully shy, or so completely maladjusted to their social environment that any attempt at expression may destroy their self-concept. The person who is usually the butt of all jokes, who is "put upon" by other, more aggressive individuals, but will not make any defense, suppresses emotional hostilities because he cannot do anything else.

Tension resulting from this inability to release frustration or resentment gradually builds up to a point where the individual may be unable to handle it, and some collapse may occur. At best, suppression is a method of escape from uncomfortable or untenable positions and in its mildest form, is exhibited by the overcautious person who is cautious, not because of his lack of knowledge in the particular situation, but because of any possible criticism which may accrue from replies or actions taken. The overcautious person never does things on impulse. In the main, he is steady, conservative, and perhaps successful, but he is usually rigid in terms of personality and thinking.

The recreationist recognizes that the method of suppression is one frequently utilized by people attempting to adjust to group mores and traditions. However, he attempts to encourage self-expression, particularly emotional expression, by recreational activities, as long as such expression is not belligerent and does not interfere with group interaction.

Repression. Repression is suppression in its most extreme form, with the added factor of non-awareness of the behavior. Thus, the individual denies to himself any thought or action which he actually had or did, as though it had never existed. The individual is so horrified by his thoughts or acts that he strives to forget their occurrence by telling himself that they never happened. Repression derives from feelings of guilt or shame resulting from conflicts between ideas and ideals.[8]

The most negative aspect of repression is that the feelings of shame and stress remain within the individual and perhaps increase in time. There is no acknowledgment of the cause of tension because the individual tends to forget specific attitudes. Having repressed a fearful thought, the individual may deny that he ever had that thought, particularly if the thought

---

7. L.W. Doob and R.R. Sears, "Factors Determining Substitute Behavior and Overt Expression of Aggression," *Journal of Abnormal and Social Psychology,* Vol. 34 (1939), pp. 293-313.

8. R. H. Price, *Abnormal Behavior Perspectives in Conflict* (New York: Holt, Rinehart and Winston, Inc., 1972), pp. 40-41.

represents something which he considers sinful or at fault. Since the thought is repressed, he will have to live within a frame of reference which consistently places him in contact with the fear from which he is trying to withdraw. In refusing to confirm what he fears, he continually undermines himself and exposes himself to excessive strain.

The recreationist is in no position to treat or even to diagnose repression in any individual. He will, however, begin to understand individual behavior within group structure as he notices patterns of conduct emerging from daily experience with the person. Only where there is long-term association will such suspicions be identifiable, but there is little likelihood that that can occur unless there is an overt expression from the subject.

With the exception of those recreationists who actually work in therapeutic situations, long-term association with any individual on a professional basis is extremely rare and may even be nonexistent. While knowledge of human behavior and its causes is extremely important for better communication, its application remains academic. Nevertheless, from the standpoint of mental hygiene, such knowledge is worthwhile if only to make the recreationist aware that such anomalies exist in human personality.

Fantasy. Fantasy is one outlet for suppressed feelings. The individual who finds himself inadequate in some activity in which he would like to participate makes up for his deficiencies by daydreaming about them. In his dreams he becomes the champion, hero, great scholar, or other outstanding character with all the skills and abilities which he does not in fact possess.[9]

Fantasy, or the projection of wishes, is not harmful in itself. Wishes may actually serve as the stimulus for later action. When fantasy draws the individual away from contact with reality to the extent that daydreaming becomes the entire focus of attention, the cycle of removal is complete. The individual who spends his time in fantasy removes himself from the immediate problem or frustration which confronts him. He also postpones the time when he must face up to the problem. In its extreme form, the individual loses contact with reality and substitutes his dreams for what is actually occurring. Unable to distinguish between what is real and what is wish, the individual travels a dark road of mental illness.

Illustrative of this need to attain satisfaction may be seen in the following hypothetical situation:

> Danny, a fourteen-year-old, was a member of the Greatful Dead, a street gang in X city. He was not particularly robust or bright, but his

9. G. W. Fisher, *The Disorganized Personality,* 2d ed. (New York: McGraw-Hill, 1972), pp. 147-149.

older brother had been a member of the gang, and so he had been accepted. His activities were mainly those of the follower. He went blindly with the group. He was never able to hold his own with any member of the gang in any activity. A rival gang had invaded the "turf" of the Greatful Dead, and a "rumble" or fight was scheduled. Danny was not aggressively minded and had been a fringe participator in previous clashes with other groups. When the two antagonists met, Danny held back, merely watching. After the fight, with some members on either side getting hurt, some of the Greatful Dead questioned Danny about not taking part. Danny was very vague in his replies but finally came out with the story that he had been in the middle of the fight, had beaten one of the opposing gang members, and had, in fact, done more than any other member to rout the opponents. He continued to expound this story, although everyone knew it to be untrue. It was assumed by this recreationist that he actually believed what he said.

From the above, it can readily be understood that the adjustment to the group situation was simply too much for Danny to handle. As conflict, tension, and thwarting increased, he became incapable of coping with his own inadequacies in the group. As a result, his break with reality came when he could no longer carry the burden of stress to which he was subjected. He saw himself as he wanted to be in real life and wove a story around the fiction of his wish. In this fantasy he gave himself the opportunity to become heroic, to gain status, to glorify himself. This dream proved so satisfying and compelling that he substituted it for the facts in the case. Although the recreationist was not present at the time of the gang fight, word reached him concerning Danny's behavior. He was successful in persuading Danny's mother to let the boy see the school psychologist for examination. After the referral, Danny was placed in the municipal diagnostic clinic for observation and was found to have developed marked schizoid symptoms of the paranoid type.

Rationalization. Rationalization is escape from thwarting by redefining the situation which gave rise to the frustrations in such a way that the individual's needs are satisfied without further action. It is a special form of daydreaming that is quite overt and may be verbalized to reinforce the reinterpretation.[10]

An individual frequently resorts to rationalization in order to adjust to some situation: a lowering of aspirations if goals are set too high; an instance of "sour grapes," where failure is excused on the grounds that "I really did not want it anyway." The individual who fails to achieve some

---

10.   L. A. Pervin, *Personality: Theory, Assessment, and Research* (New York: John Wiley and Sons, Inc., 1970), p. 233.

object may rationalize his failure in order to conceal from himself and others the real reasons, which may be considered shameful, weak, or inferior.

This may be seen in the racial prejudice which is found everywhere. Blacks may be denied equal opportunity or service because they are considered inferior by Caucasians. The following illustration is indicative of such bigotry:

> Mr. K is resentful of blacks. The basis for this bias stems from one occasion when a black worker was granted a position which K thought he should have received. Mr. K realizes that the black happened to know more about the work than he did and does not represent all of the blacks in the world. Nevertheless, K experienced such frustration at the denial of the job in favor of this member of a minority race that he was not able to recognize the facts. He has therefore adjusted to this emotional strain by rationalizing his complete rejection of blacks in a way that justifies his stand. He claims that all blacks are potential miscegenists, and he is thus protecting the purity of all white women from sexual attack. In this way, K defends his self-concept. First he placates his original frustration at losing a position; second, he presents what he thinks is a more acceptable argument than mere jealousy.

Each of the foregoing mechanisms the individual uses to adjust to group living situations and protect the self must be understood if the leader is to deal with them. All of these aspects of interpersonal behavior are encountered over and over again in every conceivable social condition. Only when these compensatory behaviors are recognized will a leader be able to guide individuals within a group to grow in self-awareness and function smoothly as a part of the group. The leader can assist individuals in achieving success, thereby reducing frustration and creating an adjustment that is mutually satisfying to the group and the individual.

On the positive side, the inner self can perform the task of maintaining the individual's real, not neurotic, identity as it interposes itself between him and the process which neatly attempts to gain conformity to mores. Where the inner self is not submerged or threatened by an individual's association with others, it appears as individuality, the manifestations of one's uniqueness in contrast to the beliefs, biases, and values which we hold in common with others. The inner self enables the individual to cope; it is the mechanism by which a person learns to adapt to and exist cooperatively with others in society as he attempts to attain the maximum development of his own personality and abilities.

The External Self

How we appear to others and how we think we appear to others are manifestations of the external self. A person is capable of painting several different self-portraits for the benefit of particular relationships with others. Indeed, people could produce a complex array of social images if they were not regulated by common values. A person's conformity to commonly held values is vital to group life if social efficiency is a valued goal. The external self recognizes the expectations others have for one's social and psychological behavior. It is the external self, for example, which allows leaders to empathize with followers and thus see themselves as others see them; this ability enables them to comprehend the impact of their actions as they are experienced by others.

The potential for variety in the presentation of the external self is always present, and deviations from the expected have an important influence on the ways in which a person relates to others. Fortunately, one's concept of how he thinks others see him and how they really see him can, and do, generally coincide. Sometimes, however, these images are so dichotomous that there is no commonality whatsoever. To the extent that the view of how others perceive us and how they actually perceive us is congruent, we can achieve greater communicability between ourselves and others. As communication increases, so the achievement of durable social goals increases. The hazard to the individual who conforms completely with social mores is that uniqueness may be lost; to the individual who conforms not at all, contact with reality may be lost. The total self, then, is formed by these two interdependent yet dissimilar components. The degree to which an individual will be able to integrate these components and develop a personality, or self-awareness, is dependent upon relationships with other people. Only through association with others is personal growth possible.

COMMUNICATION, INTERPERSONAL RELATIONSHIPS, AND LEADERSHIP

Self-awareness is a product of interpersonal relationships; without the latter, selfhood could probably never develop. The education philosopher, Philip Phenix, renders this explanation for interpersonal relationships:

Human personality can develop only through association with other persons; there can be no personal growth in isolation. It is not merely that other human beings constitute a favorable environment, giving protection, enjoyment, and instruction. They play a more fundamental role than that. Other people are essential because the relationships the growing person has with them are actually constitutive of the self. A person is not a self-contained entity which happens to be related to other persons. The relationships enter into the very being and essence of the personality. A self is not a thing-in-itself but always and necessarily a person-in-relationship. This does not mean that when no overt interaction is occurring betwen persons, selfhood disappears. The constructive role of the interpersonal simply means that the self, whether alone or in company, is what it is largely by virtue of the encounters experienced with other persons. There would be no self had solitude been the only experience.[11]

The self reveals itself as we contact others and interact with those who assume some significance in our lives. Our chief method for gaining such association is through the communication process.

The Significance of Communication

Communication is basic to human life and association. It is probably valid to state that without communication there would be no human beings as we now interpret the phrase. There would, most likely, have been no human communities without communication. Communities and association have developed only as wants and needs were expressed by commonly understood sounds. Without the cooperation that is necessary for human communities to become organized, interpersonal relationships could never be formed. Effective leadership is achieved when another person's cooperation in accomplishing a specific objective is obtained through the process of communication.

For the moment, let us consider communication as a process and how it affects interpersonal relationships from which leadership may derive. The process of communication cannot be readily understood until language comprehension is attained. Language is the essential form of human communication. If language were nonexistent, there could be no remembrance of the past nor conjecture about the possibilities of the future. Without language, the range of man's universe would be completely minimized. Beyond its definitive function of directing one's attention to a person, place, thing, or idea, language promotes the formation of ideas about things, their qualities and properties. Language permits abstraction, revealing a universe which is superior to personal experience. If we had to depend upon personal experience for knowledge, we would be limited indeed. Abstraction allows learning about things, people, and places which we will only experience vicariously. We begin to know as we verbalize: "Man, the talking animal, not only talks but he talks about talking."[12]

Language is necessary to the formation of interpersonal relationships and, by extension, of groups. The group's aims, standards, expectations, and attitudes are directly related to shared communication. Language is

---

11. P. H. Phenix, *Philosophy of Education* (New York: Henry Holt and Company, 1958), pp. 193-194.
12. M. L. DeFleur and O. N. Larsen, *The Flow of Information* (New York: Harper and Brothers, 1958), p. 31.

the instrument by which groups may be formed and maintained. Initially, language creates role relationships which may be viewed as status molding. How one person addresses another assists in defining relationships.[13] Secondly, language opens the way to group acceptability and accessibility. Unless the individual uses the terminology (jargon) of the group, which has a tendency to reassure, support, and indicate common attitudes and values, the individual seeking membership may be rejected.

Of course, there is unspoken as well as verbalized language. It is a speech of gestures, facial expressions, physical symbols, and signs. All of these constitute a quite distinct language which transmits information as effectively, if more subtly, than does speech. Because the very essence of social existence is founded in the communication process, both verbal and symbolic, the art of communication assumes major proportions in the development of interpersonal relationships and the possibility of emergent leadership. A great deal can be learned about group adhesion from attention to the language and communication pathways utilized by the members. It is equally important to understand that both social reality and group viscidity can be altered by language.

Personal Involvement

If leadership is the gaining of cooperation from another, then communication is certainly the indispensable way in which it is elicited. Communication proceeds on several planes. One plane, perhaps the simplest, is the transmission of information between persons without any emotional exchange whatsoever. This may best be exemplified by a passenger asking a bus driver about advantageous stopping points closest to his destination. It may be observed as a professor provides some historical or scientific fact to a class. Such transfers of data should not evoke emotion and therefore are accepted easily in response to generalized needs for information. If there is a language barrier, however, all communication stops, becomes frustrated, and may terminate in hurt feelings or reinforced stereotypes.

A second level of communication might be explained in terms of mutual dependencies, such as those which typically occur in organizational contexts. On this plane, associations between superiors and subordinates may involve relational problems concerning norms, judgments, opinions, and attitudes. These can be reduced by the expectations of each party about the behavior of the other. If status-casting differences are confirmed and accepted, and value variations and rewards are in agreement with these differences, then communication and its outcome — cooperation — can

---

13. D. M. Schneider and G. C. Homans, "Kinship Terminology and the American Kinships System," *American Anthropologist,* Vol. 57 (1955), pp. 1194-1208.

occur without too great an expediture of effort.

The most complicated level of communication is that which involves interpersonal relations. Here strong emotional ties become significant. The consequences of an encounter may produce results ranging from complete harmony and accord to outright distrust, hostility, misunderstanding, and aggression. In the former, the self-appreciation systems and relevant values of the parties concerned are consonant and reciprocally supportive. In the latter, the inability to communicate results in a threat to these systems either of both or one of the individuals involved.

In the complex of human communication all three levels may be operating simultaneously. When this happens the course of understanding between individuals is precarious. What is said by one person to another may conceal true meaning or suppress experiences which seem threatening. Twisted meanings may occur, the explanations of which cannot be consciously perceived by the individual. What is received by the other party may or may not be consistent with reality. When this happens, there is a denial of truth or little truth to be shared.

Leadership and Communication

Happily, this state of distrust or anxiety is not general and can be rectified. The act of communicating meaningfully is so necessary in carrying on the normal course of human endeavors that the process must be facilitated. Here the art of leadership comes into play. How the communication process can be improved and how self-systems and empathy are connected to communication are questions which will now be addressed.

Communications Concepts

Communication begins with a source. Where a message originates and how effective the transmission will be depend upon the credibility of the sender. The quality of the source is not always significant, but the credibility of information is augmented if there are compatible records from other sources. On the other hand, it is suspect if inconsistencies develop. Successful transmission is secured by easy access to communication networks.

The substance of the transmitted information also plays an important role by its effect on the receiver. Messages can be biased by reporting only one point of view, by distorting meanings through connotative word usage, or by lying. An associated aspect of slanted information deals with the effect of anxiety-provoking messages. One study suggests that strong fear statements have a diminished effect upon the listener more than do moderate ones.[14] Messages which reach a conclusion or press home a

---

14. I. F. Janis and S. Fleshbach, "Effects of Fear-Arousing Communications," *Journal of Abnormal and Social Psychology,* Vol. 48 (1953), pp. 78-92.

particular point of view seem to be more acceptable than those which place the burden of drawing conclusions upon the receiver. Repetition of content appears to be most effective with those who have not had broad exposure to prolonged education or those without great mental ability because of the opportunity to appeal to the lowest common denominator.

Directed thought is one of the more effective devices for gaining influence. This method employs existing wants, attitudes, and values instead of establishing new ones. It is easier to exploit something with which an individual already identifies than to have to build a case for an unfamiliar value. Thus, if an individual sees himself in the role of conservationist, it is relatively simple to involve that person in a cause which espouses environmental protection. This, in turn, may lead to further participation in activities dealing with mass transportation, the restriction of nuclear power plant construction, offshore oil drilling operations, use of pesticides, abolition of the federal Highway Trust Fund, or to the passage of legislation affecting the use of private property. Depending upon the person's original sense of values and degree of concern, influence may be achieved in terms of coidentification.

Bales' investigations into the implications of communication deal with informative or tension-releasing communication.[15] According to him, interpersonal communication is intimately bound up with a homeostatic process. It appears to be composed of alternating informational efforts which create tensions between group members and tension-releasing communication which alleviates the stress. It is probable that the relative balance between these facets of communication is significant for persuasiveness. As with mechanical systems, the behavior of a person occupied with interpersonal communication influences and is influenced in turn by the behavior of others. When individuals interact, communication occurs against a mutual background of interchanged information in which reciprocal feedback is continuous.[16]

Interpersonal Communications

Communication is related to almost every side of social existence. One's attitudes and values are group oriented. An individual is usually not receptive to communication which diverges from the norms of his group. Messages are transmitted in the group by the group's opinion leaders. When communication is a component of the leadership structure, the flow is not from source to receiver, but from sender to an intermediary (opinion

15. R. F. Bales, "The Equilibrium Problem in Small Groups," in T. Parsons, R. F. Bales, and E A. Shils, eds., *Working Papers in the Theory of Action* (Glencoe, Ill.: The Free Press, 1953), pp. 111-116.
16. M. Argyle and J. Dean, "Eye-Contact, Distance, and Affiliation," *Sociometry*, Vol. 28 (1965), pp. 289-304.

leader), who then passes it on to the receiver. Opinion leaders serve as evaluators, determining what messages will be transmitted and analyzing the content for interpretation as they send it along.[17]

Human communication is a reciprocal process which depends upon the language of speech and symbol for interpretation, intensification, and clarification. In human communication, information which is returned to the organism so that adjustments can be made to maintain a steady state (negative feedback) is employed to ensure continuity in interpersonal relationships. On the other hand, positive feedback demands modification and interrupts equilibrium with the environment. This is true for the individual as well as for the group. For example, there are several states of group change which have been commented upon by Lewin and others. There is a steady state where no change is noticeable. This is seen as a balance between positive and negative arguments or influences. Equilibrium can be altered either by employing pressure in the required direction, or by reducing opposing arguments. In the first instance, the new state would be attended by stress. In the latter case:

> If the resistence to change depends partly on the value which the group standard has for the individual, the resistence to change should diminish if one diminishes the strength of the value of the group standard or changes the level perceived by the individual as having social value. It is usually easier to change individuals formed into a group than to change any one of them separately.[18]

In relation to any aspect of human communication neither positive nor negative feedback is harmful. Each serves a specific function which is determined by the given situation. Thus, negative feedback is necessary when stability is required and positive feedback has value when modification of behavior is needed. However, when either form of feedback operates to the exclusion of the other or persists unabated, then potential disorganization is likely and growth and development cannot take place.

Change within the individual, a group, or an organization comes from acquiring new ideas, outlooks, responses, and behaviors in relation to other people, places, things, and situations. This learning is based upon the individual's intellectual ability and interest, and overcoming those barriers to learning erected by healthy skepticism or a lack of self-acceptance as illustrated by defense mechanisms. To be effective, learning in

17. E. Katz and P. Lazarsfeld, *Personal Influence* (Glencoe, Ill.: Free Press, 1955), p. 45.
18. K. Lewin, "Group Decision and Social Change," in G. Swanson, T. Newcomb, and E. Hartley, eds., *Readings in Social Psychology* (New York: Henry Holt & Co., 1952), pp. 459-473.

interpersonal situations requires a stabilized relationship and modification on the part of the followers. In interpersonal relationships, negative feedback concerns how one's behavior affects others, while positive feedback deals with how the individual should act. The following hypothetical situation exemplifies this concept:

A group of boys at a playground requested that they be allowed to have a cookout at the barbecue pit fireplace. Several of these youngsters met with the recreationist in charge. When it came to deciding the menu, frankfurters were suggested as the main course. One youngster reminded the others that two of the other boys were Hindus and were not permitted to eat meat. Another boy stated, "Let them eat meat like everybody else! It won't hurt them."

The recreationist suggested that it would be an easy matter to provide a meatless substitute for the two Hindus. The rest of the group thought that this would be the best thing to do. The cookout was successful. The two Hindus had potato pancakes while the others ate hotdogs.

The recreationist, as a leader, must help people to accept the diversities of custom and religion or ethnic traditions of others. In this way, the young can be assisted to become relatively receptive to differences among people. Although the recreationist's suggestion worked in this situation, it might have been better for all concerned if there had been a discussion by the entire group. This latter circumstance may have provided the gaining of some insight and an accommodation in which all might have shared.

Interpersonal communication is a mutually supporting process which has as its goal an interchange of messages between two or more people so that each can understand the other at the most personal levels. Where emotions are concerned, the problem of understanding becomes the relationship itself. Attention is placed on the intricate defense mechanisms and self-concepts of those involved. Since the individual is motivated to maintain his own integrity by deep-seated internal forces, he can facilitate this effort for the other person by his own self-perception and empathy. Newcomb and others state:

Communication is the form of interpersonal exchange through which, figuratively speaking, persons can come into contact with each other's minds. The mechanism of communication includes the encoding, through symbols, of information; the behavioral transmission and the perceptual reception of those symbols; and their decoding. Following the exchange of a message, if the exchange has been sincere and reasonably accurate, transmitter and sender have more nearly the same information about one or more referents of the message than before. Such equalization of information is not the goal of communication; it is only a relationship between the participants, usually not recognized by them, through which the motive satisfaction to which communication is instrumental can be attained.[19]

LEADERSHIP AND BEHAVIORAL CHANGE

In order to persuade others to follow, there must be some sort of voluntary desire to coordinate efforts and cooperate for mutual benefits. Cooperation, on occasion, necessitates modification in interpersonal relationships. The leader's skill enables positive change in others. He must also recognize the necessity for modifying his own attitude and behavior if he wants to become a leader. He would have to apply his knowledge and capacity to ensure change through interpersonal relations. When personal modification is involved, the individual must appreciate the desirability for transformation. His conduct should confirm his ability to redefine and recast his attitudes. Personal change results only when the individual wants to change. Learning procedures, which are intimately associated with the communication process, follow.

We understand others in terms of our own needs and outlooks which we learn from our personal experiences. People exist in conformity to what we think they are and what we have come to anticipate from them. What we believe about others colors our attitudes and affects our behavior toward them and their behavior toward us. Our competency in interpersonal relationships is directly observed by our attitudes and conduct toward others which are received or felt by them and to which they react. What are attitudes and how may they be modified through leadership? Sherif states that:

Attitudes refer to the stands the individual upholds and cherishes about objects, issues, persons, groups, or institutions. The referents of a person's attitudes may be a "way of life"; economic, political, or religious institutions; family, school, or government. We are speaking of the individual's attitudes when we refer to his holding in high esteem his own family, his own school, his own party, his own religion, with all the emotional and affective overtones these terms imply. We refer to his attitudes when we say he holds other groups, other schools, other parties, or religions in a less favorable light or at a safe distance (as "safe" is defined by his attitudes).[20]

Of course, possessing an attitude means that the individual takes a

19. T. M. Newcomb, R. H. Turner, and P. E. Converse, *Social Psychology: The Study of Human Interaction* (New York: Holt, Rinehart and Winston, Inc., 1965), pp. 219-220.
20. C. W. Sherif, M. Sherif, and R. E. Nebergall, *Attitude and Attitude Change: The Social Judgment-Involvement Approach* (Philadelphia: W. B. Saunders Co., 1965), p. 4.

position for or against some issue or object. Leadership brings pressure to bear by helping the learner to recognize his internal patterns of emotions and attitudes toward himself and others and, where necessary, providing remedial measures so that inadequacies can be overcome. For deficiencies of knowledge, educational methods are applied. Changing a person's social behavior by strengthening his ability to encounter others is a difficult process. Frequently, modification of behavior means that the individual must divest himself of certain habitual ways of thinking as well as altering specific attitudes which he has about himself and others. Additionally, the social learner will have to utilize other experiences in which he has had more competency. Recreationists often have a direct opportunity to contribute to social learning and attitude change, as illustrated by the following postulated situation:

Nine year old Ljubljana, who had recently come to the United States from Yugoslavia, was having difficulty gaining acceptance among her peers at the neighborhood recreational center. When she tried to learn an American folk dance, she was confused by the rapidly-spoken English directions of the instructor. The other children laughed because she made wrong turns and was unable to follow the directions.

The recreationist assembled the dance class after the lesson and asked if any of the children had ever seen a traditional Slavic dance. When they said that they had not, she explained that these dances were far more complex than the simple folk dance they were trying to learn. Knowing that Ljubljana knew some Croatian dances, she asked her to demonstrate for the class. Ljubljana executed the dances gracefully and well. The rest of the children admired Ljubljana's dancing and asked her to show them how to do the steps. They soon discovered how difficult it was to learn something completely foreign to their experience, even when the instructions were given in their own language.

From an admiration of her dancing there developed a new respect for their Yugoslavian playmate. Fortunately, the recreationist knew of the skill which Ljubljana had. It was relatively easy to show the other children her uniqueness without a great deal of moralizing or explanation. Particularly when working with children, the recreationist-leader's approach should be to accentuate the positive by bringing out the individual's skill, knowledge, or talent. Such things are recognized and appreciated almost immediately.

Behavioral change is founded upon intensive and prolonged interaction between the individual to be changed and the change agent. This is a process which enlists the personal concern and willingness of participants. As the individual becomes more ego-involved and identifies with the process, effectiveness is greatly enhanced. The person learning to alter social behavior must initiate such change. Unless modification is perceived as valid and significant, the learner will not alter his self-image.

Change originating from within necessitates a particular type of association between the leader and the individual undergoing change. Initially, the leader has to assume that the person to be changed has the ability to effect change; he then becomes the focus of all effort for any attempt at attitudinal modification.[21] The thrust for change and the ability to comprehend one's own emotions and perceptions are an internal problem and may be understood vaguely, if at all, by the person effecting change. The same may be stated about any behavioral change relationship, whether of the individual or group type. As Kemp indicates:

> Leaders can help members to recognize that some resistance is a fact of life and to distinguish between resistance which may prevent one from understanding and resistance which appears as rationalizations for disregarding insight. Members can be helped in the use of productive imagination to diminish or eliminate the underlying fear. The group will eventually perceive that basic to various forms of resistance is the fear of change. The leader hopes to develop a psychological climate in which resistance is accepted and understood and the fear of change reduced.[22]

This idea of modification is founded on the belief that the nature of man is rational and the self is a special and unique presence which moves through an uninterrupted sequence of existence. This affirms that existence is absolutely personal and only the individual has the capacity to differentiate, from the continuum of his experience, those components which are in accord with and sustaining of his self. If external forces are encountered which appear hostile to the unity of the self, protective devices are raised to thwart their effects, unless the individual's desire to know is so powerful that it overcomes reticence and succeeds in suppressing such defense mechanisms. The desire to know is a superior instrument for modification. The role of the change agent or leader is to provide the kind of support which will enable the follower to reduce those defense mechanisms that can obscure attempts to examine flaws in the self-structure. The leader acts circumspectly, offering assistance and occasionally becoming the model which the follower attempts to emulate.

Instruction for Change

All interpersonal relationships occur in some group situation. In attempting to effect change within the individual the leader resorts to certain facilitating methods which can have a positive impact on the follower's attitudes toward himself and others. A most significant

---

21. C. Rogers, *On Becoming a Person* (New York: Houghton Mifflin, 1961).
22. C. G. Kemp, *Foundations of Group Counseling* (New York: McGraw-Hill, 1970), p. 190.

technique is instruction through which the follower is made aware of the outlooks, values, and referents of the group, with the leader as model. In this way, greater sensitivity to the self may be initiated. Self-awareness is vital if the individual is to have an opportunity for expanding his range of experience. This invariably increases the efficiency of interpersonal relationships, uncovering the capacity for personally satisfying encounters within the social milieu. Each encounter contributes to self-understanding and unity. Even negative experiences may be accepted as a perfectly normal aspect of existence if similar experiences have previously been assimilated in the self-structure. The ability to acknowledge and appreciate the presence of positive and negative facets of our self enables us to see that others also have the same characteristics. However, it is the totality of self that is a matter of consequence.

As a corollary, if the extent of openness to experience is to be maximized, there must be a subsequent increase in data from experience which the individual is capable of recognizing as being coherent with his self-structure. As self-awareness is heightened, protective mechanisms are minimized, feelings of personal cohesiveness and consistency are augmented, and contact is made with reality. As the self-system is an outgrowth of social experience, it may be changed by social experiences that assist the individual in reassessing and scrutinizing his aptitude for adjusting to situations which appear to menace his self.

Under the domination of genetic variables, internal pressures, and environmental constraints, the self-system is constantly changing throughout the life span. In this encounter between one's self-structure, one's heredity, and one's external circumstances, conflicts are alleviated either through adapting their origins to an existing idea of self or through altering the self-system, which requires the integration of new concepts associated with similar changes in the self-structure. Above all, the process of reconciliation and accommodation should be positive and developmental. Unfortunately, some people are stultified by the inadequacies of previous experience or by contemporary social standards and values. The process of personal growth which would subscribe to the formation of a better interpersonal environment becomes frustrated by defensive behavior. On the other hand, the substructure of self-continuity may be coupled with inactivity, thereby slowing the rate of change in the self-structure to the extent that it cannot satisfy the requisites for competent behavior in specific circumstances. In these instances, the change process needs to be provided with new directions or given new impetus. Problems which may arise as a result of inability to change may be observed in the following instances:

The director of X Recreational Center thought it would promote better intergroup relations if an occasion were arranged where members of minority groups could become acquainted. The recreationist suggested an intergroup dance between the teen-agers at his center and those of another center. The date was set, an orchestra was employed, and invitations were sent to the youths of the other center. The night of the dance, the teen-agers of the host center arrived first and danced among themselves while waiting for the other teen-agers to arrive. When the guests finally did arrive, they were ushered into the gymnasium where the dance had already started. The guests paired off with one another and danced exclusively among themselves for the rest of the evening.

During the evening, the recreationist in charge made several attempts to stimulate some interchange between the two groups. A few of the hosts invited girls from the other center to dance, but they were rebuffed. After some refreshments were served, the visiting teen-agers left the center. Far from promoting better intergroup relations, the activity may have actually worsened them. Poor planning resulted in a hardening of attitudes.

A better procedure might have been arranged if a committee from both centers had actively participated in planning the evening. The activity should not have begun without all parties in attendance. There should have been some kind of mixer event scheduled first. Exclusionary practices could have been frustrated if diversionary activities had been planned so that intermingling would have been mandatory. Intergroup contacts are not facilitated through dances. The setting has proved to be too formidable and formal. Dance requires overt behaviors from age-group members who are typically reserved among their own friends, no less among comparative strangers. Other activities, previously planned, such as sports contests, exhibitions, and so on, might have been a more productive lead-up to the dance.

Instructional Consequences

The entire range of instructional technique is geared to behavior modification through the promotion of critical and social skills and, sometimes, by heightening self-perception and altering personal attitudes toward the self and others. Modifying behavior by augmenting an individual's knowledge about particular issues, things, and concepts is typical of all educational procedure. With the assimilation of more factual information, different behavior may be likely unless the additional information is in some way qualified by a condition of related attitudes or biases pre-existing in the self-structure. Those people with the intellect and the desire can learn almost any non-emotion-provoking skill. Where there are emotional aspects to learning, however, opinions about, attitudes toward, or referents conditioned by the social environment act as screens, changing perceptions, and inducing behavioral outcomes conformably. Normally, the individual's behavior results from an intricate mixture of positive and negative attitudes based upon experience and such immediate influences as situation or position for which reason the connection of attitudes to behavior is not easily understood.

This connection has been established in any number of ways by psychologists. Behavior, capable of being observed by others, is more plastic than attitudes. Cultural standards frequently require conformity to certain expectations whether the individual actually approves or not. Thus, we sometimes overlook or do not comment upon obvious inaccuracies made by one person in company to avoid embarrassment, even though we may wish to correct misrepresentations. To add to the confusion, attitudes do not always take priority over behavior. They occasionally change in consequence of behavior. Attitudinal modification may also result from some experience where sudden insight is gained.

This network of associations between attitudes and behavior inevitably affects instruction. It may be seen that certain attitudes concerning the disclosure of one's feelings may be pernicious to learning. There is no way to understand how worthwhile or authentic such feelings may be unless they are revealed and information about them is interchanged. Such exposure and exchange may best be brought about in small group situations where role-playing is employed as a learning method. Jourard has indicated that self-disclosure may be the essential factor for acquiring self-knowledge. He states:

> Through my self-disclosure, I let others know my soul. They can know it, really know it, only as I make it known. In fact, I am beginning to suspect that I can't even know my own soul except as I disclose it. I suspect that I will know myself "for real" at the exact moment that I have succeeded in making it known through my disclosure to another person.[23]

Attitudes are more open to change when the individual is committed to an interest and finds himself involved in an equivocal situation. Let us say that the person has undertaken a role-playing assignment. In such a situation, the group's expectations require the revelation of the inner self, and if we determine through feedback that attitudes are inconsonant or unaccountable in relation to our self-concept, we become anxious. If the social situation is empathic and the concern is strong, defensive behaviors may be avoided as the individual attempts to subdue the disagreement or the sense of vagueness which confounds him.

---

23. S. Jourard, *The Transparent Self: Self-disclosure and Well-being* (Princeton, N.J.: D. Van Nostrand and Company, 1964), p. 10.

The results of modifications of self which derive from different instructional methods — case method, role-playing, discussion groups, self-study, T-groups, etc. — will differ with the stage of concentration.[24] Where the focus remains on a record of experiences concerning other people rather than on the person who is learning to change, perceptual modifications may be anticipated in social conduct as participants relate to the social circumstance in the group. Cognitive alterations will also occur in the participants' comprehension of social and psychological phenomena. Group members will develop such fundamental skills as observing, analyzing social conduct, and taking pertinent action. However, until the leader introduces the group members, or individual, to an intensive regard of personal attitudes and emotions, modification of values and subsequently of personal inner behavior will not occur. Thus, cognitive alterations may take place which affect the social self, but not the subjective self.

Sustaining a reduced state of personal concern, a typical representation of the case method and role-playing techniques, is simultaneously more beneficial and less gainful in comparison to more comprehensive kinds of personal instruction. The instructional environment may be intentionally designed to handle inner values and attitudes that comprise formidable barriers to necessary personal growth and development. The result should be more effective behavior. The particular aims of instructional methods are to modify personal values, enhance interpersonal skills, and augment the effectiveness of groups in gaining their goals. Sometimes effort centers on only one of these objectives, sometimes several, and often on all at the same time. Therefore, the consequences of instruction are associated with positive modifications in cognition, communication skills, openness to experience, emotional adaption, and sensitivity.

The Formulation of the Modification Process

Modification is a process which insists upon the development of the individual's capacity to modify himself through a unique form of association between the leader (catalyst) and the person or persons to be changed. People do have the ability to learn new ways to perceive and behave as they respond to an empathic and interpersonal environment. Although individual personality has probably been crystalized by the age of twelve (some psychologists say it is an even earlier age), there is no need for any individual to remain trapped at some indeterminate point, always answering to situations in ingrained childhood ways. People must discover their own capacities as they interact with others. Humans tend to coordinate their efforts and act cooperatively when they perceive

---

24. R. D. Mann, *Interpersonal Styles and Group Development* (New York: John Wiley & Sons, 19 — ?), pp. 9-33, 76-79, 163-178.

supportive and enabling behavior in others.

The fundamental assumption is that man's inclination toward positive behavior can be guided and made to predominate. When individuals are offered the opportunity, they can reach logical conclusions about themselves and, in coordination with others, participate in helpful and encouraging relationships. Among the techniques which can be employed to good effect are those which tend to reflect the learner's self-motivated approaches to acceptance, openness of communication, a supportive psychological atmosphere, and innovation. The application of these attributes to normal interpersonal relationships in group life is a necessary concomitant.

Finally, group participation in the decision-making process is a corollary to what is typically thought of as the practice of democratic principles and the utilization of interpersonal references as the basis for such practice. It is concerned with the decentralization of authority and widespread acceptance of group-based ideas, plans, and programs. It is apparent that this signifies the need among members of a group or personnel of an institution for personal attention and involvement in the expression of group or organizational aims and the various ways they are to be achieved.

SELECTED REFERENCES

Abrahamson, M., "Position, Personality, and Leadership," *Psychological Record,* Vol. 19 (1969), pp. 113-122.

Back, K. W., *Beyond Words: The Story of Sensitivity Training and the Encounter Movement* (New York: Basic Books, 1972).

Berscheid, E. and E. Walster, *Interpersonal Attraction* (Reading, Mass.: Addison-Wesley, 1969).

Byrne, D., *The Attraction Paradigm* (New York: Academic Press, 1971).

Jacobs, T. O., *Leadership and Exchange in Formal Organizations* (Alexandria, Va.: Human Resources Research Organization, 1971).

Jones, H. R. and M. Johnson, "LPC As a Modifier of Leader-Follower Relationship," *Academy of Management Journal,* Vol. 15 (1972), pp. 185-196.

Merton, R. K., "The Social Nature of Leadership," *American Journal of Nursing,* Vol. 69 (1969), pp. 1614-1618.

Patton, B. R. and K. Griffin, *Interpersonal Communication: Basic Text and Readings* (New York: Harper and Row, 1974).

Sedwick, R. C., *Interaction: Interpersonal Relationships in Organizations* (Englewood Cliffs, N. J.: Prentice-Hall, 1974).

Wheeler, L., *Interpersonal Influence* (Boston: Allyn & Bacon, 1970).

CHAPTER FOUR

The Effects of Domination, Power, and Influence

In any discussion of leadership, whether concerning the field of recreational service or any other enterprise, the effects of domination, power, and influence must be understood. There is a close enough association between these three terms to cause some misconception.

DOMINATION AND SUBMISSION

Domination is control of others by virture of superior force. Domination is brought about by such actions as manipulation, threat of loss of security (e.g., personal safety, economic capability, freedom), naked aggression in the form of physical violence, imprisonment, and even the loss of life.

Dominance may be structured and generally accepted as a cultural manifestation, as typified by parental control over children or the control of the lower by the higher ranks in military and paramilitary organizations. Yet in these circumstances, as well as in corporations or organizations, dominance stems from and operates within the context of social interaction. To state that one individual is dominant suggests that there is another acting in a submissive position. Fromm offers a most compelling statement concerning domination and submission:

> The common element in both submission and domination is the symbiotic nature of relatedness. Both persons involved have lost their integrity and freedom; they live on each other and from each other, satisfying their craving for closeness, yet suffering from the lack of inner strength and self-reliance which would require freedom and independence, and furthermore, constantly threatened by the conscious and unconscious hostility which is bound to arise from the symbiotic relationship.[1]

Domination is essentially the capacity of an individual to control the decision-making functions of one or more people. Such restraint suggests the stifling of personal expression, indulgence in destructive criticism, and

---

1. E. Fromm, "Values, Psychology, and Human Existence," in D. E. Hamachek, ed., *Human Dynamics in Psychology and Education* (Boston: Allyn and Bacon, Inc., 1970), p. 666.

insistence on conformity to established and routinized ways.

Why will some people enter into a relationship where one person dominates them? There are several possible reasons. An individual may view another in light of some previous experience and seek out a parental surrogate or authoritarian personality in order to cope with the present situation. There are individuals who believe that to offset their low-status position within an organization, they must somehow ingratiate themselves with, or assume a submissive attitude toward, an individual higher in the hierarchy. This subordination of self is performed so that they may obtain a form of protection, status by association, or a sense of security.

Among the basic factors to be considered in any study of dominance is the need, drive, or ambition of an individual for dominance and the associated desire of another to be submissive, revealing the personality of each. There is the presupposition that individuals who "go along" will not have the personality that would ever permit active opposition to domination. Obviously, such domination can only be thought of in a social sense, rather than in the physical sense of force or its threat. Under such circumstances, submission is involuntary. Social domination, on the other hand, requires a desire to submit.

Abnormal desires for dominance have long been acknowledged. The individual who needs constant recognition has this need. The Napoleonic complex appears to be a compensatory behavior for those who feel the need to make up for their short stature. Perhaps other perceived physical limitations may be a factor contributing to the ambition to gain mastery or command in order to counteract feelings of inferiority. An individual's abnormal need for dominance may also be the outcome of early childhood experience in which extraordinary parental domination emerges in later years as an effort to dominate others.

A normal desire for dominance does not offer such a facile explanation. Certain cultural pressures (for example, success and the perquisites of success accruing from accomplishment in work life are highly regarded in western society) can produce an inclination for mastery, motivating individuals to compete for rank, prestige, or power. The desire to assert oneself is a learned response to environmental forces which tend to assist in the development of personality as the individual matures. Family life, peer relationships, societal demands, and personal tendencies are bound in determining the amount of each person's appetite for dominance.

Conversely, the need for submission, both normal and abnormal, is comprehensible when parent-child relationships are explored. Babies are born helpless and in need of physical support. Only among human animals is the period of immaturity and dependency of such long duration. In fact, many societies mandate continued dependency of the young upon the adult population even after there is mental and physical capacity for self-care. It is not surprising that people become so completely habituated to submission. Just as individuals learn to become dominant, they also learn to become submissive. To the extent that submission, or in this case dependency, is enjoyable there is a corresponding attitude that being protected and cared for is extremely advantageous. In normal situations, however, there will eventually be an attempt to break away from parental control and achieve personal independence. When this occurs varies with the personalities of the individuals concerned. Some seek autonomy at a relatively early age, some after reaching the age of majority, and some never leave the nest.

As the individual matures and develops there is a consequent ambivalence — it is the conflict between the desire to submit, be protected, and cared for (with all its associations of pleasant security and disagreeable restrictions) and the vaulting determination to be free (with all of its satisfactions and unattractive responsibilities). The manner in which this contradiction is resolved will probably relate to the ways in which our parents behave toward us and will also indicate the extent to which an individual will want to play submissive roles in the social groups or organizations which he joins.

Social Domination and Human Development

A child with a particular hereditary endowment will mature, differentiate, and have a concept of self only to the degree that his social milieu permits. Domination denies the social expression of others, hinders inspiration, thwarts impulses to perform with enthusiasm, and assaults the integrity, position, and the equity of another to think and act as an individual. How may domination be explained insofar as growth and development are concerned?

Acceptance. There is little or no such thing as perfect accord in human relations. Perfect agreement would necessitate absolute understanding of the aims and wishes of others as well as one's own. Because each of us has difficulty in verbalizing personal desires, it is inconceivable that others would have complete understanding of us. Even with excellent human relations, each person contributes some problem to those within his social sphere. Each person finds his own initiative somewhat reduced by the well-intentioned actions of others, but each of us takes a great deal of such discommodity as a matter of course. We continue to have affection for friends and to appreciate them, without holding a grudge for minor irritations. Acceptance permits those involved to reveal an inner self without the need for defensive mechanisms.

Interpersonal behavior based on acceptance is likely in a relationship where individuals may become more intimate and gain better understandings of one another and still maintain their individuality. This is really an ideal relationship. For development, differentiation can be maximized when an individual is recognized and appreciated for his uniqueness at an early age.

*Avoidance.*In families where the offspring are emotionally secure, the children are able to discuss any issue whatsoever with their parents without recrimination. Unfortunately, some families have neither established the rapport nor the opportunities for such discussions. It is little wonder, then, that children learn very early to be especially cautious and discriminating both in the subject matter which they discuss and in the behavior which they disclose to their parents. When one person is required to reside in close proximity to another, and realizes the other tends to frustrate freedom to act, that person will avoid confrontation but will otherwise be himself. This form of behavior supposes that the domination is so overwhelming that it cannot be accepted, and protective countermeasures must be taken. Keeping back information from one's parents or conducting discrete conversations with one's peers are typical of such a relationship.

In the acceptance and avoidance patterns of dominating relationships, response to comparatively mild inconvenience which impinges on one's own spontaneity is not sufficient to divert energies from fundamental objectives. If it is necessary to be less than candid or to hide ideas, there is probably going to be less understanding in the relationship. Nevertheless, this kind of behavior is found in relationships where there is neither a breach nor conflict. In both of these situations adaptations may be made so that domination cannot interfere with the essential purpose of the individual.

*Opposition.*When domination reaches a peak where it can no longer be avoided without a substantial change in life style, integrity, or individuality, it must be actively opposed. The relationship is then characterized by open conflict, the inception of the negative spiral in human behavior. Dominance breeds dominance (opposition), which tends to magnify the level of conflict rather than diminish it. It reduces understanding to such negligible proportions that it forces the combatants to employ deceit so that they may assault each other with more strength People who lie to others usually do so as a form of self-protection in a contentious relationship.

Some adults mistreat children and act in ways that would seem shocking by any civilized standard of behavior. Name-calling, physical abuse, sarcasm, and rejection are imposed. It is not amazing when the subject of this abuse finally has had enough and actively begins to oppose such treatment. Then another round of abuse is begun. With resistance there is further aggression. This promotes more hostility and opposition. The only way out of this spiral is to stop the counterproductive behavior which initiated it and seek solutions to the conflict. Domination must be obliterated and greater understanding substituted.

Submissiveness. When an individual realizes that opposition to domination can only meet with personal catastrophe, he is inclined to submit. Submissive behavior reflects a much more reduced level of will than does opposition. Submission presents an outer appearance of agreement or agreeableness, which persons in authority find pleasant or actually work to attain. In so doing, they squeeze every vestige of spontaneity out of the individual and leave a passively conforming, manipulable object in place of a vital human being. Adults frequently misinterpret a child's shyness and submissiveness for agreement. What they do not comprehend is the child's fear of self-expression because of recrimination or retaliation.

Breaking the Spiral of Domination

The most direct method for abolishing the negative spiral of domination is to accept people for what they are. For instance, both the timid and the hostile person are fearful. Both are in conflict with their surroundings. The basic difference between the two is that the hostile person is less fearful.

The method for dealing with timid, withdrawing, and conforming behavior is to augment the individual's expression of self and will. As self-expression increases and domination decreases, the timid person will undergo a stage where he is irritating to others. He will come to resemble the aggressive person for a while. During this period, he will develop high initiative, but will remain in low accord. The negligible accord, however, forms environmental obstruction to his high initiative, and the negative spiral comes into action. The method for stopping the spiral in which the hostile person finds himself requires acceptance. Accepting the individual as a person, even while disapproving his conduct, tends to minimize for him the perceived threat. With the threat reduced, the individual no longer needs to destroy his environment. Naturally, it takes time before the individual realizes that the danger to himself has been reduced.

Accepting the individual as a person helps socially integrative involvement, since it initiates association that was not available before. Socially integrative behavior promotes a positive cycle. When such behavior is exhibited, corresponding behavior in one's companions occurs. The rapport that results effectively ends the negative spiral. Indeed, the whole process which induces harmonious interpersonal relations and rejects protective behavior opens avenues to understanding both the self and others which may preclude domination.

Hero-worship is another type of submission. The idolizing of chosen individuals and the search for great men to guide the destinies of nations has had a long history. Among the writers who have concerned themselves with this form of submission is Thomas Carlyle, who wrote:

> Find in any country the Ablest Man that exists there; raise him to the supreme place, and loyally reverence him: you have a perfect government for that country...what he tells us to do must be precisely the wisest, fittest, that we could anywhere or anyhow learn; the thing which it will always behoove us, with right loyal thankfulness, and nothing doubting, to do so.[2]

The worship of heroes and the search for an infallible person to proffer support and protection in times of stress is an adult expression of an infantile attitude toward one's parents. During periods of stress, some people become overwhelmed. They long for the time when they could run to their parents for security, and so seek a dominant person — a surrogate parent upon whom burdens may be unloaded. Reliance upon such an individual requires the same idealization with which small children sometimes picture their parents. *However it is rooted and for whatever reasons it is called upon, domination has no place within the process of leadership.*

Persons sitting at the apex of power may dominate, command, or direct, but unless those who are led have the freedom to follow or not to follow, there is no personal leadership. Without the voluntary features of "followership" there can only be subservience. Paul Pigors crystalized this concept when he wrote that the denial of choice breeds domination which is the antithesis of leadership.[3]

POWER AND SOCIAL CHANGE

Social power is the ability of an individual to effect intentional modifications on the behavior of another. To the extent that one is motivated to act and complete an activity instigated intentionally by another, it can be said that social power is present. The important underlying factor is *intent.*

Typologies of Power

Humans are motivated by acquired attitudes, ideas, ethics, and convictions, and conduct their behavior in interpersonal relations in consonance with them. Such extra-personal forces as religious belief,

---

2. T. Carlyle, *On Heroes, Hero-Worship and the Heroic in History* (New York: Thomas Y. Crowell Company, 1840), pp. 259-260.
3. P. Pigors, *Leadership or Domination* (Boston: Houghton Mifflin Company, 1935), p. 20.

political creed, and philosophical reference have power to influence behavior. While the individual may possess personal power which he employs to gain his objectives, he is also the object of these extra-personal forces.

A second set of powers are those which are economic in nature. Economic power is based upon the possession of property or other wealth and is conditioned by the social controls of custom and law. Hierarchical power is a third type which accumulates from the social or positional status that individuals enjoy within the organizations to which they belong. A fourth concept of power is that which is based upon compulsion or physical force. Within these forms of power are other manifestations which require elaboration. Among the forces which tend to influence behavior are moral power and intellectual power.

Nothing is innately wrong with the word "power," but it has often been used with a monstrous connotation. To many people, power conjures visions of autocracy, secret police, awakenings in the middle of the night to the thundering summons of a rifle butt, and the enslavement of millions of people by political, economic, or military means. Many think of power in terms of brute force, cunning, hatred, and injustice, with some Machiavellian character pulling the strings to which mindless puppets are attached. On the other hand, just as there is power for evil, there is also power for the right, the ethical, and the good.

The attainment of power — authority and influence — may seem to corrupt so that application of power is immoral, but what the individual brings to the power structure determines its use. The ethical nature of the personality will limit the betrayal of human values. Character pollution by power is not inevitable; only when a morally weak or pathological personality achieves power is it turned toward depraved ends.

Physical Power. The usual concept of physical power is brute force. Because of this widely held view, it is generally regarded negatively, but the utilization of pure physical power has both a positive and negative meaning. While sheer physical force has rarely accomplished anything of lasting inner value, it also represents the capacity for action. Movement of things or people to achieve goals or results is an attribute of physical power.

In terms of influence with people, a structure or form must exist beyond force in order for physical power to have acceptance. The concept of legitimacy may be employed to rationalize force, as in police power for public safety.

Human beings may be beaten into submission; they may be made into any mold or pattern under duress. Unless the threat of punishment is continually applied, few individuals willingly respond. They may be compelled to serve a cause, and they will serve, but only as long as the lash, the bayonet, or arms reinforce the demand. Human will, once it realizes any freedom, can never voluntarily assume a slavish position.

Moral Power. Morality may be conceived in terms of general rules, regulations, or behavior customs to which human society knowingly adheres and which are ethically significant. Moral behaviors are those which abide by socially approved conduct. Morality, therefore, is based upon ethical relationships, upon knowing what in a given culture is right and what is good. This knowledge is based upon freedom and individual decision, coordinated with criteria for evaluating possible courses of action. The worth of every decision hinges upon the understanding and analysis of the several choices presented. All available information is gathered so that each person may have the opportunity of deciding what has value in the light of social acceptance.

Morality must not be confused with conformity; it is concerned with value systems which determine free action, rather than the development of specific accepted forms of conduct. The practice of ethical activities is based upon what is good and therefore of value to the individual and to society. Hypocritical and sanctimonious efforts at morality, which in effect disguise selfish tendencies, are not moral regardless of how good such behavior appears. Morality is vitally concerned with more than surface conduct.

Moral force is influential because it produces the most valid of possible behavior systems. The rational frame in which morality operates precludes baseness; in the long run it will consistently win over those activities for which there are no justifiable supports. Morality exercised within the human community seeks optimum coordination of human effort in the production of the good life for all. One form of recreational problem with moral overtones may be observed from the following:

A black recreationist was assigned to work with two white recreationists in a predominantly white neighborhood. There was some concern as to how she would be accepted by those who utilized the neighborhood recreational facilities. The supervisory and center staff were hopeful that the transition for the new staff member would be smooth and that the community would come to accept her.

Following a discussion of neighborhood attitudes and possible prejudices, the new recreationist was asked to be as active as possible in the program. It was decided that, whenever possible, the other staff members would answer a request from a child with the statement: "I can't be with you now, but Ms. McKinney can. She is the lady over there. Just go over and ask her."

As a result of this procedure, the black recreationist was accepted by the children and few racial incidents flared. In a short time the entire neighborhood came to accept Ms. McKinney and she was a valuable member of the staff.

The idea of power is somewhat estranged from the connotation of morality. In the power ethic, the test of goodness is whether or not a thing succeeds. The good is that which brings desired results. Unfortunately, this power ethic is one which supports immorality in the practical sense, but which may be perfectly valid in any test of truth. Dictators justify their employment of unholy means by pointing to the ends which they achieve. According to the ethic of power, such a view is acceptable. Yet any activity which is reprehensible cannot be called ethical. Murder is unethical. Killing in time of war is condoned, although the act itself is unethical, because this behavior is thought to serve an ethical end. Morality refers to the decisions which are reached on the basis of knowledge of consequences. Thus the ends, even if they are worthy and valuable to society as a whole, and not just to a select few, never justify the means which appear to be or are a violation of ethical practices.

Violence against any individual or group is unethical as such. However, in our society, violence may be supportable in certain cases. Among these are: punishment of a criminal for acts committed against society, destruction of armed might in defense of a particular system, killing during wartime, and suspension of certain civil rights as a preventive against rebellion. While these are actions which cannot be considered ethical in themselves, they may be warranted in terms of the ends which are achieved for the entire human community. Immoral means deny noble ends. Where the individual breaks the law to expose injustice or maltreatment, that person willingly accepts the possibility of punishment in hopes of gaining justice. One may not break the law with impunity and expect amnesty.

It would be outrageous even to consider ethical those actions which dictators have generally resorted in consolidating their position. Racism, genocide, nationalism, and aggression have been used to destroy people and places. The "ends-justify-the-means" argument must be carefully weighed in the light of human dignity and service to humanity.

Those who have placed truth upon the altar of expediency also adhere to the power ethic. In the case of pragmatism, however, moral actions are taken into account and concepts are tested. The clearest statement of this idea was made by William James:

> True ideas are those that we can assimilate, validate, corroborate, and verify. False ideas are those we cannot. That is the practical difference it makes to us to have true ideas; that, therefore, is the meaning of truth, for it is all that truth is known as.[4]

---

4. W. James, *The Meaning of Truth* (New York.: David McKay Company, 1909), pp. v-vi. Reprinted by permission.

Intellectual Power. The third variety of power is intellectual power, or knowledge of what must be done. Inherent in this aspect of power are technical skill, social power, and self-realization. Intellectual power has as its aim the control of natural and material things, other persons, and the self. Intellect is clearly associated with power because its use provides knowledge, and knowledge is the path to power. The content of what is known is the essence of what can be performed or obtained. Applied intellect is one method of swaying others toward the leader's desired goals. Unless it is guided by ethics, intellectual power degenerates into manipulation.

Control over other persons may be explained as social power. Intellectualization is necessary in the development of language and the art of communication. By these means, the development of rational powers of persuasion may occur. Influence grows out of the impact which intellect has on specific feeling. For example, tremendous pressure is exerted upon those for whom we have affection or who have affection for us. The ability to sway behavior because of the interdependence of affection is one of the more powerful instigators to action. Also, through such personal relations, opinions and attitudes may be changed.

Power and leadership

It requires abililty to persuade others to follow voluntarily a plan of action which requires attitudinal modification or a change in behavioral patterns. An individual with power does not need this ability if he can coerce others to follow. His power may stem from what he is or what he does — he may either have means at his disposal or hold an authoritative position from which he may issue commands. A powerful person who controls group objectives can immediately reinforce his demands on the behavior of others by providing or withholding rewards or punishments. If group members are not stimulated to achieve their objectives, the control does not produce power.

Coercion occurs when individual members of a group openly, not privately, comply with the demands of another. Nevertheless, the restriction on their own free choices may produce discontent, frustration, and hostility. The weaker members of the group may simply withdraw from an untenable stituation, or the membership may become so frustrated that they react in ways which tend to reduce efficiency and effectiveness in carrying out assignments. Another outcome is that members may counteract by forming a new group. The latter is illustrated by the following postulated situation:

> The teen-age center in a changing neighborhood in X city became the focal point of ethnic rivalries. A group of Puerto Rican youngsters found themselves outnumbered by the older, established white

Protestant majority. This created significant friction and resulted in fighting and severe injuries.

The Puerto Ricans decided to leave the center rather than face continual harassment and possible bloody conflict. The director of the center maintained contact with these former members and when the Puerto Ricans organized a rock group, he helped them secure an audition with a recording company. A rock concert was held at the center with the Puerto Rican group as the main attraction.

The group was well received and continues to appear at the center on occasion. Although the Puerto Ricans were accepted as talented performers, they are not really integrated as center members. Such status has never been accorded since their withdrawal.

In retrospect, the wisdom of having the minority group withdraw in the face of threat is questionable. It is likely that other ways could have been found to permit contacts between the two groups. Initial meetings might have been much more easygoing until familiarity broke down some of the obvious biases. Withdrawal, in this situation, seems to have strengthened the alienation between the groups.

Discussion of power frequently includes the employment of sanctions. In his statement on power, Easton offers the point that a more particular, and therefore a more useful, consideration of power would incorporate the two dimensions of intention and coercion to the usual understanding of power as social causation. He writes:

> To give power any differentiated meaning we must view it as a relationship in which one person or group is able to determine the actions of another in the direction of the former's own ends. Furthermore, and this is the aspect that distinguishes power from broad influence, this person or group must be able to impose some sanctions for the failure of the influenced person to act in the desired way. Power, therefore, is present to the extent to which one person controls by sanction the decisions and actions of another.[5]

Leadership is distinguishable from power. Strictly speaking, all leadership acts may be exemplifications of power because the leader enables aims or objectives to be gained and, further, provides directions for such attainment. How then do power and leadership vary? The essential factor is the reaction of the other person to an attempt at influencing. In the power relationship, the person who has minimum power is restricted in his choices of behavior and performance; he literally loses his options to act when the possessor of high power compels him to participate in selected

---

5. D. Easton, *Political System,* (New York: Alfred A. Knof, 1953), pp. 143-144. Reprinted by permission.

activities which he ordinarily might not have done. Thus all decision-making is extra-personal to the individual with low power.

In direct contrast to this situation, leadership offers unrestricted options to the potential follower. Leadership acts are those which try to persuade others to act in a certain way despite the fact that there are alternatives. Leadership is a process that attempts to foster the idea that one form of behavior or course of action is better than another by indicating which possibilities are more relevant, practical, or beneficial. The recipient of this information is in the position of accepting or rejecting the propositions. If group members accept ideas and act accordingly, they have been influenced. The most important point is that the decision to act or not to act lies entirely with them.

INFLUENCE

Influence is defined as the capacity for one person to convince others to act in the achievement of some desired end without the exercise of sanctions. Insofar as leadership functions in the same way, it is equatable with influence. Influence has to do with one person's attractiveness to or for another and the subsequent interaction that occurs in obtaining modified behavior through convincing communication. Compulsion plays no role here. Influence is at work when one person undertakes certain activities, voluntarily, at the request of another and adopts the object of the activity as his own or modifies his behavior in order to live up to the expectations of the influencer.

In its connection with leadership, influence is that which a leader wields as he communicates with others in the attainment of specified aims. Since this social relationship is based upon acceptance of leader-directed ideas by others, the leader functions by activating other individuals and stimulating them to perform in ways that he, or the group, has decided upon. This is, in fact, the power of influence.

Influence and Power

A leader is placed in a position of extreme power through his influence with others.[6] This capacity for stimulating action is a most important attribute of the leader, since his influence rests on acceptance.

An often stated claim is that influence requires the use of power. This implies that any attempt at influence would mean the imposition of power over the individual who was influenced. In the sense that this idea is being promoted, the words influence and power are not synonymous, whereas in

---

6. K. Lewin, *Field Theory in Social Science* (New York: Harper, 1951), pp. 40-41, 176-187, 224-228.

our definition influence is a form of power.[7] Another specious idea is that appointed leadership, authority granted from some institutionalized structure, must engage itself in the enunciation of power. Actually, appointed leaders must take account of group structure which may furnish support for resistance to the autocratic employment of power. The power to evade unrestrained demands lies with the group, and this resistance must be recognized as a significant reaction.

Influence attempts of an appointed leader are usually appraised by the group in terms of some generally accepted benefit for the group's goals. In the continuity of leadership, especially by an imposed leader, careful attention must be paid to the interpersonal relationships which are affected by the impact of the leader's power.

While leadership operates within bureaucracies, institutions, prescribed procedures, and hierarchies, it also operates in the more spontaneous setting of emergent human interactions, activities, and opinions. The central focus of activity for the leader, regardless of setting, is the informal or natural organization, which includes interactions with people as they go about their routine tasks. Goal-striving activity supports the dynamic interchange necessary to the social structure of the group, and animates interpersonal relationships. It is here that leadership is most effectively practiced, and here that the leader must utilize his ability to shape and modify the course of human behavior and guide it to beneficial ends.

Influence and Interpersonal Behavior

Among the interrelational processes that are involved with influence are emulation and compliance. Emulation or imitation is any behavior which resembles another person's behavior and to which it is a response. Imitation is not a generalized tendency. It is similar to other kinds of responses that are made in relation to other people in that it satisfies certain motives or reflects particular attitudes.[8]

Imitation resembles all other behavioral expressions because it incorporates the basic psychological processes of motivation, perception, and learning. The act of imitation excites interpersonal perception which recognizes that the behavior being imitated tends to satisfy some desire on the part of the imitator. Imitative behavior is most probable under those social conditions where some skill or characteristic behavior is wanted. As for interpersonal relationships, an individual is likely to emulate another when he perceives qualities of superiority which are admired as well as

7. J. M. Burns, *Leadership* (New York: Harper and Row, 1978), p. 12.
8. A. Bandura, "Influence of Models' Reinforcement Contingencies on the Acquisition of Imitative Responses," *Journal of Personality and Social Psychology,* Vol 1. (1965), pp. 589-595.

attitudes that reflect enough similarity to his own to make the model a repository of confidence.

Compliance is an interpersonal response which depends upon the perceived requests of somebody else through direct communication. It is no overestimation to assert that routine compliance is the fabric from which most, if not all, social existence is produced. It is difficult to conceive of a society in which the common courtesies are excluded. These social compliances exert influence on and elicit response from the daily interactions which permit people to tolerate the ebb and flow of human events.

The socio-psychological aspects of emulation and compliance are universally familiar. Of particular interest are current understandings which interacting persons hold in common: anticipation that one of them will offer and the other will be the recipient of assistance or security. Such perceptions are typical of established role relationships and deal with the internalization of standards.

Of no less significance are associations of interpersonal attraction. In this kind of relationship influence is likely to be accepted from an individual to whom one is especially drawn. It might be stated that this attraction almost causes the one who is pulled to relinquish some control over himself. In such a relationship, some power is inherent in influence. For corresponding reasons, influence which is likely to be accepted will probably be offered by someone who is drawn to the recipient of the influence. This reciprocal process enables those who need help to accept help thereby making for a satisfactory interpersonal combination.

Influencing others is often made easier by the perceptions and attitudes of those who will be influenced if they identify in some way with the potential giver of influence. When individuals identify with someone else they may be more susceptible to influence by the respected person. It must be noted, however, that not all inordinate tendencies to be swayed by another's influence derive from ego-involvement; one may, for instance, enthusiastically accept another's influence without any desire for emulation.

The circumstances in which influence occurs are:

1. Intrinsic fascination in the behavior indicated or suggested by the person with influence.

2. Amount of captivation by the would-be influencer's perceived qualities, skill, and reliability, as well as one's own desire to gain favor.

3. Necessities imposed by the interpersonal relations between the influencer and the one influenced within an existing hierarchical structure.

If one of these aspects exists to any great extent, acceptance of influence is highly probable despite either the absence or presence of other conditions. If all are present, there can be no question that influence will be accepted. The converse is equally true.

Influence and Mutual Reinforcement

All interpersonal relationships are, in effect, participation in the exchange of influence. Let us consider those situations in which two or more individuals influence one another identically. One situation immediately brought to mind is the effect that crowd stimulation has upon the individual. No matter the instigation, the behavior of the crowd may cause a change of behavior on the part of the individual, who in turn adds his behavior in response. Each behavior elicits additional behavior.

Within the group situation, the kind as well as the degree of behavior exhibited by group members is frequently influenced by their interaction with one another. When the norms of any group affect membership behavior, there is a mutualized influence operating. The effects on the nature or the type of conduct expressed can be ascribed to group reinforcement. Mutual reinforcement reflects interpersonal processes wherein group standards are developed, agreed upon, internalized, and strengthened among individuals who are members of the group.

Such interaction includes communication and interpersonal experience subject to several conditioning forces. There is the immediate relationship of mutually reinforced influence involving two or more individuals in which there is exchanged communicative capability by all parties concerned. Each participant acknowledges the other as a possible communicator and is stimulated to transmit information about some commonly held idea or activity. Even the act of originating communication opens the potential of the initiator entering the sphere of influence of another's reaction. If, moreover, the first party is unqualifiedly attracted to the second, he is susceptible to the latter's influence within the bounds of his attraction. Attraction signifies that one finds laudable traits in the individual toward whom one feels drawn, and close relations with such a person beome extremely satisfying. If the attractive person's assistance is in some way needed, he is in a position to exert all the more influence on the requestor, either by granting or withholding the required aid. A relationship of mutually reinforced influence is established to the degree that two or more persons have such perceptions of one another.

Another variation affecting the quality of behavior is consensual communication. If two or more persons are conscious of the fact that they will be fraternizing in some context — as team members, club members, group members—each will experience some hesitancy or doubt if signs of mutually accepted meanings are nonexistent. The more such individuals are thrown together and the greater the necessity for them to work together, the more vital is an acknowledgment of reciprocal agreement on conditions pertinent to their united efforts. Consensus is a prerequisite of their affiliation, and the determination that they can agree on commonly held ideas or interests is very satisfying. Therefore, each will be attentive to any manifestations that express some associated understandings. When members conform to their conscious awareness of accord by feedback information, revealing their perception and confirmation of agreement, consensus is accompanied by reciprocity. The process of forming shared attitudes and perspectives is generally coupled with much testing and accident, but sooner or later, through the practice of attitudinal modification and of simple revelation of mutual consensus, some level of communal group-related attitudes results through prolonged contact.

Commonly held attitudes tend to become internalized. This happens in communication dealing with experimentation and reaffirmation: group members show each other, through their respective actions, not merely what they believe to be appropriate behavior, but also what they expect normal behavior for group members to be. Any behavior which typifies the membership becomes normalized over time, accepted as standard, and is displayed in any number of ways. Thus, habitual dress, mannerisms, activities, meeting places, reading matter, etc., come to be reinforced and accepted by group members, while other behavioral expressions are discouraged, disparaged, or otherwise disapproved. In this way, subtle and not-so-subtle information about group behavioral standards are expressed. Everyone who accedes to the norms, particularly if it is done in a positive, predictable manner without subsequent depreciation, is thereby strengthening them. Similarly, each implied admonition at some deviation from the norms also works to sustain them.

Such group reinforcement essentially relies upon an interpersonal response of reciprocal- and self-reinforcement. As each individual member of the group finds it satisfying to receive the approbation of other members so his norm-accommodating behavior will probably be strengthened, either by the approval of others or, if he has assimilated the norms, by living up to his own expectations. This sets a standard for other members who see it. While it is not unknown for some group members to conform to group norms in a superficial manner, group viability requires, in very fundamental ways, concurrent self-and reciprocal support. Without such simultaneous reinforcement of self and others, group norms could never be established and there would be neglibible group stability. The entire concept of reciprocal- and self-reinforcement is essential to prolonged group life. The net effect of such standardizing results in mutual influence.

SELECTED REFERENCES

Filley, A.C. and A.J. Grimes, "The Bases of Power in Decision Processes," *Proceedings of the Academy of Management* (1967).

Goodstadt, B. and D. Kipnis, "Situational Influences on the Use of Power," *Journal of Applied Psychology,* Vol. 54 (1970), pp. 201-207.

Gray L.N., J.T. Richardson, and B.H. Mayhew, "Influence Attempts and Effective Power: A Re-examination of the Unsubstantiated Hypothesis," *Sociometry,* Vol. 31 (1968), pp. 245-258.

Hersey, P. and K.H. Blanchard, "The Management of Change. Change and the Use of Power," *Training and Development Journal,* Vol. 26 (1972), pp. 6-10.

Ivancevich, J.M. and J.H. Donnelly, "Leader Influence and Performance," *Personnel Psychology,* Vol. 23 (1970), pp. 69-77.

Kipnis, D. and R. Vanderveer, "Ingratiation and the Use of Power," *Journal of Personality and Social Psychology,* Vol. 17 (1971), pp. 280-286.

Sampson, R.V., *The Psychology of Power* (New York: Random House, 1968).

Shiflett, S.C. and S.M. Nealey, "The Effects of Changing Leader Power: A Test of Situational Engineering," *Organizational Behavior and Human Performance,* Vol. 7 (1972), pp. 371-382.

Wood, M.T., "Effects of Decision Processes and Task Situations on Influence Perceptions," *Organizational Behavior and Human Performance,* Vol. 7 (1972), pp. 417-427.

PART II

The Leadership Process and Group Dynamics

CHAPTER FIVE

The Nature of Leadership

L eadership is a learned ability through which other people become aware of the person attempting to lead, recognize the information or idea which he is trying to present, and move or act on the basis of the idea toward some predetermined end. Leadership, therefore, is ability, process, and product. It is an ability because the potential leader must have the intellectual awareness to perform in ways which attract others. It is a process because interpersonal relationships are developed and certain behavioral changes are brought about. It is a product because the processes initiated by the leader and developed among group members result in satisfying goals. A leader, consequently, may be defined as one who has unusual influence with others, a proposition supported by McFarland.[1]

> The term "leadership act" is used to designate a pattern of interpersonal behavior in which one person attempts to influence another and the other person accepts this influence. Such a definition of leadership has several implications. The first is that whether an act is one of leadership or not depends in part on the degree to which others accept it. Leadership is not defined here as a quality inherent in a person, nor in an "act" pure and simple. Leadership exists in the relationship between two people. Note furthermore that in terms of this definition the person engaging in the act of leadership must have an intention to influence. That is, he intended to communicate to others, and hoped that they would accept his ideas.[2]

Leadership is based upon influence. Influence rests on three basic principles: the leader behaves in ways that gain personal recognition, in ways that assure comprehension of his ideas by his followers, and in ways that stimulate action toward a goal.

---

1. A. S. McFarland, *Power and Leadership in Pluralist Systems* (Palo Alto, Cal.: Stanford University Press, 1969), p. 154.
2. E. Stotland and L. K. Canon, *Social Psychology A Cognitive Approach* (Philadelphia: W. B. Saunders Company, 1972), p. 530.

Recognition

The leader has certain criteria to live up to. The first step in achieving influence is to gain recognition or to arouse the interest of prospective followers. Once stimulated, most people grasp and react to ideas which are presented to them, particularly when an appeal is made to their self-interests.

Enthusiasm and a genuine feeling for the ideas he is espousing is probably the best basis from which the potential leader can sell himself and his ideas. When the individual actually believes in his project, when he sees it as an attainable ideal, when he experiences and captures the excitement that such a vision has for him and passes it on to those who may follow, he is well on his way to establishing influence with others.[3]

This ability to transmit enthusiasm is a tremendous advantage in gaining attention and recognition. In addition to an enthusiastic presentation, a person bent on attracting followers must make an offer that appeals to the appetites of those he desires as followers by using his knowledge of those appetites. On a level which they can understand and appreciate, he plays upon their sympathies, pride, intelligence, emotion, or bias. He implies, suggests, persuades, reiterates, inspires, and infuses vitality into those whose attention he gains.

Among the techniques a would-be leader might use as he seeks recognition are the following: 1) implication; 2) logical persuasion; and 3) repetition. No universal principle can be laid down as the proper use of these techniques — a leader chooses those which are most effective in a given situation.

Implication is often used to strengthen or renew confidence in the leader. For example, a hint of popular support, whether valid or not, may do more to enhance the leader's idea or movement than any exhortation. The leader implies that the majority of people support him; thus he becomes a symbol of the common good and basic human values. His listeners, in order to associate themselves with the common good and basic human values, need only identify themselves with him. It is a subtle form of flattery. A leader must convince would-be followers that he is one of them, that he can represent them because he can be identified with their needs, emotions, and goals. If listeners feel that the leader's approach is too radical, too divergent from accepted mores or ways of doing things, they will surely reject his attempts to lead.

Logical persuasion is a technique used by the leader to present an idea in such a manner that its refutation becomes associated with overt bigotry.

---

3. E. Hollander and J. Julian, "Studies in Leader Legitimacy, Influence, and Innovation," in L. Berkowitz, ed., *Advances in Experimental Social Psychology,* Vol. 5 (New York: Academic Press, 1970), pp. 33-69.

The technique requires the compilation of information with such precision and attention to fact and detail that the transmission of this information to an audience indisputably weights the case in favor of the leader's cause. But before a leader can use such irrefutable logic to persuade his audience, all eventualities or available alternative courses of action must be explored in order to anticipate their consequences. All data pertinent to the problem at hand must be analyzed and material must be refined for ease and thoroughness of presentation. Probable objections to the idea must be studied and possible courses of action determined for overcoming such objections. A typical case illustrates this concept:

A low-income housing development, staffed by the public recreational service department, had a predominent black population. When a survey indicated that many residents were interested in crafts, a class was scheduled. All who expressed an interest were invited. The first meeting was attended by fifteen blacks and eight whites. After the meeting, the recreationist, who was black, was asked if there were any white instructors on the staff. He received the impression that the white women would not return if the staff were all black.

The recreationist here was alert to the numerical majority of one racial group. He realized that this might lead minority group members to withdraw. He knew that he had to give the white minority a sense of security.

The recreationist managed to recruit a white volunteer to assist with the group. At subsequent meetings the white proportion of participants increased and the entire group enjoyed the crafts course. White children also came to the recreational center and participated in a variety of activities. Adults returned for other activities and soon a successfully integrated program existed.

The recreationist knew that it would be desirable to move slowly and gain the group's confidence. He determined that the first activity had to be successful. By adroit tactics he gained acceptance, overcame resistence, and was able to persuade formerly reticent individuals to be more forthcoming.

Logical persuasion is a direct appeal to listeners through public speaking, debating, literature dissemination, and publicity through the communications media. Information based on fact and logic and imparted in a stimulating manner is a most valuable technique for persuading an audience and obtaining lasting influence.

Repetition is a technique a leader can use to impress a specific concept upon an audience. The validity and reliability of this technique is evidenced by its long and continuing existence. Among the various groups that frequently use repetition are educators, political officials, the clergy, the military, businessmen, labor unionists, and, most assuredly, advertisers.

Educators have used the repetition of facts as a basis from which to enable students to relate particular bits of knowledge to other fragments. Athletes are trained by drilling themselves in fundamental physical movements and in patterns of movements. This same process is the basis of military drill, and musicians, too, are trained in this manner. Through drill and incessant practice, habits are acquired and an automatic pattern of response is set up. The mass media demonstrate how repetition of a single idea — say, a particular brand of soap to buy — over a period of time will so focus the audience's attention on the brand that it becomes familiar in the average household. Once such attention is attracted, it is only a matter of time until a great many of the audience acquire the habit of buying the familiar brand rather than one they have never heard of. The influence exerted by repetition is often so strong that the buyer may disregard differences in price, quality, and quantity when making a purchase.

Candidates for public office also use — and misuse — repetition to attract the attention of the electorate. Although repetition can be used to subvert the audience's intelligence and lull them into failing to exercise their critical faculties, it is an equally powerful technique for stimulating the mind. Repetition of a new idea gives the individual a chance to assimilate it and to examine it in detail; an idea that is accepted on the basis of careful and intelligent analysis is likely to be more durable than one that is merely parroted.

Comprehension

After the leader has attracted attention and achieved recognition, he must devote energy to ensuring that the audience comprehends his message. Their comprehension, whether gained on an emotional or intellectual level, is the next essential step in influencing them toward action. An appeal to the emotions is a style of leadership that has proven highly effective in stimulating the achievement of short-term goals. The dangerous aspects of this technique are, of course, manifold. The leader who seeks to influence his listeners by appealing only to their emotions is likely to play also upon their fears and insecurities, causing them to abandon reason and act in ways harmful to themselves and others. Adolf Hitler's infamous career as head of the Nazi government is a classic example of the adverse effects of gaining audience comprehension through appeal to the emotions.

An appeal to the intellect, on the other hand, can lead to audience comprehension of a more lasting nature. Even unfamiliar or radical ideas presented logically and defended rationally may win followers. An idea that is accepted on the basis of critical analysis is likely to become a firm conviction and thus a strong motivator of direct action. Witness the following case:

In one community where several low-income housing projects were situated on the outskirts of a middle-income Jewish neighborhood, there was little contact among the teen-agers living inside and outside the housing project. Both groups attended the same high school. Mutual distrust and continued isolation threatened to develop into serious confrontations.

Two community centers served the low-income project and the Jewish community. A joint staff meeting was arranged between the recreationists of each center. Out of this conference grew plans to form a teen-age council which would serve as a meeting ground for all of the teen-agers concerned. The primary function of the teen-age council was to find ways for contact to be made between various of the minorities represented and to develop recreational activities for potential participants.

After the council was organized, it sponsored a block party. Limited contact produced further efforts along the same lines and other successful recreational activities were programmed. From initial enjoyment there grew better relationships and intergroup cooperation between formerly isolated groups.

When an individual finally decides in favor of something by a process of reflection, introspection, and reasoned inquiry, the notion is more likely to remain with him indefinitely. He will probably be highly stimulated to follow with action the thought that required intellectual exercise. The process of ratiocination urges on participation. When insight is gained into the fundamental principles which originated the concept, there will be more readiness to support it.

This is the most important part of comprehension. It allows the receiver to understand not merely what is going on or being said, but why it is so. When, at last, communication is achieved, the results are mutual satisfaction, acceptance, and agreement upon common objectives. This, of course, is a main component in the configuration that is influence.

Intellectual comprehension as a component of influence is illustrated in this situation taken from the report of a supervisor in the field of recreational service:

As a recreational personnel supervisor in a large municipal department of recreational service for X city, I learned that neighborhood participation at a particular facility within my jurisdiction had deteriorated to the point of nonexistence. My problem was to rebuild interest in the activities and program conducted at the facility, utilizing the workers then available.

My first step was to determine the exact nature of the recreational experiences being offered at the agency in relation to the expressed desires of neighborhood constituents. Armed with this knowledge, I held a series of individual conferences with the facility's personnel in order to learn what they understood their responsibilities to be to the community, the agency, and the program.

The results of the conferences indicated that almost all of the workers were at a loss to explain the obvious deficiency of the program, that personal difficulties between workers were an impediment to the program, and that several new workers felt completely discouraged because no in-service preparation was available to them. All of these factors pointed toward a lack of direction, enthusiasm, and cooperation on the job.

I initiated a weekly group supervisory conference designed to facilitate the free flow of ideas, appointed two of the older and more experienced workers to aid the newer employees in becoming oriented and educated on the job, and began a systematic overhaul of the recreational presentation at the center. Within three weeks the effect of the new administration was being clearly demonstrated.

I introduced a professional bookshelf into the agency. I discussed, at the weekly worker-group conferences, the basic concepts for which the agency was created. I spoke about the part that each worker played in the provision of recreational services to the people of the community. I told my people about professional ethics, conduct, and that each of them had the need to represent the agency to the public. I pointed out the fact that their personal reputation was enhanced or destroyed as the public identified them with a successful or poorly operated facility. The presentation of valid reasons for the present personnel program and the necessity for each worker to feel that he was actively contributing to the betterment of the entire department and consequently to the field as a whole apparently turned the tide.

Later, individual workers took more interest in their appearance and manner in giving information or in instructing particular activities. Activities were better planned and scheduled. The means for communicating ideas were facilitated, and workable ideas were used and commended. Every worker seemed to respond to this appeal for dedication to the job in the service of the community, and increased participation at the facility resulted.

Directed Action

The last component of influence, perhaps the most important, is directed action. Whatever techniques the potential leader has used to capture the attention of his audience and make them comprehend his ideas, only if the audience then acts on these ideas can leadership be said to have occurred. The chain of influence is complete only when individuals are so convinced and inspired by what they have heard that they take direct action toward a goal.

Getting others to act is no small task. The potential leader must be able to judge when the climate is right for action and assume the responsibility for inducing such action. He does this when he accepts or undertakes a specific task which he feels will result in the attainment of a given program he has in mind. Implied in his acceptance of this responsibility is risk of failure and attendant deterioration of any influence which he may have had up to the crucial point of initiating the action.

Among the responsibilities of the individual who guides others to a specific goal are: such an achievement must be made valuable for those who follow; no matter what the end in view or the reason for its selection and advocation, the leader still must observe moral and ethical boundaries for the benefit of his followers and the social order in which they exist. If he neglects either one of these responsibilities, he will run into difficulty. If he overlooks the welfare of his followers, they will overrule him and his dictates, and thus his influence will be nullified. If he oversteps the lines of good taste, judgment, or morality, the society in which he resides will obstruct and probably destroy or disperse his power. Further, he will do damage to his followers by leading them into trouble. In any case, his value to the group and to himself will be lost.

Basically, goal-striving or task-accomplishment plays an important part in the preservation and spirit of membership within a group. Any activity which speeds action toward a particular objective and lends itself to the continued maintenance and solidarity of the group in question serves to strengthen the influence of the leader.

The fact that the group will react to consolidate any gains it has achieved, especially when threatened by some type of conflict or pressure, means that movement toward a valued end will be more highly motivated and easier to bring about in emergency or stress conditions. One of the methods by which the leader may bring concerted action to an objective which he has in mind is to create situations which will cause action. The leader is obliged, therefore, to produce an atmosphere which is favorable to his aims.[4]

Situations and Leadership

Problems call for behavior which will effectively alleviate painful or apparently insoluble circumstance. The individual who successfully discovers the solutions for emergencies or obstructions which block goal realization enhances his influence with the group. Invariably, leadership functions most frequently in groups which are confronted with uncomfortable or anxiety-provoking situations.[5]

---

4. F.E. Fiedler, *A Theory of Leadership Effectiveness* (New York: McGraw-Hill Book Company, 1967), pp. 181-196.
5. C. Gibb, "The Principles and Traits of Leadership," *Journal of Abnormal and Social Psychology*, Vol. 42 (1947), pp. 267-284.

The movement of people toward a specific goal requires several types of behavior. One of them is planning for activity, which is a basic function of leadership. A carefully worked-out scheme, analyzed for possible errors and systematically viewed for other possibilities, is the initial step. The margin for mistake must be minimal. Where feasible, all details should be given thorough consideration before any direct action is contemplated. Thus, through the collection of highly relevant information and the sifting of fact and evidence from distortion and half-truth, a composite picture of the immediate situation is drawn. Selecting the one best route, whose consequences can be least detrimental to the group or whose results will place the group in the most defensible position and proximity to the goal, is necessary prior to calling for action.

Gaining Involvement

Perhaps the most valid method a leader can use to initiate action is allowing his followers to participate in the decision-making process. A group is most likely to expend time, money, or effort toward objectives which they choose and with which they identify. A first step in initiating action on any program is to help the participants see the connection between the proposed goal and themselves. Helpful techniques are appeals to community pride, personal philanthropy or altruism, ego-building aspects of involvement in a project, patriotism, or an appreciation of aesthetic, cultural, or historic factors. An attractive goal may have intrinsic value — economic gain or aesthetic, cultural, social, educational, or physical enhancement — or it may have symbolic value such as mastery, prestige, affection, reputation.

Directed action hinges upon the motivational elements in human behavior. People are most motivated when there is any threat to their equilibrium: physical, self-image, or basic-needs. If a goal can be related to one or more of these factors, and the potential followers persuaded that unless they act the goal will be lost, action will usually result. Many a successful leader has motivated action by appealing to primitive drives: the need for food, the avoidance of pain, the need for self-preservation. Reward incentive is another powerful motivator.

A leader may also use the present interests or experiences of his group members. The leader need only relate his ideas to these existing interests, and action upon those ideas will follow. For instance, knowing of the interest of citizens in the provision of community recreational service, he can expect to gain support from them for the organization of a public recreational service department. Immediate interests are usually practicable for initiating action. Once the action is underway, momentum will impel further action.

Appeals to psychological, social, and intellectual needs are also very successful in stimulating action. Ego-involvement may be the most important of the intellectual motives for action. In this case, the goal is presented in such a manner that its attainment will enhance the individual's self-concept, personal worth, and ability. The ego becomes a part of the goal whenever the individual feels that a part of him is identifiable with or attached to the consequences of goal attainment. The leader must use extreme care in applying ego-involvement as a spur to action, and be able to distinguish between those objectives which are meaningful to his followers and toward which they will strive, and those which have little or no meaning to them.

An interesting example of how the leader may utilize ego-involvement as motivation is examined in the following excerpt from the central files of an executive in the field of recreational service:

The community in which I had recently been employed had had a series of bond-issue defeats. The community was quite wealthy, since the average income of its citizens hovered around the five-figure mark. Inability to surmount these failures to pass any bond issues relating to community recreational facilities of any nature had finally forced my predecessor to resign.

This was my second year in the community, and I found that unless an increase in capital expenditures was made, almost half of the program based upon the utilization of physical facilities and spaces would either have to be abandoned or drastically curtailed. As superintendent of public recreational services, my legal board empowered me with the authority to seek capital funds for the construction, development, and expansion of physical facililties relating to the park and recreational services function. My only problem was how to obtain favorable consideration and action for this promotion by the citizens of the community. This is what I did:

With the help of my limited staff, I drew up a financial plan consistent with what was needed for the present needs of the community as well as for future growth of population, metropolitan trends, and area annexation. We brought together all of the information that was available, detailing such items as the economic base of the community, land-use patterns, age, sex, occupational status, and the educational experiences of the citizens. I called upon other community agencies, such as the school system and police department, fire, and health services. I had access to and used the City Clerk's office for such information on land appraisal and value, subdivisional lines, zoning regulations, and all of those pertinent items that might prove useful in the implementation of a master plan for the evaluation and development of recreational facilities, equipment of a capital nature, and land acquisition. Although I was not prepared to call for bond-issue elections until a year from that time, I was going to schedule all events and leave nothing to chance.

Once the basic information was collected and analyzed, I felt reasonably secure and attempted to put the second phase of our timetable into operation. This involved the presentation of our procedures to whomever we could get interested in the community.

I lined up speaking engagements with most of the social, civic, professional, and service organizations in the community. I felt that these groups might be our best bet for arousing support for this endeavor, since most community-minded people generally belong to these clubs. My presentation to the people in these groups concerned several points. First, there had to be a logical explanation for the expenditures that we were considering. Second, the reasons for having recreational service had to be enumerated. Third, I wanted to involve personally as many of these people as I could in taking part in the campaign which was to come.

I utilized the data which had already been collected by my staff, including charts, maps, and mockups of the proposed developments. To this I added information concerning population increments, metropolitan trends, and economic productivity which would support our proposals. I spoke about recreational needs that people have; about the growing leisure in the community; about the services that a public recreational agency provides for all age groups. I told them about human growth and development and the educational, cultural, social, and aesthetic values to be found in recreational experiences.

Then I pointed out the economic gain that could accrue to the value of land from being adjacent to or across from community and recreational parks or other facilities. I further spoke about the benefits that convenient and well-supervised playgrounds would have on the children of the community. Since the facilities were planned so that no child would have to cross a major traffic artery or go more than one-quarter mile to reach a playground, the safety of participants was taken into consideration. Playing on dangerous streets would be avoided. Mothers would be able to take their children to nearby and very accessible locations, planned for their comfort and enjoyment.

Finally, I explained that the proposed development would enhance the community setting, beautifying blighted areas and acquiring green spaces and recreational places which would be preserved for the health, education, and welfare of the citizens of the community for as long as they wanted it.

With this phase out of the way, I received commitments from several members of each group who pledged their support and assistance. My next objective was to form committees which would function as the campaign machine to sell the bond issue to the entire community.

With participation from the local P.T.A., denominational groups, business and professional clubs, civic, and service organizations, I was able to organize the five committees needed to administer the campaign. There was a planning committee, which met to discuss and get a better understanding of the community's recreational needs, so that a detailed budget could be made for financing the recreational plan. This group worked as a steering committee, which coordinated all the efforts of participating groups working on the campaign. A budget committee was responsible for estimating the total cost of the campaign and raising the funds necessary for carrying it out. We had a public relations committee, responsible for disseminating information to the public. A neighborhood person-to-person committee was formed. Its duty was to knock on the door of every registered voter within the community and solicit a yes vote on election day. Finally, a transportation committee was mobilzed to see that every voter had transportation to and from the polls, if he so desired it.

Every organization in the community supported the issue. With our detailed plan of coordinated action and each individual's taking a part, a record number of voters turned out on election day. As a result, over $1,872,496 was voted by more than a three-to-one majority.

What had turned the trick? Simply the utilization of people in a planned effort to attain a specific objective. The desired end was already determined, but the people of the community had to be stimulated to achieve this end. Once the citizens listened and were persuaded by the logic of the idea, it was a matter of providing identifying symbols which would bind them to the tasks and serve as the motive power in gaining this goal. The attractiveness of the original concept, the clear analytic presentation, and the ego-involvement which this project had for those who became interested carried the plan to a successful conclusion.

While several techniques were used in achieving the desired goal, it was not until the personal factor was brought in that people responded to the task. Although logical exhortation, repetition, and some emotional appeal was tried, the point that actually impelled action was ego-involvement. Individuals were made to feel that their contribution was more important than anything else. The whole matter became one of reputation, integrity, and personal identification with the success of the bond issue. Reinforcement came with the assignments and the progress made each day the campaign operated. Rivalry between civic organizations was forgotten as each group worked to meet the indicated need. Everybody performed to some extent. Achievement of the predetermined goal was accomplished. Leadership was exhibited. Action was the result.

SELECTED REFERENCES

Dyson, J. W., D. W. Fleitas, and F. P. Scioli, "The Interaction of Leadership, Personality, and Decisional Environments," *Journal of Social Psychology,* Vol. 86 (1972), pp. 29-33.

Evans, M. G., "Leadership and Motivation: A Case Concept," *Academy of Management Journal,* Vol. 13 (1970), pp. 91-102.

Fiedler, F. E., *Leadership* (New York: General Learning Press, 1971).

Gibb, C. A., ed., *Leadership* (Baltimore, Md.: Penguin Books, 1970).

Harrison, C. W., J. R. and D. J. Rawls, "Differences Between Leaders and Non-Leaders in Six-to-Eleven Year Old Children," *Journal of Social Psychology,* Vol. 84 (1972), pp. 269-272.

Hastorf, A. H., D. Schneider, and J. Polefka, *Person Perception* (Reading, Mass.: Addison-Wesley, 1969).

Hornaday, J. A. and C. S. Bunker, "The Nature of the Entrepreneur," *Personnel Psychology,* Vol. 23 (1970), pp. 47-54.

Knowles, H. P. and B. O. Saxberg, *Personality and Leadership* (Reading, Mass.: Addison-Wesley, 1971).

Yukl, G. A., "Toward a Behavioral Theory of Leadership," *Organizational Behavior and Human Performance,* Vol. 6 (1971), pp. 414-440.

CHAPTER SIX

The Origins of Leadership

E ven in the simplest circumstances, as when a group begins a discussion which will result in a decision of some kind, a leader appears to be required. Actually, it is very difficult for a group to act or verbalize except through a designated member. If everybody speaks or acts simultaneously there will be general confusion. For the group to act in concert or display cohesion, it is vital that individual members speak for it. Some one person must articulate the necessity for order, the techniques to be employed to reach goals, the acceptance of the means for achievement, and the decision to act. When the purposes of the group require greater diversity of activity and, therefore, more cooperation and coordination, the fundamental need for a leader will be heightened proportionately.

The leader emerges in one of several ways. Initially, the members of a group may become aware that one individual serves it more effectively than any other. Such acceptance may be completely predictive or mere estimation. It may come in consequence of experiences which various members have had. The member of a group who first suggests some plan of action that agrees with other members for achieving satisfaction of needs may collect a following for varying lengths of time. The member of a group who is known to possess a skill, knowledge, or other means which is required to solve a problem confronting the group may be called upon and expected to perform the leadership role.

Leaders also develop because a person who desires some end may not be able to achieve it without assistance. If he can influence others to participate then his objectives will be met. In the process, an act of leadership has been performed. An individual who wishes to lead may purposefully seek an appropriate group, but he may also discover that unless he is perceived as one who can provide increased need satisfaction or offer solutions to problems, there will be no followers.

Thus, leadership in all its manifestations is a symbiotic relationship between the leader and his followers.[1] But what determines who leads? How does a leader attain that position? Does every individual occupying a leadership position actually lead?

---

1. E. P. Hollander and R. G. Hunt, eds., *Current Perspectives in Social Psychology,* 3d ed., (New York: Oxford University Press, 1971), p. 500.

Problem-Solving and Leadership

The leader steps into a situation that requires attention and enables others to act with or toward some purpose. The recreationist is supposed to be a leader. In fact, this is the work title by which most program-or entry-level workers are identified.

Leadership is an explicit understanding and interaction between the person placed in the position of leadership and those of the group or other individuals who are his followers. The leader must also attempt to reconcile whatever differences in opinion there may be. When there is a divergence of opinion, a test of leadership develops.

Leadership is often a product of crisis. Crises, however, need not always be thought of in terms of great peril, revolution, or any other catastrophic event. They may be little-known incidents which have no particular significance to anyone outside the situation. They may occur over school grades, team tryouts, dramatic endeavors, or attempts at creativity. They may occur in the church, in the home, in the community center, or on the playground. They may come in the guise of time, money, effort, or personality. The person who solves critical problems is a leader.

In the field of recreational service, crises always occur. A problem in one area is no sooner solved than two others spring up to take its place. Resolving such problems is the responsibility of the recreational leader.

HOW THE LEADER IS DETERMINED

There are at least four conditions which can promote the creation of leadership in any given group situation. The one most usually found in the field of recreational service is appointment by some form of authority. This is generally made on the basis of technical competency, with or without the consent of subordinates or potential group members. The next instance is election. This is quite different from appointment. The elected leader is one who has received his sanction directly from those who are his followers. The third is emergence, a leader who comes to the fore as a result of a crisis or who, because of his dominant attitudes or forceful behavior, enlists the support of group members despite other claimants. The fourth possibility derives from an individual's infallibility and charisma. Through the popularization, usually by the efforts of a vocal and zealous few, of an idea which captures the imagination of a great majority, the ideal figure is made leader.

The Appointed Leader

The recreationist functioning as a resource or technical advisor is appointed to his position. Whether or not he is a leader, in the true meaning of the word, or merely performs in a "headship" capacity remains to be seen. A true leader is one who has such influence with others as to motivate them toward a particular goal. The recreationist may very well function in this way. However, it is not usually from selection by the group that the recreationist derives his influence, but rather from the auspices of the agency for which he works.

The appointed leader generally has some professional requirement to fulfill, perhaps as a technician, teacher, administrator, or performer. Whatever his role, his assignment comes from some source outside the group with which he will be working. Thus, the appointed leader brings with him an aura of control and authority vested in him by the agency. He must function despite the possible handicap of being placed with a group that does not want him. With appointment come obligations. He must perform within the framework of agency policies; he must attempt to influence a group with whom he works; he has no choice in the selection of his group members, but must provide them with professional service despite any negative personal feeling toward them.

The obverse is that the appointment carries with it the prestige of the agency and its sanction. Group members are more likely to look upon this leader as an individual with the special talents, skills, or techniques to help them function. His word may stop conflict; he may be looked upon as the mediator when argument flares. He may become the security or supporting figure to self-effacing members. He may, of course, simply become an object of intense dislike. The latter is a possible outcome when the appointed leader has usurped prerogative. Generally, however, an ambivalent reaction is the one which the appointed leader must face.

The leader, no matter how he tries, cannot always be good, kind, gentle, and permissive. There are times when his understanding of the need of the group-as-a-whole obligates him to act in ways which may deprive one or more members from having things "their own way." Surely some hostile feeling will result from such conflicts. However, the same individual who expresses hostility at one moment may well change as the condition of the group changes. This is a part of the dynamics of group life.

The appointed recreational leader performs his functions within the community in relation to certain cues which are a part of the environment. He learns by what he hears, sees, and experiences. From his observation of the individuals with whom he works and the community in which he serves, he begins to formulate a modus operandi for the particular situation. The following factors are those which influence the recreationist as he attempts to fulfill his professional obligations:

1. The community fabric involves socio-economic-political considerations, ethnic factors, and religious aspects. The life of the

community, with its tradition, mores, cultural standards, and social institutions, does much to limit or extend the recreational leader's possible service. Such intangibles as class, race, education, and the like may allow or prevent certain individuals entering a particular group. Coming from the "wrong side of the tracks", so the speak, may effectively bar persons from acceptance in organizations or cause caste lines to develop which necessitate the organization of certain agencies within one section of the community and not in others. All of these interacting forces play a part in influencing the role of the appointed leader in any recreational agency setting. How the community sees itself will unquestionably have direct bearing upon how the leader will be able to conduct himself or provide the services which he knows are necessary. An unsympathetic or nonsupportive community may cause undue hardship and create conflict situations for him. In such instances, he must create a favorable atmosphere through the use of logical persuasion, education, negotiation, and all other means at his disposal in attempting to enlighten the community so that what he is doing will receive adequate public support and acceptance. Where the community is receptive to his work, his opportunity for professional service is unlimited.

2. The agency's policies and activities concern such diverse facets as rules and regulations of operation, function or responsibilities, and scope. Depending upon the type of agency — school, club, public recreational department, welfare department, church, or private organization — the recreationist will perform within its frame of reference. If the agency feels that it should operate in a group-work capacity or offer a wide variety of activities which are open to all or a few, it will radically affect the leader's role.

3. The agency's facilities will have a marked effect upon the work of the recreationist. The type, number, and adequacy of agency facilities will also attract or repel specific individuals. This reaction may be a limiting or inclusive factor in terms of the leader's effectiveness.

4. The kind of group with which the recreationist is placed will, in large measure, influence his role as a leader. Whether or not he will lead in a direct manner, work through others within the group, play a resource role or an observing role, or function as an arbitrator will depend upon the interests, needs, abilities, and limitations of the individuals within the group. The amount of help which the group will accept from the leader, as opposed to what it actually needs, and the skill and efficiency of the recreationist himself will certainly restrict or extend the range of leadership functions and responsibilities. If the recreationist is a true leader and understands his position in relation to that of individuals in the group, his confidence, talent, and competence will be

"on the line," and will be continually tested.

All of these conditions may well create the boundaries and special circumstances beyond which the appointed leader may not go. His appointment is based upon specific professional qualities. He must function to the extent of his professional knowledge and skill, limited only by the immediate policy of the agency, the support of the community, the makeup of the group to which he is appointed, and his concept of service within the recreational field.

Crisis situations critically illustrate the leadership adequacy of the recreationist in the group setting. The appointed leader moves into a crisis with complete awareness of why such a condition exists and what must be done to control or remove it. He looks upon conflicts as a challenge to his knowledge and technical skill. The reactions of group members to such a strained situation provides insight into individual and collective needs. The leader observes and evaluates behavior in reference to group structure or other norms which are available. From these views of individual and group behavior, he may draw certain conclusions about participating individuals and thereby place himself in a position where his technical knowledge or understanding of those individuals would be useful to them. By enabling others to handle extraordinary situations which may be beyond their experience or ability, the leader affords them the opportunity to help themselves.

Realizing that conflict is simply a question of points of view, experience, or knowledge about particular values, the leader is better able to give support and encouragement where needed. His obligation is to sustain his group members and help them to achieve desirable patterns of behavior in dealing with unaccustomed emergencies or predicaments.

The Elected Leader

The elected leader may not be a leader at all; he may be brought to the position of leadership through popularity, accident, design, or tradition. Such an individual could very well be a real leader, his popularity reflecting his ability to influence others, but this is not necessarily true. Our society is quite aware of popularity polls and how they may place into office or position an individual who is neither qualified nor, in fact, a leader. Fortunately for recreational programs, the recreationist is seldom, if ever, elected to his position.

Some elections are really popularity contests based upon so-called values which have little or nothing to do with leadership. For example, a candidate for public office might proclaim the fact that he belongs to a certain religious denomination, is married, has children, loves dogs, is a veteran, and is a member of a number of service clubs or fraternities. Few of these facts have any bearing on his qualification to hold office. They are simply a means of creating a popular image of the candidate, running on a "common man" approach rather than on his demonstrated qualifications to hold the office.

Election by popularity can be achieved if the candidate can force himself to shake as many hands as he can reach, kiss babies, or say the things which people want to hear, even if he does not believe them himself. Typical of this situation is the following example:

> The Recreationist Majors Club at X College was about to elect officers to administer and operate the Club for the academic year. A senior student campaigned vigorously for the president's office. She made many promises. She indicated that, if elected, she would design a calendar of activities, have interesting meetings on topical subjects, make sure that the monthly newspaper was produced, and see to the general management of the Club. These promises included a certain amount of recruitment for new Club members. She was vivacious, intelligent, made friends easily, and was considered excellent material for the presidency. As a leader, she was a complete failure. She not only failed to live up to her campaign pledges, she completely ignored the Club in favor of other less arduous assignments. What resulted was a deterioration of the Club program, demoralization of the membership, and the realization on its part that it had "been taken."

Popularity is, after all, a matter of taste. Friendliness and the common touch may appeal to many people, but they are not a guarantee that the elected office holder will be a leader. Fortunately, they are sometimes coupled with leadership ability, in which case the judgment of the electorate will have been justified.

Elected leadership through accident rather than plan is a common occurrence. We have all known cases in which an individual just happened to be present at a time when an incumbency opened and, in desperation to fill the position, the "powers" took him because he was the only person upon whom all factions could agree, he compromised enough to be acceptable, or he was a "good old Joe."

As Haiman has noted:

> Any observer who has watched the emergence of leadership in a fair sampling of social situations would be a remarkable analyst indeed if he claimed to see important explainable forces at work in every case. Let us frankly face the fact that on a multitude of occasions, leadership falls into the laps of those who simply happen to be in the right place at the right time. They do not necessarily have any special characteristics or

native endowments, they are not created by an urgent situation, there is no tradition at work — they simply happen, willy-nilly, to get in the way when the roles of leadership are assigned. There is good reason to believe that some of our less eminent American presidents came to office in this way. It also happens frequently among young children in classroom elections, where Sally happens to be elected because someone nominates her first. It sometimes happens in adult committee meetings, where someone casually says, "Well, Jack, why don't you act as chairman?" and ipso facto, Jack has the job.[2]

The accidents of outliving competition, seniority-based jobs, or birth may contribute to the combination of happy incidents which propel an average person into an elected position of leadership. Civil service incumbencies, a one-party system of politics, union activities, military positions, and family-operated enterprises are all part of this insidious system which tends to promote the incompetent over the qualified. Invariably, also, death opens the way for position in the accidental race of leadership. The dullest, most mediocre, least inspiring of individuals may rise to a position of leadership simply by staying alive longer than his co-workers. The seniority system may be an excellent protective device against corruption, but it is also the best way of promoting unqualified persons to leader slots and discouraging the qualified. If no one else is available, the electorate must place into office those who cannot, by any stretch of the imagination, be considered leaders.

The accident of birth is another contributing factor in the promotion of mediocrities. Family firms, in order to maintain control of the corporate enterprise, rely upon dynastic principles in order to retain the prerogatives of management. Thus, the unqualified son of the chairman of the board may very well be elected to an executive position and then assume the mantle of leadership. Perhaps he is merely the figurehead, with the shadowy form of an administrative assistant to give him informed substance, but, to the world at large, he represents leadership for that firm or industry.

The Emergent Leader

Situations determine the rise of the natural or spontaneous leader. A combination of emergencies and the lack of a determining influence to shape a course of action may arouse latent leadership. Leadership potential is always present within a group. Whatever triggers this leadership performance lies within the needs of the group, any crisis which threatens its continuation, and the individual personality involved.

---

2. F. S. Haiman, *Group Leadership and Democratic Action* (New York: Houghton Mifflin, 1951), pp. 16-17. Reprinted by permission.

The indigenous leader, one to whom most or all of the group members gravitate for direction and affection, has the central role of the interrelational process in the group. Direction and affection are the two motivational forces which stimulate followership. Direction includes not only guidance and goal-setting, it very likely contains such force features as physical strength and economic, social, or status factors. For instance, leadership in children's groups is usually associated with the most physically capable, biggest, and consequently strongest group member. He is in a position to implement his goals by coercion or by means of the members' belief in his strength and skill. He is worthy of emulation and has influence with them.

In children's groups, leadership status is sometimes seen as the "pecking order," the position or status within the group. The expression is taken from the barnyard, where the more aggressive fowls get the grain and the passive or cowardly chickens, relegated to the end of the line, receive only the leftover crumbs. We see this type of behavior in "bullies," who by their strength and aggressiveness gain their ends at the expense of others.

Status through fear is not leadership but a form of dictatorship. Nevertheless, the indigenous leader may be highly authoritarian and obtain his position through the imposition of an impressive physical, economic, or social strength. Such an individual would neither be elected nor appointed but would emerge in a leadership position because of his forceful personality or through his use of power.

Coercion does not necessarily characterize the indigenous leader. Affection and its associated components may also merit admiration and influence others. If the group chooses to entrust its structure to one individual, then they believe in him and want to follow his advice. His personality, just as forceful as that of an authoritarian, is of a different stripe. He wields his influence with others because he has demonstrated that his ideas are either the best or that they are most acceptable to the common interest of the group-as-a-whole. The emergent leader's role is created from a group's need. An aggressive or forceful personality or the possession of knowledge, which can determine the outcome of a situation, may be the stimulus which prods a group to act.

But what of the recreationist in the emergent-leader picture? Surely it must be obvious that the professional is not an indigenous leader, except perhaps among his peers. Why then has this section been included? Basically, because within groups with whom the recreationist works, there usually are natural leaders. If the recreationist wants any influence with members of these groups, he must find it indirectly through the central person of that group.

In general, natural leadership is generated through personal relations. Two examples of the indigenous leader's strength within the group are illustrated as follows:

A state correctional school for girls in one of the midwestern states employed a program director. During the summer, one of the recreational activities was a campfire program which included all of the girls in the school. Some of the girls indicated by their actions that they were dissatisfied with the activity and did not want to take part in it. However, since this was an all-school program, they had to be at the campfire and could not remain behind in their dormitories. One group in particular was vociferous in their protests against this activity and would neither cooperate nor give any valid reason why they should not.

The program director, realizing that they would receive little or no value from an activity which they appeared to dislike so intensely, called the group together and attempted to determine a reason or reasons for their adverse reactions. There was no reason given. The recreationist knew each of the girls and was quite aware of the girl who controlled the group.

The indigenous leader was an individual whose main attribute was that she was bigger and stronger than the other girls in her dormitory. However, she had a very pleasant personality, was a model student, and cooperated with the school authorities in every way. She had been placed in the institution because she had borne a child out of wedlock. Having been adjudged delinquent by the courts, she was sentenced to the state correctional school until she should come of age.

Her size, together with a warm and friendly nature, naturally pushed her into a leadership position. The girls all liked her, and she was the confidante of them all. The director asked her what she felt was causing the difficulty. She replied that there was nothing vicious behind the girls' lack of response; it was simply that they felt the activity was for younger children and that they were too "sophisticated" to participate. Upon learning this, the director recalled the group and was able to demonstrate successfully that the campfire activities may include singing, dramatics, pageants, picnics, and game or sport activities, depending upon what the participants wanted and how accomplished or adept they were in learning skills. With the knowledge he gained from conferring with the natural group leader and by working through her to direct the group into the activity, the program went off with slight interference.

The Leader as Facilitator. Here, one can see the problem that a recreationist faces when working with a formed group. Invariably, he must determine who the central person is and attempt to guide the group indirectly. He must prevent conflict between himself and the indigenous leader if he expects any positive help in influencing the group.

Although the professional can discern an indigenous leader or leaders within a group, his functions are quite different from those of a direct leader. Regardless of the situation, the recreationist must always be a guide. However, when working with indigenous leaders, the professional has an even more sensitive role to play. He must be a facilitator, one who helps or enables members of the group to achieve satisfying experiences.[3]

As a facilitator, the recreationist is available to give technical advice or assistance to the group when it lacks experience. He aids in the development of group cohesiveness, individual self-realization, membership awareness, and comprehension of personal ability or limitation. He may further enable the group to perceive any internally divisive forces or those which hinder the group from attaining complete accomplishment. He usually aids the group to formulate its structure and the indigenous leaders to understand their obligations and to function in a way that will further group goals.

Situational Forces. Another illustration of the professional's role in coordinating the influence of the indigenous leader with that of his own may be seen from the following case:

> The executives of a southern region decided to form a group which would represent the professional recreational agencies. They organized an association. The first president elected was one of the older superintendents, who had developed the original recreational department in the region. He was authoritarian in his methods. Individual members of the group may have had cause to dislike him, but they collectively deferred to him. Everything which he suggested was executed, and his word on any matter was the final decision.
>
> He was succeeded in the presidency by his closest cohorts. As the years went by, other recreationists joined the association, and newer members were elected to the presidency and enjoyed official status. However, the original first president still ruled the roost. His aggressive behavior, personal opinions, and knowledge made him the acknowledged leader. He was successful in forming, within the association, a small hard-core clique which invariably voted the way he wanted questions to be decided. Thus, he controlled the direction which the organization took, although theoretically the president was elected to direct the group. In any matter, his ideas were solicited in order to gain acceptance.
>
> One member of this group found it was necessary to request funds for a scholarship. The president of the organization was opposed, as were some of the more influential members. Simply by going through the

---

3. T. M. Newcomb, R. H. Turner, and P. E. Converse, *Social Psychology the Study of Human Interaction* (New York: Holt, Rinehart and Winston, Inc., 1965), pp. 473-486.

natural leader of the group, after showing why the scholarship was beneficial both to the association as well as the recipient, this member was able to obtain an affirmative reaction to the request. However, instead of bringing the question up for vote, the member asked the indigenous leader to raise the point. With no conflict whatsoever, a unanimous approval was gained.

In this situation, there was no problem in identifying the central figure of the group. Only by aligning this individual with the course the member wanted was there any chance of achieving it. Without the approval of the indigenous leader, there would have been only a slim possibility. Once he was committed to the member's ideas, success was assured. In order to get the group to agree on an idea and then act to realize it, it was mandatory that the indigenous leader be persuaded to lend his support. It was no gamble to call a vote after he requested that the money be donated.

It should be obvious that almost any action may be accomplished through indirect leadership when the figure to whom the group defers is utilized. Guiding such a person may be performed on the basis of logic, personal gain, dedication to a cause, or appeal to the ego. This latter technique may be used when the natural leader considers himself an elder statesman or enjoys playing a father figure.

Appeal to the ego must be carefully considered. Such an approach places the user at a distinct disadvantage. It requests some sort of favor, and the petitioner must be ready to donate something of value in return. This can lead to complications, unless the professional really understands the individual with whom he is dealing. Arbitrariness on the part of the indigenous leader can completely wreck any chance for guidance of the group.

When the recreationist is working with an individual who views himself as a father figure, he must be shown that following the line to which the professional adheres is the one which will be most satisfying to the group and to its central person. Perhaps the most valuable strategy is to wait patiently for the indigenous leader to expose his feelings toward the idea which the professional has in mind. Once the natural leader expresses himself, it is easy to shape a course which may appear to coordinate with his, but which in reality may be completely different.

Such a technique has been used by many. It simply consists of repeating what the individual has stated, making an affirmative reply, and then adding another idea. Such a process may sound like this: "I feel that our group should concentrate its efforts on the production of a community field day." "Your idea for a community field day is excellent, but don't you think that a little theater group might serve a better purpose at this time? A community field-day program would be much more beneficial to the participants if it were held later."

Stated in such ways as to praise the original contributor's idea, there is more likelihood that the new thought will be accepted. In general, such a response will be received with good will. The indigenous leader's reception of this type of reply will be one of reciprocity: either he is placed in a position of acquiescence or else he appears to be unnecessarily harsh or, at the very least, ungenerous.

Leadership is a conditioning process which affects followers in their continuation of sanctions of power upon a single individual as a leader. When a person has demonstrated his ability to overcome a seemingly impossible problem by decision and influenced action, he achieves some notoriety and becomes the focus of attention. Future expectation of the same sort is entrusted to him. The cliché "success breeds success" is not to be taken lightly when individuals are influenced by another's apparently miraculous talent to alleviate difficult conflicts.

The situational leader will survive in the leader role as long as the unexpected is expected. Those who have followed will follow again. As long as a suspicion remains that the chosen individual may be able to surmount hazards or seemingly critical situations, he will retain leadership. Thus, the leader's influence over his followers grows with each successful achievement. In a word, they are conditioned to accept an individual as a leader in direct ratio to the number of critical situations which he solves. Knickerbocker has succinctly explained this process:

> The leader may "emerge" as a means to the achievement of objectives desired by the group. He may be selected, elected, or spontaneously accepted by the group because he possesses or controls means (skill, knowledge, money, association, property, etc.) which the group desires to utilize to attain their objectives . . . . However, there will be no relationship with the group — no followers — except in terms of the leader's control of means for the satisfaction of the needs of the followers.[4]

Leadership and Success. Unless the leader attains the goals which he and the group tend to accept as their own, his influence with the group will wane. If he is to retain the position of leader, his activities must be recognized as those which contribute toward or enable the accomplishment of desired ends. The durability of the indigenous leader lies with his continued success. The recreationist must recognize what is ipso facto a dictum of the group: there are many leaders within any group. Thus, the recreationist cannot always depend upon the same individual in any one group to have the same degree of influence upon others. He must therefore

---

4. I. Knickerbocker, "Leadership: A Conception and Some Implications," *Journal of Social Issues,* Vol. 4, No. 3 (1948), p. 33. Reprinted by permission.

continually observe the shifting patterns of relationships within the group in order that he may correctly work through the current central personality. Should he misjudge who holds influence with the group, his plans may not only be thwarted, but his rapport with members may be damaged. One necessity in any group situation is knowledge of changing attitudes or shifts in alignment. The sociographic image must be kept constantly at the fore.

The achievement of success makes little difference to the leader's incumbency. Where knowledge is the only answer to difficulty, however, individuals are less prone to place their faith in the expert with whom such knowledge resides unless qualifying factors are also present such as potent personality and approachability to followers' needs. People crave the dynamic rather than the studied technique. Decisive movement which stimulates seems to be the foundation upon which leadership rests and survives.

The Charismatic Leader

A leadership role may be created from the need to respond to a superhuman source of strength. Such charismatic leadership may stem from a vague idea or an overpowering concept with overtones of spiritual guidance. It can be personalized in a man or made metaphysical in a thought.[5]

Charisma is conceived as a mystical power which raises the owner to godlike status, if not actual divinity. It is the power to perform miracles which the ordinary man lacks the ability to do. Generally, charismatic leadership develops from a verbalization or frequently repeated idea which is purported to have been originated by one individual. Regardless of the idea itself, which is usually a powerfully worded or deeply meaningful message, its continuous repetition may place the mantle of leadership upon the shoulders of the originator, or upon someone who can utilize the idea to his advantage.

This mode of leadership is not born of an individual who influences others, but some striking message or philosophy. The concept is invariably directed at a particular group, but as time passes, it receives a much wider dissemination until it becomes the underlying foundation or rationale of whole populations. Such influence is of the longest duration. Continuity of this form of thinking contains power for the protagonists of the idea long after the inventor has passed from the scene. In fact, where an idea becomes the focal point around which a unique scheme of life is born, the occasioner may be deified by the followers. This process is exemplified by the

---

5. I. Schiffer, *Charisma: a Psychoanalytic Look at Mass Society* (Toronto: University of Toronto Press, 1973).

originators of some of the world's great religions, whose exponents have raised the creative thinker to a state of godhood. Similarly, political thinkers have been accorded charisma.

The charismatic leader is one who either makes pronouncements with the fanatical conviction of infallibility, or one who creates the impression of indispensability through the decision-making process. The success of the mystic is dependent upon the particular need of the would-be follower. Basically, such a need is found in man's insecurity. When a relatively weak or insecure person finds in someone a protective or supporting figure, he leans heavily upon that support. He romanticizes such a figure and idealizes him to the extent that he is ready to grant him the powers of divinity, if that individual will just point the way toward salvation. Salvation comes in many guises. It may be in terms of life after death, economic or political security, a way to ascribe all weaknesses to someone else, a place in the spectrum of society, money, independence, or something called world domination. Any of these may be the panacea upon which the individual is willing to raise another to the position of leadership.

Whether the leader justifies the faith of his following makes little difference after the position has been attained. Even where charisma is simply mass hysteria or a figment of the would-be follower's imagination, the legend is at work. Thus, infallibility, the "sure hand of God," or incredible wisdom is attached to the person forever after.

One aspect of charisma may be observed among children's groups where a counselor, coach, or beloved teacher is the recipient of an adoration almost bordering on love. Idolization of an attractive person is frequently experienced in recreational service settings: camps, schools, hospitals, playgrounds, and centers. In some adult groups, overreliance on a recreationist who has a magnetic personality and recognized technical skill occurs. This is particularly true when adult members desire to participate, but abdicate responsibility for making difficult choices. The group membership may view the recreationist as charismatic especially if he is a problem-solver or his advice and guidance usually result in success.

The Charismatic Father Surrogate. Faith in some paternalistic figure is the solution which man has always utilized to gain comfort and security from the stress of life. Most people have a simple philosophy, which they construe as "live and let live." This is a policy of allowing anything to occur, just so long as it does not jeopardize the personal freedom of the individual. Ironically, this policy of isolation is one that abets tyranny and connives to make human freedom impossible at any time. The strain of having to enter another's dominion in order to determine whether one's personal liberty is being denied flies in the face of what most people consider their basis for living. This is a strain which many cannot face, and thus they deputize another to do it for them.

The characteristic of avoiding or vacillating over decisions, which many do because it is easier and does not entail the sacrifice of friends or good will, paves the way for a charismatic leader to arise. The escape from reality, postponement of decisions, and entrance to the world of irresponsibility bear just one consequence — the relinquishment of power into the hands of a leader,[6] Kretch and Crutchfield have indicated this point quite well:

> The leader serves as a perfect focus for the positive emotional feelings of the individual; he is the ideal object for identification, for transference, for feelings of submissiveness. Psychoanalytic theorists have stressed this exceedingly significant feature of the relationship of the leader to his followers, and there seems no doubt of the major role that it plays in accounting for the tremendous powers of certain leaders in special group circumstances. Roosevelt and Hitler undoubtedly served as compelling father-figures for many of their followers.[7]

As long as individuals are willing to grant responsibility to one who is looked upon as infallible, the flight from reality and personal security is irrevocable. The follower rarely or never questions the leader's judgment, for to do so would bring about a general questioning of the entire structure of faith which the follower has built. Aside from opening up doubts as to the dogma for which the leader stands, it tends to weaken the follower's system of values and casts aspersions of heresy upon him. The character of one who would elevate another to divine status militates against any questioning. But, beyond this factor, lies an even more insidious reason: it would cause the individual to question his personal rationale for believing and undermine his abiding faith. It could mean that the individual would have to break away from his complete identification with the leader. It might even mean that the follower would have to deny the premises which have sustained him, make his own decisions, and take responsibility, not only for his actions, but for others as well. Those who need the support of an all-powerful figure could never bring themselves to act in ways which might require responsible activity.[8]

Surely recreationists are neither charismatic leaders, nor are they likely to be working with those who are considered to have charisma. However, human nature being what it is deliberately finds the path of least resistance in its attempt to reduce conflict. One of the methods which the human community utilizes is the placement of authority so that it does not have to think or act. Such authority is construed as charismatic leadership.

---

6. S. Hook, *The Hero In History* (New York: John Day, 1943), pp. 14ff.

7. D. Kretch and R. S. Crutchfield, *Theory and Problems of Social Psychology* (New York: McGraw-Hill, 1948), p. 421. Reprinted by permission.

8. J. V. Downton, Jr., *Rebel Leadership Commitment and Charisma in the Revolutionary Process* (New York: The Free Press, 1973), pp. 209-237.

SELECTED REFERENCES

Argyle, M., *Social Interaction* (New York: Aldine-Atherton, 1969).

Aronson, E., *The Social Animal* (San Francisco: Freeman, 1972).

Bathory, P. D., ed., *Leadership in America: Consensus, Corruption, and Charisma* (New York: Longman, 1978).

Berkowitz, L., ed., *Advances in Experimental Social Psychology,* Vol. 5 (New York: Academic Press, 1970).

Geis, F., R. Christie, and others, *Studies in Machiavellianism* (New York: Academic Press, 1970).

Jaffee, C. L., S. A. Richards, and G. W. McLaughlin, "Leadership Selection Under Differing Feedback Conditions," *Psychonomic Science,* Vol. 20 (1970), pp. 349-350.

Loye, D., *The Leadership Passion* (San Francisco: Jossey-Bass, 1977).

Morris, C. G. and J. R. Hackman, "Behavioral Correlates of Perceived Leadership," *Journal of Personality and Social Psychology,* Vol. 13 (1969), pp. 350-361.

Vroom, V. H. and P. W. Yetton, *Leadership and Decision-Making* (Pittsburgh: University of Pittsburgh Press, 1973).

CHAPTER SEVEN

Foundations for Group Dynamics

The recreationist is usually appointed to a professional position on the basis of demonstrated ability, specific knowledge, and dynamic qualities that indicate some talent in organizing or administering broad programs of activities in the recreational setting. Such an individual must then prove his real ability to lead as he encounters his peers and works with people in the community. The recreationist must be capable of guiding and directing participants in such a way that they derive the utmost benefit and satisfaction from their recreational experiences. In this way the recreationist may gain influence with others through their voluntary availability to him. Because the recreationist works almost always in a group situation, this chapter will focus on the nature and characteristics of groups.

BASIC ASSUMPTIONS ABOUT GROUPS

The combination of leader and followers creates the entity known as a group. People seem to have an affinity for all kinds of groups. It appears that the group is the structure through which most individuals feel they can best achieve their goals. The fundamental feature of such an aggregation of people is that they have *chosen* to join together. No extra-personal pressure has required any individual to become a member of such a group. Conversely, persons who are institutionalized are not considered a group, although they may voluntarily affiliate themselves with groups which they either form or join within such institutions. Initially, an individual forms, affiliates with, or remains a member of a group because he realizes that he can gain his objectives more easily by being a part of the group than he can by remaining outside it. Among the benefits accruing to group involvement are a diminution of personal costs, a magnification of effort toward personal goals impossible to achieve alone, and a reduction in the friction or painful experiences that may follow solitary action; among the objectives are security, affection, enjoyment, status, political power, and social influence.[1]

1. L.S. Wrightsman, *Social Psychology in the Seventies* (Monterey, Cal.: Brooks/Cole Publishing Company, Inc., 1972), pp. 400-401.

Qualities of Groups

First, groups are self-evident and pervasive. Although groups need not endure forever or even retain the qualities that they reveal at any given time in any given social system, they nevertheless exist wherever a collection of people live in proximity. Even the most confirmed individualists, such as members of the so-called "counter-culture," form groups which are characterized by a life-style, speech, dress, music, habits, heroes, and slogans which are as regimented and routine as are conforming patterns of any division of society. *Second,* groups marshal potent stimulants that create effects of transcending significance to individuals. A person's self-perception is highly influenced and reinforced by the groups with which he identifies such as family, peers, religious organizations, and professional associations. This also affects the manner in which others respond to him. Affiliation with a particular group may be the climax of a long-anticipated desire or the most disappointing and troublesome ordeal; serious distress and personal humiliation often accompany either rejection or compulsory affiliation by a group. *Third,* groups may occasion both positive and negative outcomes. Just as the individuals who comprise a group's membership may sometimes err or make poor judgments, so a group can make mistakes. *Fourth,* the dynamics of group living promote the possibility that highly beneficial effects for both the membership and society can be intentionally devised through enlightened leadership.

Most definitions of "group" contain certain restrictions. Others are so broad that every cluster of people is classified as a group. Typical of the latter is Brodbeck's definition:

> A group is an aggregate of individuals standing in certain descriptive (i.e., observable) relations to each other. The kinds of relations exemplified will, of course, depend upon, or determine, the kind of group, whether it be a family, an audience, a committee, a labor union, or a crowd.[2]

If groups were defined in this way, any coincidental gathering of people could conceivably be identified as a group. A group is more than two or more people in close physical proximity. The concept of observable relations does not obviate the need to distinguish further. Under this umbrella description, individuals collected at a corner waiting for a bus could be classified as a group. Even casual strangers walking along a crowded street might be defined as constituting a group. The habitual city-dweller learns to counteract crowded streets by making minute or gross

---

2. M. Brodbeck, "Methodological Individualism: Definition and Reduction," *Philosophy of Science,* Vol. 25 (1958), pp. 1-22.

corrections in his forward progress as he travels toward a specific destination. He is therefore behaving in response to the influence of crowd pressure and may be observed doing this.

Other equally weak and transitory relationships which, supposedly, may be thought of as interacting behaviors, are the coincidental meetings of people at theatres, stadia, or other gathering places. Each person may be there with the express idea of being entertained, learning something, or attempting to get some idea across to another party. Essentially, the fact that many people are gathered together in one place at a certain time is pure chance. While it may be valid to say that specific reactions to being in one place with many people around produces observable behavior, the interaction is so negligible and fleeting that it would be stretching this point to include these aggregations in the definition of "group."

What Is a Group?

Just as there are many explanations and definitions of leadership, so too are there many concepts of "group." In this text, we are necessarily concerned with social groups, and we define such a group as follows:

A group is made up of two or more individuals whose reactions and behavior patterns are modified because of some interpersonal relationship developed over time and created during the pursuit of some common interest, utilizing this entity to achieve satisfaction of needs.

In this concept, the group is characterized as a relational organization meeting members' needs through interaction in pursuit of a goal. Most important is the fact that behavioral changes occur because of this interaction. Each person within the organizational structure affects every other person in such a way that attitudes and behavior patterns are modified. Every person involved in a group situation is significant to the life of the group. Every member is part of a unitary image and, as such, is dependent upon the group for satisfaction as much as the group is dependent upon every member for existence. The presence or absence of any one member is duly noticed and will influence the behavior of others accordingly. Also essential to this concept of group is a common interest or goal orientation. Finally, the members of such a group can be identified by the following characteristics:

1. They exhibit psychic interpersonal behavior.
2. They look upon themselves as belonging to the group.
3. They are identified by others as group members.
4. They have internalized certain standards involving matters of shared interest.
5. They enter into a system of intermeshing roles.

6. They ego-identify with one another.
7. They are provided satisfying experiences by the group.
8. They participate in mutually beneficial activities.
9. They possess a generic view of their cohesiveness.
10. They tend to behave in a coordinated manner toward their environment.

The Relationship Between the Individual and the Group

The variety of groups is endless; they represent collections that are as diverse and unique as the individuals who form their membership. Groups vary not only in their aims but also in the number of people who compose their membership, longevity, efforts, level of formalization (institutionalization), structure, significance to their members, and in many other aspects as well.

Group dynamics refers basically to the manner in which a particular group functions. Among the variables to consider are group cohesiveness, individual characteristics which are affected by group structure and which in turn affect group structure, interaction between individuals within the group, interaction between an individual and the group as a whole, and interactions between the group and the environment. The positions members hold within the group — titled offices or status or formal assignment of responsibilities for goal attainment — are also factors. The degree to which members depend on a recognized leader, their individual ambivalence and shared ideas or feelings all play a part in group dynamics.

Degree of Individual Involvement. Anyone who is a member of a group will be influenced in some way by the fact of intimate association. The effects of membership on the individual will be directly proportional to the degree of intensity displayed by the group's various characteristics. For example, the caliber of group cohesiveness affects membership response to group achievement or failure. The more intense the characteristic in question, the more likely the members are to be ego-involved in the affairs of the group and to find satisfaction in group goal attainment. Each time such a goal is attained, a member's identification with the group is reinforced. Those groups which appear to be formed spontaneously by individuals who come together to seek satisfaction of needs without any other organizational pressure have a high level of interdependence among their members and are relatively long-lived.

Membership in a group is not always an all-absorbing interest; groups vary considerably in their impact on members' lives. The importance which an individual assigns his membership in a group contributes significantly to the importance other members assign their membership, to the performance of the group, and to its power which is represented by the kind of needs which the group satisfies or has the potential for satisfying. It is further reflected in the behavioral adjustment which would be required on the part of the member if the group were not available or if it should dissolve. The more significant group membership is to each individual in terms of beliefs, attitudes, and chief values, the more powerful the group.

Group Dependence. Having adopted membership, an individual frequently relies upon the group for many of the things that give him satisfaction. He may look to the group for social intercourse, security, affection, enjoyment, information, self-expression, self-confidence, and self-actualization. Under these circumstances, the group becomes the central repository of or instrument through which an individual gains status, mastery, or the contentment which he relies upon to make life worthwhile. Group dependence, then, is a measure of how securely an individual can rely upon the group for support and assistance in carrying out the activities which he would otherwise be unable to perform.

Group Cohesiveness. Group cohesiveness concerns a group's attractiveness for its members.[3] Most theorists agree that group cohesiveness reflects the degree to which group members want to remain in the group. Cohesiveness contributes to group strength and vigor; it augments the meaning of membership for those who have chosen to affiliate with the group. In effect, then, cohesiveness is the capacity to hold the membership, to muster their efforts in support of group aims, and to develop reaffirmation of group norms.

Among the factors that initially attract individuals to a group and cause them to remain members are friendship, homogeneity, status, leadership, and activities. Anticipation of the conviviality and agreeableness to be found within the company of those who form the group membership is a strong motive for joining and does much to ensure an absence of complaints about others and of arbitrary behavior designed to dissolve shared experiences. When an individual is highly atttracted to a group, there will be increased cohesiveness and concomitant control by the group on the behavior of the member.[4]

If members of a group share common attitudes, values, age, sex, ethnic, social and economic status, level of education, interests, and background, the group is likely to be highly cohesive; interaction among members will reinforce these shared qualities and thus promote group strength.[5]

---

3. H. Bonner, *Group Dynamics: Principles and Applications* (New York: The Ronald Press, 1959), p. 66.
4. A. J. Lott and B. E. Lott, "Group Cohesiveness and Interpersonal Attraction: A Review of Relationships with Antecedents and Consequent Variables," *Psychological Bulletin,* Vol. 64 (1965), pp. 259-309.
5. E. Barscheid and E. H. Walster, *Interpersonal Attraction* (Reading, Mass.: Addison-Wesley, 1969).

Some people may attempt to affiliate with a particular group because of the status accorded to its members. High-status groups represent power and influence, and thus lend their affiliates an aura of importance by association. Status seekers are usually highly motivated and may even undergo severe personal hardship to identify with the group of their choice.

A group's attractiveness to potential members is influenced in no small degree by the type of leadership it exhibits. Usually a democratic form of organization that promotes membership participation in decision-making processes will be the more attractive. Whether group cohesiveness is ultimately enhanced through leadership depends greatly on the degree to which group membership role anticipations are satisfied.

Some groups, particularly those that are recreationally oriented, are primarily attractive because of the kinds of activities they offer to potential members. Activities which are satisfying to individual group members stimulate interest, promote affiliation, and contribute to group cohesiveness.

One of the consequences of group life is that members are increasingly asked to assume pertinent responsibilities which can sustain momentum toward some goal. Where the individuals and the responsibilities are well matched, both individual and group satisfaction will be achieved and thus group cohesiveness will be reinforced.

Choice. The possibility always exists that a person may become a member of a group to which he has no desire to belong. For example, an individual can, during war, be forced by law to enter military service. Often, in such cases where people are thrown together against their will, a high degree of interdependency develops among them and they form voluntary groups within the involuntary group. Prison inmates are typically highly interdependent and through close and prolonged association tend to develop groups even though the initial preference was lacking. In other cases, an individual may be assigned to a specific group on the basis of some particularly observable physical property such as color, sex, or disability.

These examples illustrate various conditions producing involuntary membership. An individual may also be coerced into remaining a member of a group because others consider him a member or fear that his withdrawal might constitute a threat to them, because no other possibilities exist for him, or because of the heavy penalties he will incur if he withdraws (membership in a criminal organization is an obvious example of the latter[6]). A person who remains a member of a group for any of these reasons is likely to suffer from personal anxiety and depression and thus contribute negatively to group effectiveness. On the other hand,

---

6. Cf. M. Puzo, *The Godfather* (Greenwich, Conn.: Fawcett Publications, Inc., 1970).

compulsory association does not always result in disaffection and alienation. A collection of individuals who are forced to join the same organization may develop extreme pride, confidence, loyalty, and affection toward the group and, particularly where close interaction is required for survival, friendships of lifelong duration may develop. The key to successful cohesion in such circumstances is brilliant leadership.

Multiple Affiliations. Many individuals belong to a number of different groups. Usually the values and goals of these groups will be complementary, but occasionally they are directly opposed. People tend to avoid joining competing groups because of the obvious disadvantages in conforming to opposed sets of standards. The possibility of intrapersonal conflict and personal anxiety is not normally attractive. However, a person may have a special reason for joining such opposed groups. A counselor, for example, may seek out a T-group in order to learn more about sensitivity toward others so that he can improve his ability to relate to those he counsels. The same counselor may simultaneously belong to other organizations where individuality is less important than adherence to social codes. Although the counselor may find that these groups make contradictory demands, he nevertheless has the motivation to fulfill his membership responsibilities in each case.

Multiple affiliations may have various consequences for the individual and for the different groups to which he belongs. They may cause conflicts of interest, disaffection, and frustrated group action. On the other hand, they may stimulate new activities and creative experiences that enforce group loyalty and open new lines of communication among members. Multiple affiliations may also augment a group's contacts, disclosing new alternatives for achieving group objectives. In this way the group is enabled to perform more efficiently and offer more satisfaction to its membership. A beneficial outcome of relations between groups is quite dependent upon the number of members the groups have in common. Where typically opposed groups have common members, these members will be motivated toward reconciling conflicts so that polarization will not occur.

Group Reference. In order to understand how people establish, tolerate, and modify beliefs, particularly those beliefs basic to an individual's self-concept, it is particularly useful to study the individual vis-a-vis his group associations. Wherever an individual identifies himself with a group, a reference relationship grows; the concept of group reference is thus significant in explaining the manner in which the individual develops an idea of his relative position in his immediate social order. The group serves as a point of departure in creating value judgments and it is also a balancing force to the outside social influences on an individual's perception, understanding, and role expectations. Another facet of group relations is the degree to which the individual's behavior conforms to the norms for which the group stands. The costs or rewards experienced by the individual are the result of the group's appraisal of his behavior consistent with the group's control.

All individuals owe allegiance to one group or another. The entire environment of human society is formed through groups. Why any individual chooses a particular reference group is open to speculation; nevertheless, the influence the chosen group exerts on the individual is highly significant.

Customs and Codes. Customs and codes play an important part in the formation of groups and in indicating the actions or behavior patterns of those who make up the group. Customs have to do with the usual methods by which activities or conduct are performed. They are the "how" of behavior, the established patterns by which questions are resolved, values assigned, behavior instigated, and judgments made. Customs are the traditions by which the heritage of the group is conserved against the deterioration of time and the inroads of social pressures, changing standards, and fleeting loyalties.

Codes are the rules by which behavior is guided. They are the "why" of conduct. Codes are based upon long experience and are the systematized rules or norms which confine and define behavioral patterns in the day-to-day struggle for existence. They are the commonly accepted inhibitor of non-conformist actions and do much toward exerting pressure on individuals by demanding conforming behaviors.

Every group applies some pressure, either directly or indirectly, consciously or without awareness, through the customs and codes by which it abides. Certain groups intentionally attempt to influence member conduct in conformity with their code. Modification of beliefs and attitudes will certainly be expected from individuals who associate with sectarian, political, educational, or military groups. Such organizations are eager to impose their concepts, creeds, and image upon the new member or convert. The old member has long since absorbed the learning and has been assimilated into the group. Unanimity of thought and deed among members is part of the code. Individuals accept this condition in joining such a group; perhaps it is the reason they join. If individuals find that they are no longer able to conform to a code which they originally accepted without question, they are faced with the painful decision to withdraw from the group or be rejected for nonconformity.

Formal groups invariably reflect the conscious use of custom and code. Fraternal handshakes, secret rituals, and specified modes of dress are some symbols of conformity by which such groups pressure their members into accord and reinforce identification with the group. Informal groups also require unanimity of thought and action among members, but the pressures for conformity are not so obvious because the group does not have a rigid tradition to maintain.

Because group customs and codes are fashioned from those each member brings to the group, there is bound to be conflict of interest when different value systems collide. An informal group that is in the process of developing traditions and formalizing its structure is very likely to experience such conflicts. The outcome will, of course, affect the shape the group structure takes.

Group Formation: Types of Groups

Why are groups created? What causes a particular cluster of individuals to become a group? Why are they drawn together so that interpersonal behavior and other commonalities are a direct outcome?

Hinton and Reitz offer the following theory of group formation:

> Groups are formed in two ways — spontaneously or deliberately. It is interesting to note that spontaneously formed groups exhibit a number of characteristics distinctly different from those exhibited by deliberately formed groups. For example, the former are most frequently social, while the latter constitute the majority of our formal organizations. Deliberately formed groups also usually exhibit more structure and a more autocratic style of leadership than do spontaneous groups.[7]

Just as individuals may be characterized by specific personality traits, groups are also characterized by particular patterns which may be generalized, so that groups can be categorized and typed. There are three types of groups: the primal, the mutually consensual, and the deliberately organized.

The Primal Group. The primal group arises spontaneously from the matrix of natural society. It is the group having the longest duration — the lifetime of the member. Membership is involuntary. In structure, it is a highly formalized hierarchy with distinct functions for each member. If a particular primal group has been in existence for some time, it will have established traditions. Members are very much aware of each other even though they may be separated by time and distance. The presence or absence of each member affects all other members. This group may have one or more interests. Group members may assume heterogeneous characteristics derived from social, religious, political, educational,

---

7. B.L. Hinton and H.J. Reitz, *Groups and Organization: Integrated Readings in the Analysis of Social Behavior* (Belmont, Cal.: Wadsworth Publishing Company, Inc., 1971), p. 32.

neighborhood, and vocational differences, but the group itself is homogeneous. Even when there is severe internal discord, group members generally present a united front toward all outsiders. Members of the group may actively dislike other members, or they may harbor feelings of great affection. In every case, members are born into this group, for it is the family, the basic group of any society. No other group has the characteristics of the family, because the family combines the characteristics of all other groups. Yet without the family, clan, or tribe, there could be no society.

The family needs none of the outward characteristics of other types of groups. It survives through blood or legal ties which transcend any other interest, aim, need, or satisfaction. It stands in relation to society much as the single cell does to the living organism; it is the basic building block upon which society grows, develops, and matures.

All other groups are modifications of the family. The essential difference between the family, or primal group, and other types of groups lies in the formation or origin. All other groups are formed, formally or informally, on the basis of some central interest, need, or external pressure.

The Group Established by Mutual Consent. Many groups arise with no objective other than the pleasure anticipated from interpersonal contact. Groups such as gangs, social clubs, friendship clusters, hobby enthusiasts, and subgroups or cliques within larger groups are typically formed in this manner. The group develops voluntarily since the group's membership is based upon a process of reciprocal agreement — each person wants to be affiliated in the expressed relationship and each is accepted by the others who constitute the group. Informality is the main characteristic, with changing parameters and few defined aims or responsibilities, except that of deriving satisfaction from membership participation. In time, such groups may take on a more formal veneer as internal structure develops, tasks are assigned, and purposes are determined.

Establishing a specific group by mutual consent requires that the personalities concerned have sufficient acquaintance with one another to stimulate interpersonal relations. Largely through physical proximity enough contact is made so that familiarization can lead to acquaintance. However, acquaintance alone is not sufficient to promote the formation of a group. The establishment of a group from a particular cluster of acquaintances is probable only under certain conditions. Individuals tend to be attracted to one another if they hold common values, beliefs, or attitudes.[8] The attraction that develops among these people will be

---

8. T. M. Newcomb, *The Acquaintance Process* (New York: Holt, Rinehart, and Winston, 1961), p. 96.

strengthened if all place an especially high value on these commonly held attitudes or values.

Informal groups are characterized by a lack of ritual, tradition, established offices, or adherence to a particular creed. In addition, they are relatively short-lived, exhibit vulnerability to outside pressure, and depend upon the stability of their membership for continued existence (that is, once the group has solidified, new members are not sought and only rarely admitted).

The Deliberately Organized Group. The deliberately organized group is formed because the satisfaction of needs or interests can be derived only through concerted action. Such a group's development may be predetermined by a social agency using group experience to influence individuals toward a change in behavior, toward achievement of a particular goal, or toward unanimity of thought and conformity of action. Some characteristics of the deliberately organized group are: 1) it is brought into being by auspices seeking to further predetermined aims; 2) it has a predetermined ideology; 3) members are recruited; 4) its internal structure is hierarchical; 5) through assigned responsibilities and intergroup relations, members develop a unitary image as the group matures.

The essential condition for the formation of a deliberately organized group is the belief by one or more persons that a collection of individuals can achieve some objective effectively where solo efforts might fail. The chosen objectives are varied, but may be brought into perspective in terms of generalized categories:

1. *Task groups.* The purpose of establishing a task group is to accomplish some objective through the marshaling of personal resources and the coordination of skills, knowledge, and energy. A climbing club is a typical example of a task group. Each individual within the collection has the physical and personal resources necessary to enable the entire group to make an ascent.

2. *Inquiry groups.* The purpose of an inquiry group is to undertake responsibility for finding solutions to problems besetting the organizing agency. Through coordinated group effort, problems can be examined thoroughly and effective solutions reached more quickly than when individuals pursue their own lines of investigation independently.

3. *Social-action groups.* The need to affect the distribution of public services or to espouse causes that directly concern people's health, safety, or welfare prompts affiliation in social-action groups. They exist to stimulate change and to ameliorate social conditions for the benefit of affiliates and the people whose views they advocate. Individuals acting alone can barely dent the bureaucratic structure of corporate or governmental enterprise; through group action, a collection of people

can significantly influence the power structure.

4. *Client-centered groups.* Client-centered groups are formed by those agencies directly concerned with the provision of services to people. Individuals may approach a recreational service department, for example, and request help in enjoying their leisure through educational, social, physical, or cultural experiences. In response, the department may initiate clubs devoted to satisfying particular recreational needs.

Not only do deliberately organized groups vary in their objectives; they also display differences in organizational structure, lifetime and durability of association, traditions, rules, regulations, and established offices. But wherever a formal group exists, there also will be a ritualistic order, a definite division of functions, adherence to a specific concept or idea, and stability of conduct or the expectation thereof. Some examples of formal groups are schools, churches, political parties, military agencies, fraternal orders, civic, service, or business organizations, professional associations, labor unions, and primary interest groups (the National Association for the Advancement of Colored People or the American Legion). Also to be considered formal groups are those organized by recreational agencies, including teams, clubs, youth councils, and committees.

Whether the recreationist works with one person or many, he should perform in ways beneficial to the clients. His responsibility is to utilize whatever facilities are available through his agency to maximize service to the individual so that they may achieve in ways which are recreationally satisfying.

ROLE OF THE LEADER

The leader has many roles to play in working with individuals, groups, or in unstructured situations. He may be looked upon as a father figure or be placed in the role of enabler, teacher, or coordinator.

Guidance and Coordination

Guidance of group activities toward desirable goals, coordination of interpersonal relations, and elimination of conflicts to conserve group structure are three of the most significant measures of leader ability. The establishment of an esprit de corps allowing group members to set aside personal animosities and to resist pressures which might destroy the group, the elimination of self-aggrandizement by individuals at the expense of the group-as-a-whole, and the increase of group cooperation are the products of the leader's guidance and coordination.

Group Morale

Closely associated with group unity is group spirit or happiness. Most people will remain with a group, even when they are not achieving specific aims, if they receive pleasure from being in the company of others. Good interpersonal relations invariably satisfy the gregarious appetite. As long as sociability, fun, and friendliness are part of the atmosphere, good group morale will be the outcome. If unpleasant relationships develop after the group has been organized — friction in the form of personality clashes, cliques, lack of common experiences or education — the group may be destroyed.

Morale is the unspoken knowledge that one is part of a group-as-a-whole. It is knowing that there are others who like and are likeable. Where people feel comfortable in the presence of others, they tend to exhibit behaviors which will place them in contact with those for whom they have an affinity. Even at the risk of putting up with difficulties or inconveniences, they will attempt to take their place within the group of their choice.

But conviviality alone does not tell the entire story of group morale. The leader has an important role to play in the production of a climate free from internal strife and conducive to interpersonal harmony. The leader helps his group members feel that they are a part of a greater entity. He attempts to instill in them the pride of belonging. The ego-identification which can come from being "in" with the group makes each person feel that he or she is not alone. Support and encouragement from the leader and the assistance he gives each individual in assuming responsibilities as a participant result in personal gratification. In such a climate, the individual is more willing to work and serve, and in thus maintaining his relationship with the group, he heightens group morale. Morale is also influenced by the amount of freedom of self-expression that the individual feels. More individual freedom for self-determination results in greater self-sufficiency and higher morale. The ability to promote group morale is a measure of leadership competence. In turn, the presence of an environment where enjoyable relations may flourish contributes to leader effectiveness.

Stimulating Achievement and Productivity

Productivity ranges from getting out a prescribed number of nuts and bolts in a factory to the opening night of the community theatre's newest play. It may refer to a material product or to the satisfaction in a job well done, a festival accomplished without a hitch, an out-patient trip successfully concluded, or any of the multitudinous goal achievements.

Some groups are affected by a poor understanding of what they are seeking or where they are going and so get nowhere. Goals lack definition or description; this the leader must provide. Not only can such action mitigate disintegrating forces, it will allow a buildup of morale and a feeling of unified effort. The activity or behavior of the leader may be illustrated in terms of the functions which he must perform in order to elicit some aspect of productivity from the group. He must, where necessary, clearly enunciate the program with which the group identifies. He makes clear the objectives which members of the group have signified as being most desirable for them. He may focus the attention of the membership on some value he wants to gain, one which provides a base of agreement to which others may readily accede. Yet, simple agreement or even identical goal orientation will not attain achievement unless these goals are incentives for action.

Research in the field of human relations and leadership indicates that adequate leadership is concerned with the clarification of the goals or the reaffirmation of the objectives for which individuals become members of a group.[9] The ability to plan ahead indicates a recognition of goals. Stogdill states: "A leader then is a person who becomes differentiated from other members in terms of the influence he exerts upon the goal-setting and goal-achieving activities of the organization."[10] Gibb's research gives credence to the idea that goal facilitation is a function of leadership.[11] Carter and his co-workers grouped forty NROTC junior students in an effort to distinguish leaders from non-leaders. They found that the behavior by which a leader may be known is connected with understanding the situation in which he is placed and taking whatever action is necessary.[12] This illustrates the concept that the leader functions as an analyzer, acting in ways which ensure group goals. Cartwright and Zander have concluded:

> If one person does devote unusually great effort toward this end, or if he is especially effective in aiding the group, it would generally be agreed that he is performing functions of leadership regardless of his office in the group.[13]

The end to which these researchers speak is goal achievement. They have further maintained that if a group remains at status quo — neither

---

9. J.V. Downton, Jr., *Rebel Leadership Commitment and Charisma in the Revolutionary Process* (New York: Free Press, 1973), pp. 26-29.

10. R.M. Stogdill, "Leadership, Membership and Organization," *Psychological Bulletin,* Vol. 47 (1950), pp. 1-14.

11. C. Gibb, "The Principles and Traits of Leadership," *Journal of Abnormal and Social Psychology,* Vol. 42 (1947), pp. 267-284.

12. L. Carter, W. Haythorn, B. Shriver, and J. Lanzetta, "The Behavior of Leaders and Other Group Members," *Journal of Abnormal and Social Psychology,* Vol. 46 (1950), pp. 589-595.

13. D. Cartwright and A. Zander, *Group Dynamics Research and Theory,* 3d ed. (New York: Harper and Row, 1968), p. 308.

progressing toward its goal nor achieving any of its potential, going and getting nowhere — no leadership functions are being performed.

Leadership is seen here not in terms of personality, but from the standpoint of clarifying, analyzing, or defining goals for followers or potential followers. The leader initiates structure, communicates with the audience or group, attempts a new approach to the problem at hand, criticizes inadequacy, and counters with suggestions which will enable some positive action to occur. He moves toward his goal, coordinates activities so that duplication of effort and waste is avoided, promotes production of the achievement of objectives, and stimulates decisions for the attainment of those things which the group feels it needs for personal satisfaction.

One of the methods used by leaders to define aims for followers is the initiation of projects which develop group awareness of collective responsibility and orientation toward a goal. The leader may use his unique skill as a facilitator to bring the group a little closer to the attainment of an end and to increase productivity. This may be seen in the following excerpt taken from the records of the Danforth Community Center, a recreational facility operated by the Town of M in New York:

> The Teen-Age Council was meeting to formulate plans for a local high school group event. Each spring it had been customary for the senior class to put on a May dance and festival which would earn enough money for the senior formal, the last dance before graduation.
>
> The chairman of the Council had some difficulty calling the meeting to order, but when he had gained everybody's attention, he did not know where to begin. He was not sure who was going to be on the steering committee, where the May dance was to be held, whether it was going to be held, how the money was to be collected, or where the donated awards were to come from. On top of that, everybody had his own ideas as to how the dance should be run. The Council bogged down from an oversupply of talk and an undersupply of directed action.
>
> The recreationist, acting as resource person for the group, did not take any action at this point. He waited until he was asked his opinion. When everybody had finished having his say, the group still had not come to any decisions. No one was sure where responsibility lay. After the first flurry of talk, the suggestions rapidly dwindled and the council members sat looking at one another.
>
> Finally, the chairman turned to the recreationist and asked for a suggestion. The recreationist pointed out that there had been several ideas advanced which were quite good. He recapitulated some of them. Then he asked that the chairman recall to the group what the purpose of the May dance was and why the festival was being promoted. Once this

had been done, the recreationist explained how the ideas already given could be utilized to meet the stated objectives. Without actually telling the group how to solve their problem, he had the secretary write down the various needs which had to be taken care of before the dance could be given. Then he waited while committees were formed to be responsible for tasks concerning arrangements, decorations, invitations, cleanup, solicitation for donated door-prizes, money collection, etc. When all this was completed, the group was able to work out the details of the festival which would follow the dance. Thus, as soon as the real objectives of the meeting were made clear, group action followed.

The next example is that of an individual who, for personal reasons, attempted to block group goals so that action could not take place. The incident occurred at a midwestern state school, a minimum security detention institution for girls adjudged delinquent. The school is set up in ten separate dormitories; the administration building serves as school facility, auditorium, and recreational center:

The recreationist was asked to organize a recreational activity which might interest all of the girls and take into consideration the wide variety of talent and skill which was represented in each dormitory. A "Skit Night" was developed: each dormitory, at its own request, would have the recreationist as a resource person for four days and put on some sort of show or skit on Friday evening for the entire school.

The first three skits were quite successful. All the girls worked hard to make their demonstration a success, and they enjoyed the preparation as much as the performance. Some unofficial competition developed between dormitories, which reflected the group spirit which the girls felt for their particular dormitory. The fourth week, however, the group which had requested permission to stage a skit suddenly decided that it could not perform, although the request had been voluntary. Since it was too late in the week to notify another group to participate, the recreationist called the dormitory girls together and attempted to discover the hindrance.

The girls were reluctant to talk, but one, Miss Y, asked questions about what could be put into the show. Several other girls also started asking questions, and ideas were soon generated. It was apparent that Miss Y had some pet project which she wished to inject into the skit. It turned out to be a "black-bottom" dance, and, by the way she described it, it was highly erotic, if not completely indecorous. The girls were finally able to table Miss Y's dance and to settle on a pantomime to a piece of popular music.

Miss Y's aggressive and hostile attitude became more distinct as the planning sessions went on. She attempted to block every idea which was put forward and predicted dire results, including embarrassment and loss of face for the other girls. Her remarks made this clear, and she again proposed her dance.

The recreationist asked whether Miss Y would like to take the lead role in the pantomime. She accepted and the production proceeded more quickly. One day before the show was scheduled, Miss Y announced that she was dropping out. Fortunately, one of the other girls had rehearsed as understudy and was able to perform with great success.

Behavior of this type is an attention-getting device. Miss Y exhibited hostile behavior to the recreationist and threats of physical retaliation against those who did not support her proposals. Some covert homosexuality was part of her behavior. It was only when the recreationist was present that the group was able to achieve any kind of movement toward the production of the show. Her presence lent support to the girls. She acted as a buffer between them and Miss Y whose attitude clearly showed a need for the affection which she desired, but could not get from the girls. To her way of thinking, attention-getting behavior was equated with affection. The recreationist suspected that there were underlying reasons for the behavior and suggested referral to the resident psychologist for clinical examination and appraisal. The group's efforts were rewarded, and the satisfaction which the members received from being able to reach their goal was worthwhile. At least one serious emotional problem was discovered and helped.

A third illustration deals with the achievement of goals through the ownership of specific skills or knowledge which others in the group do not possess:

The supervisor in charge of program personnel assigned the production of the annual "Little Olympics" to several playground workers. This event was a combination track, field, and novelty activity which had been run with varying degrees of success in past years. The special event never failed to draw fewer than 500 boys and girls from throughout the city as participants. When a week had passed without any action on promotion of the event, the supervisor began to investigate. To her consternation, it was discovered that not one of the playground personnel had ever performed in a field day; they could not effectively coordinate the activities which were to make up the program.

With so little time left before the event, the supervisor organized and set up all the activities which were to occur, including the opening and closing ceremonies, and the judging, timing, and scoring systems of the events.

With this example as a guide, the subordinate workers were

marshalled into the program and were able to give close support after details of their functions and responsibilities were mapped out. The event was successful when measured by the number of participants who enjoyed the activities and to the extent that it went off on schedule with a minimum amount of confusion, and with each worker carrying out his or her assignment.

From the above examples it is clear that a leader is one who can perform in ways which will alleviate bottlenecks. He has the necessary skill to handle problematic situations efficiently and effectively under pressure. Followers can see that he is ready, willing, and able to pitch in and work in order to produce the results expected from a professional. His performance supports others and aids them in emulating his efforts, thus improving their skill as group participants. As they gain confidence in their own strength, they will gain the respect of others while carrying out the obligations group membership thrusts upon them. The indigenous leader has to make decisions in order to lead; the professional leader decides only when group members cannot decide for themselves.

The recreationist's functions range from a peak of complete authority, in situations where group members are out of touch with reality, to extreme laissez-faire, where the members are creative, productive, actively participating, able to determine their own best interests, and able to attain the goals they have devised. The recreationist may serve in the capacity of *director,* one who assumes complete control of all decisions when group members are not able to act for themselves. This may be seen in mental hospitals, in children's groups where the development of group members is limited, or with retarded individuals. The recreationist functions in the capacity of *supervisor* when group members can make decisions but, because of some behavioral lapses, immaturity, or atypical social norms, their judgments are poor. This may be seen in penal institutions, with some children's groups, or in some hospital situations. The recreationist functions as an *agent provocateur* when group members are apathetic. He stimulates members and provokes ideas. He is the sparkplug which ignites the thought processes of members so that they want to act. This form of leadership is observed in some young adult and children's groups. The recreationist functions as a *teacher* or *coach* when group members want to perform but have neither the skill nor experience to draw upon. Here the recreationist demonstrates, illustrates, and teaches the skills necessary for member performance. In other group situations the recreationist may serve only as a *resource person,* handy to have around when a technical situation comes up which the group cannot handle, but only acting when called upon to do so. In this case, the group members have the needed skills, knowledge, and experience to sustain them. The recreationist stays out of the decision-making except when asked.

In the foregoing situations, it may be that the recreationist's functions vary within any group, or his role may remain stable throughout his association with the group. Whatever the situation, his decision to act or to abstain from acting will bolster the development of individuals within the group through their relationships as members of the group. Thelen has stated:

> All groups have some sort of leadership, whether they know it or not. The amount of leadership is roughly proportional to the rate of change of agreements or group culture. "Good" leadership is indicated when the decisions and actions of a group become more in line with reality, and when there is minimum effort devoted to achieving this adaption.[14]

Although Thelen is oriented toward the point of view which assumes leadership to be entirely an intra-group function, it is quite logical to say that without decision-making, no group could achieve its goals, nor even differentiate goals. Decision-making as a leadership function tends to help the group gravitate toward reasonable choices. The group will retain an individual in a position of leadership only so long as his judgments prove correct.

SELECTED REFERENCES

Aronoff, E. and A. Masse, "Motivational Determinants of Small-Group Structure," *Journal of Personality and Social Psychology,* Vol. 3 (1971), pp. 319-324.

Dyer, W. G., *Modern Theory and Method in Group Training* (New York: Van Nostrand/Reinhold, 1972).

Halloman, C. R. and H. W. Hendrick, "Adequacy of Group Decisions as a Function of Decision-Making Process," *Academy of Management Journal,* Vol. 15 (1972), pp. 175-184.

Indik, B. P. and F. K. Berrian, *People, Groups, and Organizations* (New York: Columbia University Teachers College Press, 1968).

Shaw, M. E., *Group Dynamics: The Psychology of Small Group Behavior* (New York: McGraw-Hill, 1971).

Steiner, I., *Group Processes and Productivity* (New York: Academic Press, 1972).

Stogdill, R. M., "Group Productivity, Drive, and Cohesiveness," *Organizational Behavior and Human Performance,* Vol. 8 (1972), pp. 26-43.

---

14. H. A. Thelen, *Dynamics of Groups at Work* (Chicago: University of Chicago Press, 1954), p. 298. Reprinted by permission.

CHAPTER EIGHT

The Risks of Leadership

Western civilization has flourished as a result of what one might call the entrepreneurial spirit. All the advances in the various fields of human endeavor—economics, exploration, medicine, electronics, marketing, education, psychology—have been made by persons willing to take risks in order to achieve their ends. An entrepreneur by definition is a person who, with considerable initiative and risk, manages or organizes any enterprise, although common use relates the term most often to business.

Risk-takers are an integral part of every group, subgroup, or culture in western society. A true entrepreneur, recognizing the risks inherent in a given situation, first seeks to minimize these risks by careful preplanning. He collects all information concerning the object of his attention and carefully evaluates and analyzes these data. He brings his extensive knowledge and background of experience to bear. Unlike the gambler, the entrepreneur never relies on mere chance. His decision to act reflects risk, to be sure, but calculated risk. Overall is his need to better existing conditions, to challenge the status quo.

Recreationists who would be leaders must exhibit these entrepreneurial qualities. The recreationist is committed to providing individuals with the most valuable recreational experiences possible; the value is assessed by what the individuals derive from these activities, not by the activities in themselves. In order to achieve his purpose, the recreationist often must challenge the established order and risk jeopardizing his position in the community and in the agency. Within the agency, the recreationist's innovative efforts may be seen by fellow workers, as well as superiors, as the recreationist's attempts to better himself and his reputation at the expense of theirs. A well-rounded and creative new program is sure to emphasize any defects in existing programs. Ironically, the recreationist can probably expect the most opposition to innovation from those people who would most benefit by the program. He faces the large task of educating and influencing the public to cease relying on routine experiences, rewarding only because they are familiar. He must also get voters to pay their money, in the form of taxes, to support these services. Those opposed to raising taxes usually form a highly articulate and vocal opposition.

The methods the recreationist uses to approach his agency colleagues, on the one hand, and the community his agency serves, on the other, will reflect the quality of his leadership ability. If the recreationist is to accomplish his purpose and give the service for which he is employed, he must, like the entrepreneur, be prepared to take calculated risks. The process may often be slow, and the recreationist must judge when the right moment arrives to risk setting his plan into action.

RISKS TO THE LEADER

The Leader As a Target

If a group is without specific ethnic, religious, or racial characteristics, individuals who wish to cast aspersions on the group will have a difficult job unless they find a target for their denunciations. The leader of any group provides the ideal target. He stands out and is easily identified. He is vulnerable because he can be separated from the mass of people whom he leads and singled out as a living symbol of the group and its ideas. The leader becomes a focal point of criticisms ranging from mild disagreement on issues of policy to rabid verbal attacks on his character and even, occasionally, attacks on his person.

Thus, by virute of their position, leaders are constantly open to attack. This is one of the hazards of leadership. Leaders must be adept at handling the various forms of hostility directed against them. Those who cannot tolerate abuse run the risk of engaging in petty skirmishes and losing sight of their long-range goals. Leaders cannot afford to yield to the temptation of hurling accusations and verbal abuse at critics. They must rely on truth and good judgment to vindicate their policies, even when critics resort to subtle forms of slander or even outright character assassination. A true leader can only undermine his position by descending to the level of such antagonists.

Hidden Enemies

One great hazard to the leader is false friends: individuals who profess loyalty and support when in reality they are subverting the leader's aims and seeking to remove him from the leadership position. Leaders often risk their position by relying upon the loyalty of people who have in fact become disaffected.

Hidden enemies form a core of dissension and pockets of resistance, active and passive, to the leader's objectives. Such people usually occupy privileged positions within the organizational hierarchy and have the leader's confidence. From this vantage point, they exert tremendous influence upon the unsuspecting leader and thus represent a serious threat to his power and position. Often the treachery of such false friends is not uncovered until it is too late and the leader has lost the support of his loyal followers.

Recreationists are not immune from hidden enemies. Although recreationists can usually assume that their colleagues are in general supportive rather than antagonistic, inadequacies within the recreational program or the agency, or personality conflicts with those who operate it may cause some persons to become disaffected. The disaffected individual can become the nucleus around whom others of the same opinion gather. These people may air their criticisms openly and solicit support for a change of leadership or even abolition of the agency.

Critics such as these are a serious threat to the recreationist, but the threat they pose is open. The greater threat comes from disaffected individuals who work covertly, giving the leader no opportunity to confront his opposition. A person hostile to an agency, for example, is in an ideal position to discredit it or to limit its functions and scope if he or she can be appointed to the legal board or commission under which the agency operates. The following case illustrates subversion of this sort:

> The teen-age center in a southern town had been giving the local branch of a national youth-service agency considerable competition. The recreationist in charge of the teen program was extremely competent and continually originated highly attractive activities. Unable to accept the intense competition which the center afforded, the youth agency director gave as little cooperation to the center as possible. When he determined that lack of cooperation could not damage the center's program, he became a member of the community's inter-agency council and consistently attempted to hamper his rival's activities while seeming to offer assistance and material support. The recreationist did not realize that his program was being undermined until the director had actually persuaded seven of the council's ten members that *his* organization should be given complete control of all youth activities within the community, with the center to act only in a subordinate role. His sub rosa activities were quite successful; within a very short time, the teen-age center was discontinued as a separate agency and its functions merged with the other. Naturally, there could not be two executives, and the former teen-age center director was discharged.

Here one can see what pettiness and envy can do. There is no community that cannot support several recreational agencies if cooperation produces good coordination.

Polarized Factions

With decision-making comes the division between those who will follow the leader, supporting his aims and ideas, and those who will not. When a leader, confronted with two opposing paths which have equally vigorous support among his followers, decides to take one path rather than the other, he is cetain to split the group into those who commend his decision and those who, to varying degrees, deplore it. The latter group may become completely antithetical to his objectives and methods.

Inherent within the decision-making process, then, is the potential for self-destruction. Every statement, direction, or procedure which the leader untertakes is likely to be distasteful to someone who may feel it a matter of principle to oppose him as effectively as possible. Unless the leader is extremely careful and discreet about his plans and operations, he may find that excessive hostility is beginning to develop in the form of opposing factions. This is one of the perils of leadership.

The recreationist also faces this peril, often from individuals who seek to gain advantages at the public's expense. For example, polarized factions may arise over the placement of parks or other recreational facilities which are likely to enhance the value of adjoining or abutting lands. There is always some pressure placed upon the recreationist by home or property owners when such plans are drawn up. Since the recreationist must consider population density, population movement, and many other factors in order to provide the best possible service to the community, he may have to override the wishes of some property owners so that the greatest membership of the community can benefit.

Another area in which the recreationist may incur organized opposition is in the employment of community members for work in the agency. Unless the recreationist protects himself from various forms of community pressure and establishes an impartial and defensible program for hiring help, he may find himself accused of unfair labor practices by some segment of the community.

Sometimes, just by establishing a particular activity, the recreationist can simultaneously establish a faction that opposes him. For example, there are still communities in the United States where dancing is considered immoral and taboo. In other communities, prevailing religious beliefs dictate that activities may not be carried out on specific days of the week. Whenever the recreationist chooses to disregard such local mores, he takes a risk. In seeking to enlighten the community and perhaps uproot prejudicial attitudes and outmoded beliefs, the recreationist is certain to arouse a determined opposition.

Negative Propaganda

Nothing is as harmful as the lie with a modicum of truth. And no statement is more difficult to combat, for the grain of truth gives the lie substance and makes it believable. A half-truth cannot be immediately disavowed on the basis of its patent absurdity. Across-the-board denial of a statement which is half-true will refute the truthful parts of the statement as well as the false. To issue no denial at all is tantamount to admission. Thus one is faced with making a denial fraught with explanations, which sounds equivocal and is less forceful than the original accusation.

The leader can answer a deliberate half-truth only with the whole truth, phrased with absolute clarity and precision. The only defense in the face of half-truths is complete and valid justification for the plans or action under attack and the rationale on which they are based. There is no better counterthrust to distortion than a well-delivered presentation of actual facts.

The recreationist must fight constantly against prejudice and distorted facts. His best preventive weapon is the maintenance of good public relations between the agency and the people of the community. The basic objectives of public relations are aiding the agency in gaining and holding public friendship and respect, tailoring all agency practices and policies to coincide with the best possible interests of the community, and reaching every individual within the community with the complete and true story of the agency and its essential and professional functions in the life of the community. Through such measures the recreationist can reverse negative propaganda. Public relations help the recreationist to offer better service by: 1) discovering and listing all groups, or segments of the public, whose opinion is important to the agency; 2) ascertaining the attitude of each of these groups toward any or all phases of the agency's operations; 3) introducing such reasonable adjustments in the agency's policies and procedures as are necessary in order to make a more favorable impression on the public; and 4) explaining and interpreting for the public the policies and practices of the agency and any other feature of its activities which the public misunderstands or in which the public shows interest.

RISKS MADE BY THE LEADER

The Compromise of Principles

The moment of decision is always the great test of a leader's character and ability. The temptation to choose the path of least resistance is often very strong, as is the lure of self-aggrandizement. The cost is compromise. The leader who is truly dedicated will remain true to his principles in the face of all odds.

Although a leader may find it expedient to make concessions to a stand he has taken, he must bear in mind that one concession may lead to further alterations of his plans, and may even undermine his integrity. Concessions cannot be made lightly; each must be examined in the light of principle. The recreationist is well warned against this danger. He must remain alert to avoid subordinating integrity and ethics to expediency. Subversion is best eliminated when open communication and truth (or at least the facts) are established and maintained.

Once the first step is taken against what is in the best public interest, it may become relatively easy to allow oneself to be talked into further concessions until there is nothing left for the public. A poignant reminder is offered by the concessions which have been made to park and wilderness areas. Spaces and lands now used, or potentially useful, for recreational purposes are rapidly succumbing to developers, road builders, and shortsighted individuals who overlook the inherent value of such areas in favor of monetary rewards.[1]

One of the primary principles of the field of recreational service is conservation of recreational spaces and resources for perpetual use by the public. Recreationists have an obligation to protect wilderness areas, parks, and other open areas from encroachment by vested interests, or even those who seek to construct public edifices. In allowing any part of an open space or park area to be utilized for purposes other than recreational activity, the recreationist may be setting a precedent and, in effect, conceding that such areas may ultimately be used for construction. The first compromise in principle leads to further concessions in fact. After trees and grass have been uprooted and torn away, they can never be replaced. One need only look at urban sprawl to realize that where open and wilderness spaces have not been protected, the ever-widening spread of municipal development invades formerly beautiful places, replacing the flora and fauna with cement.[2] Although recreationists may have to concede some points to realtors and developers, they should never compromise on the basic principle of public-land maintenance.[3]

Arrogance

A leader may slip from the leadership role gradually, becoming a leader in name only or eventually losing his position entirely. The true leader is a person who believes in the dignity of all men; in this respect he may be termed "humble." But unless he is careful, he may allow himself to begin to feel superior to those he leads — this is the beginning of arrogance. An arrogant person is disinclined to listen to advice, believing himself to be the arbiter of what is best. Arrogance gives the leader an exaggerated sense of

---

1. J. F. Murphy, J. G. Williams, E. W. Niepoth, and P. D. Brown, *Leisure Service Delivery System: A Modern Perspective* (Philadelphia: Lea & Febiger, 1973), pp. 48-55.

2. J. N. Smith, ed., *Environmental Quality and Social Justice in America* (Washington, D. C.: The Conservation Foundation, 1974).

3. J. S. Shivers, "The Recreationist and the Environment," *World Leisure and Recreation Association Bulletin,* Vol. XIX, No. 2, March-April 1976), p. 1.

his personal worth. When he loses sight of his responsibilities in relation to those who trusted him and gave him the leadership position, he upsets the critical balance between true leadership and dictatorship. He begins to see himself as indispensable, infallible, and omnipotent; his followers as dispensable, weak, and useful only in their capacity to perform his bidding. As the leader develops arrogance, the gap between his own goals and those of his followers widens and he gradually loses influence with them. When people finally realize that they are being used rather than led, they are quick to anger and to take steps to remove the offender.

Arrogance is not a trait the recreationist can afford. He is, in the best sense, a public servant who must keep an open relationship with those whom his agency serves. When his personal relations with his constituents become poor, he will find himself out of a job, as the following case illustrates:

> Mr. B was Superintendent of Recreational Service for a midwestern state's capital city. He had been an appointed official and on the job for more than twenty years. Now that civil service had replaced the old patronage system, Mr. B was secure in his job through tenure. Over the years, Mr. B developed the attitude that he was an authority and in authority. His conduct was such that he considered his position sacrosanct. His relationship with the general public was very poor. He consistently kept people waiting in his outer office, whether he was occupied or not. This attitude gave him a feeling of importance. When anyone did get to see him, he never gave them his direct attention, but continued to sign his name or write during the discussion. He felt that his job was created for his own benefit, and he showed his feeling. He was heard to voice such statements as, "If you do not like what I am doing, have me fired." His "public–be–damned" attitude caused many people who visited his office or spoke to him over the telephone to form a low opinion of him and his department. When a new administration came into power, the recreational agency was taken out of civil service, the superintendency was abolished as a job title, and B lost his position.

The moral to this story is that courtesy and willingness to serve are excellent traits for the recreationist to cultivate. Arrogance, on the other hand, precludes courtesy and fosters antisocial behavior. Discourtesy and condescension, two attributes of arrogance, can do more to imperil the recreationist's position and undermine his agency than almost any other weakness of character.

Changing Direction

Leaders gain their influence with others because of what they are trying to achieve. Usually it is not simply the person but rather what the person stands for that draws followers. The leader may offer totally new methods of pursuing an objective, but only so long as leader and followers share a common objective will the leader be able to retain the loyalty of his supporters.

The danger of an arbitrary change in goals on the part of the leader is, therefore, readily apparent. At best, followers will be alarmed, and usually they will also be infuriated. In any case, followers will not tolerate a reversal of direction. Even if the changed goal is beneficial to them, they will see the change as a betrayal of their trust. The leader may change his stated aims only as a result of consulting his followers and gaining their approval for the change.

It can be argued that emergency or crisis situations sometimes leave no time for consultation before making an important decision that necessitates retraction from some previously agreed upon stand. Each time the leader changes direction, he must either gain the consent of his followers or, if the situation warrants, convince them of the rightness of his modification after the crisis is past. No group will long tolerate mercurial shifts, either of goals or of temperament. Followers look to the leader for stability. Although the leader may be in a better position than his followers to judge the many factors that determine the advisability of altering goals, followers still want to be apprised of new developments and be assured that they have a voice in the plans and operations of the movement. Thus the leader must maintain close communication with followers on all matters of mutual importance.

Tempo

Going too far, too fast, too soon is also hazardous to those who would lead. Unless the leader takes his followers along with him, explaining and justifying his actions to those who continually need reassurance and stimulating the understanding of those who fall behind, he will lose their interest and also his influence with them. Being an individual who talks, thinks, and acts faster than some of his followers can put the leader at a disadvantage if he allows himself to assume that everybody has his ability. When a leader is impatient to keep moving toward his objectives, he risks losing the support of the less well–informed members of his group.

The recreationist must be especially aware of the individual variations in intellect, ability, prior experiences in the group process, and any other factors which limit or restrict membership capability to perform. He must regulate the speed with which he pursues goals in order to assure that all group members comprehend his program. If the recreationist disregards the slower members of his group, he will inevitably lose their support. It may appear to them that he is neglecting them in favor of others or attempting to usurp their rights as partakers in the decision-making funciton. The following example illustrates what can happen when a leader tries to accomplish too much too quickly:

Mr. R, Superintendent of Public Recreational Service in the City of Y, determined that his community needed several new recreational facilities and areas. Upon investigation, he found that several parcels of land would have to be acquired and that a new center and three playgrounds would have to be constructed and developed in order to serve the increased population. R assembled all of his facts and figures and went before the Board of Estimate with his proposals. He needed more than $1,750,000 to complete his projects. The Board rejected his program. R decided to appeal directly to the people of his community. He simply requested that a bond issue be passed in the sum needed in order to provide additional recreational services to the people of the community. He indicated what the development was to be and left the problem up to the voters. R's program was defeated in the referendum. R could not understand why his proposals had not carried.

Basically, the trouble with R was that he had assumed everybody understood the need for the developmental aspects of his program. He had felt that this program was self-explanatory and so neglected to inform the voters of the benefits which would accrue from additional land acquisition and what their money was to be spent on. He neglected one vital factor which all leaders must take into account if they are to rally support for their objectives, and that is to take the time and make the effort to determine whether or not support is a reality. Followers must be made to understand precisely what the needs are, why the needs must be met, and how they can best be satisfied. There is a definite requirement to interpret facts and figures in such a way that they will be clearly perceived by those whose aid is necessary in gaining an objective.

The following example concerns social movement and what can happen, even to an outstanding personality, when he moves too rapidly for those who follow him:

G was brought into the growing city of P to reorganize the Department of Recreational Services. He was considered one of the authorities in the field of public recreational service administration and had been at the top of his professional career when summoned to P at quite a large salary. G's ideas were logical, attractive, and very progressive. Unfortunately, he did not bother to explain his program or the steps he was taking to his Board or to the public. He just went ahead, cutting costs here, shifting personnel there, and generally stepping on toes as he did the job for which he had been hired. However, as G worked he began to build up an intense antagonism toward his methods. He was too quick to criticize, too fast with his changes. He did his work without any preliminary interpretations, assuming that the public wanted him to perform in the manner to which he was accustomed. At the end of six months, the Board called a public meeting in response to demands made by a vociferous and aroused citizenry. The outcome was predictable. Mr. G was discharged and his contract paid in full. The epilogue to this record is that every policy and program which G initiated or had expected to produce was unanimously adopted. The replacement to G provided the same type of progressive action which G had, but also initiated a public relations procedure coordinated with his activities.

Once again, it is plain that only when the public is informed as to what the leader expects to do and how he plans to do it will they lend their support. Keeping communications open between the group and leader is vital to the influence which the leader holds. He can go no faster than the slowest member of his group in order to achieve objectives satisfactory for all.

Strength and Consistency

A leader must seem strong and unwavering in the face of crisis. Regardless of the problems or the odds which confront him, he can show no outward signs of fear or disillusionment. If he loses his composure when threatened with reversals, he will lose the confidence and support of his followers. He must have the fortitude to assume the final responsibility for whatever results from his actions: victory or defeat. Excuses for failure and attempts to shift blame immediately expose him as weak and unfit to lead.

A leader must never give the impression of defeat. No matter how discouraged he feels or how hopeless he knows his cause to be, he must appear outwardly assured of success. Only if he remains calm, resolute, and completely in control of himself will he inspire his followers' loyalty and buttress their courage. It is a rare individual who can hold up under the hammer–like blows of despair, defeat, and demoralization. The greatest hazard to the leader is not the feelings themselves but their outward manisfestations. If he seems to show signs of fatigue, disappointment, or strain, he places his influence with others in jeopardy. He must always maintain the detached look of one who is secure in the knowledge that his objectives will eventually be reached.

The recreationist also must play this confident role. He must often deal with antagonism and hostility directed at his agency, policy, or plans. Sometimes defeat seems certain as he confronts an apathetic public or a powerful branch of government that attempts to usurp his prerogatives or countermand his specialities. In order to maintain his position and fulfill his responsibility as a community leader, he cannot show fear of failure. The recreationist is often confronted with situations where he must prove himself. No matter how many times he has shown himself adequate to meet emergencies, the very nature of his job forces him continually to validate his ability. Working with small groups, for example, he must remain objective at all times. By soothing frustrations, helping members to overcome deep-rooted fears, negating prejudices, and meeting problems in order to maintain group morale and group cohesiveness, he assures the group that they can count on him. He may condemn a particular action and praise another, but it is the consistency of his attitude toward group members which provides support for the group. He is solid, dependable, never panicky. This is the strength which helps group members to stabilize their own conduct and patterns of behavior.

The recreationist as a professional worker is no less a leader among his own peers, and while fellow workers may have a somewhat greater tolerance for debilitation as the result of undue strain or hardship, they nevertheless expect dependability, consistency, and optimistic pursuit of goals from their colleagues. Thus, manifestations of depression, defeat, or default by a leader, even among his own peer group, will undermine his position and result in loss of influence.

An example of this may be seen in the following record taken from the Y department of recreational service:

Mr. T, one of the more popular recreationists in the department, was approached by a group of teen-age boys who wanted his help in building a supervised "drag-strip" where they could tune up, race, and work on their homemade cars. The boys were very enthusiastic about the possibility of having their own place for auto meets. Up to that time they had been using the main streets in the community as racing courses and had been warned by the police that further use would be met with swift punishment. Now they turned to the one person whom they felt sure could aid them. Mr. T talked the situation over with the group and initiated a club which met every week to plan the drag-strip and the activities which were to be held on it. Membership in the club grew, and there was much excitement concerning this activity. Mr. T began to check with his superiors about the possibility of organizing the type of activity which the boys wanted. He was told that the City Council and the Police Department would probably have to be consulted for final authority. When a month had gone by without further action on the matter, Mr. T renewed his request. His supervisor indicated that the probability of constructing a drag-strip was practically nil. Mr. T continued his efforts, but soon realized the futility of the proposal. At the next meeting with the boys he bluntly told them that there was no hope of realizing their objective. He said that they would only be frustrated if they continued to plan for the drag-strip. There was never a next meeting.

Mr. T's failure may be attributed to lack of foresight on the part of both his superiors and the community, but much of it may be placed at his own door. By reacting to failure in such a negative way, he completely demolished any hope that the membership of his group may have had. Had he been more discrete, perhaps a little more optimistic, he might very well have kept the club together. He was prone to accept the verdict of defeat without continuing the fight. He could have enlisted the aid of parents; perhaps he could have discussed the situation with others in the community in an endeavor to gain support for his project. Instead, he accepted a negative decision and dropped the entire matter. His feelings about the problem were very evident to the boys. They could see that he was disappointed and frustrated. They must also have realized that he was ready to give up. They could not depend upon him to carry on. Hence the entire membership broke apart, and T lost any semblence of the influence which he may have had with them. The principle is that no person in a leadership position can afford to concede that all is lost if he wants to retain his status. Once followers are made aware of the leader's pessimistic outlook, they will desert him. The leader may not win all of the time, but he must always appear to be sure of winning eventually.

SELECTED REFERENCES

Alvares, R., "Informal Reactions to Deviance in Simulated Work Organizations," *American Sociological Review,* Vol. 33 (1968), pp. 895-912.

Kipnis, D. and W. P. Lane, "Self-Confidence and Leadership,"*Journal of Applied Psychology,* Vol. 46 (1952), pp. 291-295.

Kipnis, D. and C. Wagner, "Character Structure and Response to Leadership," *Journal of Experimental Research in Personality,*Vol. I (1967), pp. 16-24.

Klein, S.M. and J.R. Maher, "Decision-Making Autonomy and Perceived Conflict Among First Level Management," *Personnel Psychology,* Vol. 23 (1970), pp. 481-492.

Miller, D.C., "Using Behavioral Sciences to Solve Organizational Problems," *Personnel Administration,* Vol. 31 (1968), pp. 21-29.

Rizzo, J.R., R.J. Hourse, and S.I. Lirtzman, "Role Conflict and Ambiguity in Complex Organizations," *Administrative Science Quarterly,* Vol. 15 (1970), pp. 150-163.

Tosi, H. "Organizational Stress as Moderator in the Relationship Between Influence and Role Response," *Academic Management Quarterly,* Vol. 14 (1971), pp. 7-20.

CHAPTER NINE

Misconceptions of Leadership

Illusions about a leader's inherent goodness, incorruptibility, rightness of action and direction, strength and steadfastness give rise to the most frequent misconceptions of leadership. Often followers are in for a rude awakening once the leader attains the eminence he seeks. History is full of instances in which people have supported a leader, raising him to power on the basis of such illusions, only to be disappointed and shocked at the outcome. On the surface, the disillusionment is directed at the leader, but it is really the process of leadership that is misunderstood. By attributing impossible qualities to the leader, people escape from the need to think and act independently because it is so much easier to appoint someone to think and act for them. To refuse responsibility is to invite dictatorship. Dictatorship, as we have seen, is the antithesis of leadership.

Infallibility

One popular misconception about an individual who is accorded leadership status is that he is infallible. People tend to assume that a leader makes only correct decisions, that his choice of methods for reaching goals reflects his good judgment, that he always knows what he wants, and that his objectives are beneficial and noble. No human is *always* right, good, accurate, and successful. Human fallibility invariably produces conflicts, questions, and unresolved situations which are detrimental to the individuals involved. Why, then, should the leader be thought to possess some mystical power which enables him to discern and achieve necessary ends? Leaders only appear to know what is right and to lead in the right direction because the group replaces those individuals who cannot successfully meet group needs. "Evaluation of leadership goes on without interruption over a time continuum; a leader is on permanent probation with his members."[1] If the leader were always right, or good, or true, such evaluation would be superfluous and leader retention would be automatic.

Effectiveness

Another misconception about leadership concerns effectiveness. It is

---

1. E.T. Reeves, *The Dynamics of Group Behavior* (New York: American Management Association, Inc., 1970), p. 131.

common to refer to the leader as effective because of the influence he wields; in fact, effectiveness lies in the process of leadership and involves not only the leader's influence with followers but also the disparate processes operating within the group and the objectives to be gained. Although the leader provides a needed resource, the group's resources are not possessed only by the leader. It is the total effort by leader and group which provides the basis for functions accomplished in the successful achievement of group aims.

Personality

The most common misconception of leadership is that leaders are born and not made. According to this myth, leaders have inherent personality characteristics that enable them to overcome what would be insurmountable obstacles to anyone else. And it is also assumed that if an individual displays some of the traits necessary for successful leadership, he undoubtedly has them all. But in fact the process of leadership is composed of many ingredients and of varied functions, part of which may be a particular set of personality attributes. It does not follow that the individual with these traits will always function as a leader. Because different groups emphasize different functions or needs, the leader's ability to adjust to changing situations will demand a high degree of flexibility.

The personality characteristics appropriate for leadership are actually determined by the perceptions held by followers. How a potential follower looks upon a would-be leader is more important, in terms of specific role expectations and satisfactions, than the pattern of traits the individual displays under examination.[2]

Research on personality traits among leaders shows enormous diversity, probably predicated on the diversity of expectations of the leader's performance. There are contrasting leadership roles. It should be recognized that the leader in distinct situations may be concerned with task accomplishment, problem-solving, providing socio-economic support, making decisions, or acting as group spokesman. Personal characteristics of a leader, including intelligence, are more apparent and more relevant to group accomplishment under circumstances of engagement by the leader than in a rigidly institutionalized role structure.

Facade

Many people still believe that a person's appearance is an indication of how successful that person will be. Another of the myths of leadership is that a person must look the part if he is to be an effective leader. For

2. J. McV. Hunt, "Traditional Personality Theory in the Light of Recent Evidence," *American Scientist*, Vol. 53 (1965), pp. 80-96.

example, the stereotypical leader is taller, heavier, and more intelligent than others; he also has a full head of hair, dresses well, looks distinguished, and generally presents the impression of immense power. In fact, leaders come in all sizes and shapes, have varying amounts of hair, dress as they see fit, and convey whatever impression their followers find worthy of adulation. An example of such a person from U.S. history is President Warren G. Harding. Elected because he looked like a man who should be president of the United States, Harding was in truth a man of mediocre abilities and easily manipulated by self-seeking persons.

Reputation, closely allied to appearance, is often equated with leadership. An individual who has a good reputation as a problem-solver, trouble-shooter, or mediator will be called upon frequently to exercise his skills. Each successful outcome enhances his reputation. The difficulty in relying on reputation as an accurate gauge of skill is that it is hard to determine on what basis the reputation has been built. Empty phrases and jargon falsely convince many followers. In such a manner an undeserved reputation for success will be reinforced. On occasion, the individual in a leadership position values his reputation so much that he indulges in unleaderlike behavior in attempting to preserve it, shifting responsibility for his own failure to others with whom he works. Such face-saving is a time-honored response to failure, but it is not the response of a leader. Once again, appearances can be deceiving, and mere reputation does not necessarily denote a leader.[3]

Nomenclature

In all leadership contexts, misuse or misunderstanding of terminology is more common than not. Indiscriminate use of the word "leader" has caused confusion about both standards and concepts of leadership. The term is applied so generally that anybody, regardless of ability, can be called a leader.

For example, the term leader is often merely a bestowed title. Although this practice is common in many professional fields, it is particularly so in recreational service. All too many recreationists are hired to the *position* of leader, regardless of leadership ability, personal qualities, or understanding of human relations. They have been hired for some technical competency or program skill and for nothing else. It is even conceivable that if the employing agency had known beforehand they actually were leaders, it would not have employed them. The common practice of giving titles to positions, rather than to the people occupying these positions, does much to maintain popular misconceptions about the process of leadership.

---

3. L. Lowenthal and N. Guterman, *Prophets of Deceit — A Study of the Techniques of the American Agitator* (Palo Alto, Ca.: Pacific Books, Pub., 1970).

The designation leader should be reserved for those who have influence with others.

Leaders are an infectious breed with strong motivations and convictions and a propensity for testing axioms and upsetting status quo. Even when the hiring authority really needs applicants with leadership qualities and abilities, sometimes little thought is given to the applicant's character, personality, or preparation for a leader's position. Too often, skill in an activity, prior experience within a position, and perhaps specific preparation are the determinants. Leadership, and the techniques this term implies, is assumed to be a part of the individual's nature which the job will cause to flourish.

Instructional Skill

Many of the personnel within recreational service agencies are employed not on the basis of personality, professional preparation, or even knowledge of the field, but on the basis of their skills in various specializations. Thus, leadership has often been confused with program and instructional skills. Having specialized skills is an important part of the recreationist's background, but his preparation does not stop there. Above and beyond program skills are those which are necessary for working and dealing with people.

Leaders approach any task and any group with the knowledge that all human beings are different and that these differences will show up in a variety of ways. On the basis of this realization, a leader will set about developing an influential relationship with the group. An instructor, on the other hand, will usually approach a group with the single idea of instructing them in achieving a particular short-range goal. It is fortunate to have an instructor who is also a leader, but it is not common.

Many, who should know better, are convinced that a recreationist can develop leadership only as a result of teaching an activity. For these people, it is inconceivable that there could be a leadership process beyond an instructional role. They believe that organizational hierarchy precludes any form of leadership that does not rely on headship.

Headship Versus Leadership

We have previously discussed the difference between leadership and headship, but it may be worthwhile to reiterate some points in this context. Headship refers to the assignment of specific functions and responsibilities in an organizational hierarchy. In such a system, it is the position rather than the person holding the position that gains respect and therefore obedience. Leadership, on the other hand, is a process in which the leader gains respect and influence and thus attains the position.

Although headship and leadership may appear to coincide in some instances, although they may not be precisely dichotomous, some characteristics of each are at opposite extremes. Headship usually implies a position within an established system which is designed to maintain the system rather than to allow natural or indigenous changes to come about. The person in the headship position is not voluntarily placed in office by a following of those whom he has influenced, but by the organization itself. Conversely, the leader is accorded his position through influence with others who have chosen to follow his direction. Thus, the essential difference between leadership and headship lies in the origin of the central figure's power.

In the field of recreational service, the distinction between headship and leadership is especially important because so many agencies and organizations exhibit a hierarchical structure. When headship positions are allowed to be filled by people who are not truly leaders, the functioning of the leadership process goes awry. For example, an appointed leader concerned primarily with task accomplishment puts pressure on subordinates to conform to the existing system and to replace their own goals with those of the system. In view of the way most agencies are structured, recreationists must be on their guard to avoid submitting to such pressure.

Conformity. From the record of X recreational agency's supervisory report, the following incident is taken to illustrate the pattern of pressure for conformity in a small group situation:

> Staff conferences were called every week at the central office of X recreational service department in a medium-sized midwestern community. One of the reasons for the staff conference was the promotion of new ideas for the overall recreational program. Each worker brought with him some project which had been found to operate well in his neighborhood center and which could be utilized by other personnel in the agency. This conference technique had worked well for a long time; now it appeared as though a breakdown had occurred. The workers complained that the weekly meeting was simply a waste of time. Morale was low, and agency activities had degenerated to "the same old things." As area supervisor, it was my responsibility to determine why this deterioration had set in to a formerly high-producing region.
>
> I sat in on one of the meetings, and it soon became apparent why morale was so low and why new ideas were not forthcoming. Shortly before this demoralizing atmosphere had started, the original group supervisor had been transferred to another position, and a new group supervisor had replaced him. Unfortunately, the new group supervisor, with a number of years' experience, was not particularly openminded when it came to accepting new ideas. As a result, his subordinates

stopped offering suggestions because they found that they were never utilized, or because they invariably received criticism for giving the idea in the first place. What had been stimulating was now a rather boring and routine meeting. Along with this routinized aspect there also developed a type of conformity to the supervisor's suggestions or implied orders. No one bothered to argue or remonstrate with any of the supervisor's ideas, although some were questionable, and there was a rather passive acceptance of what he said. This pattern was reinforced by others in the group who "fell in line" as each preceding worker patronized these opinions. When privately questioned, over a period of days, each of the workers expressed disillusionment with the staff conference method, indicated that they disagreed with much that the supervisor suggested, but felt that they had to "go along" in order to retain their positions.

The pressure to conform may represent self-preservation when an individual is confronted with an uncomfortable decision. In any conference situation within an organization where a supervisor is present, subordinates may be reluctant to voice their true opinions unless rapport is established. Unless the supervisor can assume the leadership role and establish easy communication, spontaneity will be restrained and progress will be impeded. Rapport permits relaxing of tension so that professionals sincerely dedicated to the solution of problems which affect the agency and its personnel can feel free to contribute suggestions without fear of ridicule or reprisal. Face-saving and job-saving pressures make for conformity. If the line of hierarchy is filled with people merely filling headship positions and not truly functioning as leaders, each worker will fall into agreement with the one above him, constantly increasing the pressure for conformity.

The Figurehead Versus the Leader

Even worse than the substitution of headship for leadership is the substitution of a figurehead for a leader. A figurehead is a leader stereotype, a person appointed to the position merely because he looks the part and can be depended upon to do the bidding of those who placed him in office. The figurehead is neither qualified nor competent to carry out the responsibilities which rest with his position. In the field of recreational service, the figurehead invariably represents some concentration of power within the agency because of *whom* rather than *what* he knows. The figurehead issues directives but does not dare to question principles, policies, or actions. Appointments of such people to executive positions in some recreational service agencies in recent years have produced mediocre programs, poor morale, and questionable recreational service practices. The figurehead lacks not only the necessary experience but also the daring required of a true leader.

A figurehead who masks as a leader within a recreational service agency can cause infinite confusion and discord. Because of his inability to communicate with those who must carry out his directives and his total lack of experience and information in formulating plans, he is prone to issue orders that workers find unreasonable or incongruous. Lack of coordination, duplication of effort, and the resulting tensions and frictions reduce efficiency throughout the agency. When workers are in constant doubt about the plans of the agency, morale rapidly disintegrates. Recreationists who want to achieve within their field usually withdraw from agencies with figureheads as soon as they can and attempt to locate in situations where democratic procedures are encouraged.

Indecisiveness Versus Leadership

An individual who lacks confidence in his ability to produce competent work is a liability when he holds a leadership position. Perhaps the lack of assurance manifests itself only when pressures of the job demand some urgent decision, but that is precisely the situation that most demands aggressive action on the part of the leader.

The following example shows how leadership is absent when the "leader" is insecure:

A midwestern hospital employed a staff to operate the recreational program. The director of that program had been brought into the agency by the head of the Special Services Division. Although the director had absolutely no professional preparation, the employing authority overlooked this fact because the Special Services chief specifically requested this individual.

The director had little or no understanding of the meaning of recreational activities and relied upon the use of completely passive entertainments as a mainstay of his program. As a personality, the director was innocuous, although his practice was to be as negative as possible whenever staff physicians asked that he perform some of the services for which he was employed. However, he had occupied his position for the necessary length of time to secure tenure, and he was further protected by his immediate superior. In order never to appear wrong and because he was inordinately afraid of committing some outlandish error through ignorance, he did as little as humanly possible. His first concern was that his record should not have any marks against it.

His operating principle was, "If you do not do anything, you never get into trouble," or, "I would rather take one step backward than stick my neck out and take two steps forward."

Such an attitude is antithetical to all the principles of leadership. To consider such individuals as recreationists, much less leaders, is not only an insult to professionals but a disgrace which the entire field must bear. Other professional fields have weathered the storms of quackery, malfeasance, and immorality. Other professions have protected themselves from incompetence by requiring licensing in order to practice. If licensing were required for recreational service, the illusion that a clean record is an indication of leadership would be dispelled.

Rationalization Versus Leadership

An administrator who continually justifies his errors and poor judgment by making excuses, damning bad luck, or blaming adverse circumstances and inability of subordinates is rationalizing his own incompetence. The individual who knows that he is at fault, mistaken, or completely wrong in an action or idea admits the facts and tries to correct his errors, or else he rationalizes. Rationalization is a way of subordinating truth through self-deceit; the motive is usually false pride. In order to preserve his image as a leader, such a person indulges in unleaderlike behavior. Take the example of Mr. W, administrator of a recreational service agency in one of the large municipalities in the southeast:

As superintendent of public recreational service in the city of X, Mr. W had a reputation to maintain. He felt that a man in his position should command the respect of all. Not only to his subordinates, but also to community members, Mr. W appeared to be, on the surface, easy-going, chivalrous, courteous, and kind. He considered himself to be politic and diplomatic. In reality, he was weak, incompetent, vain, and ruthless in his insecurity. He was egotistical in the extreme. One might say that he was narcissistic. Mr. W had been interviewed on agency policy regarding the utilization of public facilities by private groups. The newspaper carried reports of the interview which stated that any private group could use any facility of the recreational agency at any time if proper payment was made to the department. The Board of Recreational Service had laid down strict policy for facility use, and the statement contradicted the policy. Private funds could not be used to lease, rent, or otherwise provide space for other than departmental functions. Several telephone calls to the recreational agency apprised Mr. W of the situation, and he immediately called the newspaper in order to get retraction on the basis of a misquotation. The editor called in his reporter, and the latter indicated that his story was precisely what Mr. W had stated to him in the interview. The editor thereupon called Mr. W to inform him that the paper would stand behind the printed story unless Mr. W would admit his own mistake in giving out the statement. Mr. W refused because he said that he had not meant to be taken in such a literal manner and that he had been misunderstood. He also indicated that he would bring pressure to bear by going to the publisher of the newspaper, who was a personal friend. The result of error on the part of Mr. W produced a very poor opinion of him in the press of the community. All this resulted in his eventual resignation from his post.

Because Mr. W was so concerned with maintaining his public image which, through his own error, he had endangered, he tried to cover up rather than own up to his poor judgment. In attempting to rationalize his behavior, he finally brought himself down.

A leader faces reality rather than escaping from it. No leader can ever afford the luxury of rationalization. People occupying leadership positions who rationalize their activities further the myths and misconceptions regarding leadership prowess.

The Superficial Harmonizer

It is from the office of the chief executive in any recreational agency that the psychological atmosphere issues. If the administrator wants a highly spirited, productive organization, he must set the tone which filters down through every level within the agency. The administrator has it within his power to build or destroy morale. Whatever attitude he adopts will be the one which permeates the entire system.

Ironically, the administrator who above all desires an agency which has the outward appearance of a happy family may merely be opening the way for serious discord. It is fallacious to equate agreement with leadership. To put peace foremost, the administrator may pay a high price. Conflicts which cannot be aired may create seething dissatisfaction and even passionate hatreds. Tolerance of incompetence, unethical or bigoted acts, concessions to vested interests, and entrenched mediocrity do not permit the organization to function in the best interests of those it is set up to serve.

The don't-rock-the-boat administrator who requires mere surface harmony will often find it all too easy to achieve. Unprincipled individuals or persons who are pursuing personal goals antithetical to those of the agency are quick to seize every opportunity to contribute to maintaining surface harmony because by doing so they can best further their own goals. An administrator who is interested only in the appearance of accord is incompetent; he is not a leader. Under his inadequate guidance, dedicated professionals will be frustrated and the productivity and effectiveness of the agency's programs will be decreased.

Harmony is not undesirable, of course, but there are valid ways to achieve it. With a little more foresight and a little less self-indulgence, the initiator of agency philosophy can do much for the morale of agency personnel and at the same time promote effective service. This is the harder road to follow. It is always easier to tolerate the conditions which exist, no matter how mediocre. Below is a description of an agency with such a problem:

A federally operated agency employed as recreational director an individual whose sole qualification for the job was his friendship with the employing authority. This individual was a *busy-worker,* a general term referring to an employee who looks busy but actually accomplishes nothing because he does not work. (Such creatures are found wherever administrators overlook unqualified performance and stagnant programs. They generally inhabit technical and specialized professional fields where the need for personnel greatly exceeds the supply.) During some six months of agency operation, this person did not perform his functions nor engage in any of the tasks which were part of his routine assignment and responsibilities. It is true that he always looked busy. There were always papers on his desk; he periodically shuffled them, particularly when anybody happened to pass his office door. He invariably could be found in the snack bar or raising or lowering his venetian blind. But he did not work. All of this was known to the administrator, who did nothing about the situation. That individual still maintains his position as recreational director in the agency.

Which is better: to fight against intolerable personnel situations or to hide from the obvious decisions which must be made? It is easier to tolerate incompetence than to demand a high degree of competence from the incompetent. Typical of the administrator's rationalizations for adopting the easier position is the following: "I know his work is poor, but suppose I discharge him and obtain someone worse?" One person's substandard work is much the same as another's. Better than foisting off a completely substandard program on agency constituents would be leaving the position vacant. Not only would the agency, the field as a whole, and the public benefit, but greater harmony would surely obtain.

Below we have an example of how a don't-rock-the-boat administrator stifles leadership and betrays the principles for which recreational service stands. The example is taken from the records of a government hospital for tuberculosis in one of the midwestern states:

The recreational director had employed a new supervisor whose job assignment included the chronic and acute tuberculosis wards of the hospital. As is usual on chronic wards, where the patients are simply waiting to die of the disease which cannot be arrested, the morale was quite poor. Realizing this fact, the recreationist attempted several activities which could possibly improve morale as well as promote closer cooperation between the recreational section and medical staff. Within six months from the date of the initial employment, the professional was discharged on trumped-up charges by the director who saw the worker as a threat to his job. The threat was real, because the worker possessed the professional education and experience which allowed him to perform competently and confidently. Any comparison which might have been drawn between the two would have been detracting for the director.

Such self-indulgence on the part of an administrator discredits the entire field.

Patronage Positions

Although there are patronage systems founded upon sound principles of public administration and personnel management which put so-called merit systems in the shade, we are concerned here with the more usual negative connotation of the term "patronage." The practice of assigning patronage positions — appointing close friends or relatives to posts for which they are not qualified or for which they lack specialized knowledge — has application to any study of leadership.

In the field of recreational service, political patronage often brings an unqualified person into a leadership position. Such an appointee quickly finds out that he must hire someone who can really operate the agency and conduct daily operations of the recreational program for which the appointee is nominally responsible. When the person in the patronage position is smart enough to realize that he is incompetent, the operation of the agency can be most efficient. By employing an individual who is qualified and competent, the appointee can ensure that the program is conducted properly. Only the taxpayer is cheated because he is supporting a drone. When the political appointee is unaware of his own shortcomings, everybody gets cheated.

The following case concerning Mr. G, former administrator of a large midwestern recreational agency, gives ample support to the above assertion:

Mr. G was Superintendent of Parks and Recreational Services in X municipality, a city of 100,000. He had been designated chief executive of the local recreational department as a result of long and faithful service to his political party. The mayor nominated him for turning out the vote on his behalf. Mr. G was a typical party hack. There was no mistaking his political affiliations. His every move was designed to win approval of those who had placed him in power. He considered it his primary responsibility to place his party's name before the public as underwriting the entire public recreational program. Perhaps this was his ultimate undoing.

Unfortunately for the people of X city, Mr. G knew little or nothing about the administrative procedures or techniques involved in the operation and management of a major recreational system. However, this lack of knowledge did not hinder his efforts at all. He quickly filled key positions within the agency with local heroes who owed allegiance to him and knew as little as he about their functions. These individuals were former highschool football players who had achieved nothing further, former college players who had not made the professional ranks, or would-be fight promoters. Mr. G's concept of recreational service was the promotion of team sport for youngsters. His favorite slogan was, "Sports will keep children off the streets and out of trouble." Leagues were organized, and football, baseball, and basketball contests were seen on every hand. This was the sum of the entire program.

After six months of constant team competition, even the participants were getting a little tired of the same old routine. The outstanding athletes of the community were having a fine time, but the rest of the population began to grow restive. Complaints started to come in to city hall. Parents wanted activities in which they too could participate with their children. Parents asked where their daughters could find recreational experiences. There was some concern expressed by educators and physicians about the physical and mental anguish competitors on league teams were being subjected to. The ministerial association stepped into the picture when one team accused a second team of cheating, claiming the officials had not asked for penalties. It was later brought out that the officials were unfamiliar with the rules and regulations pertaining to the sport and had, in fact, been paid by one of the parents to look the other way when infractions were committed.

The PTA finally circulated a petition asking that the mayor discharge Mr. G and employ a qualified and competent person. So bad was the odor of his department, and so often had he claimed that his political party was behind his program that, in the following election, the opposition candidate was swept into office on a reform ticket which issued, as one of the campaign promises, the statement that henceforth the recreational agency would be divorced from politics and placed under civil service protection.

A second instance, with a happier ending, also illustrates what happens when political considerations determine who fills leadership positions. Here, however, the appointee realized his technical deficiencies and employed as his second-in-command a professional to actually administer the recreational agency:

The mayor of an east coast community employed, as the first superintendent of recreational service, a former Olympic athlete. The newly employed individual was soon found to have no real under-standing of community recreational service and relied solely upon his athletic prowess and knowledge to develop competitions. Initially, there was much favorable comment about the ex-Olympian's expertise with sport and game activities, but shortly thereafter some dissident notes were heard from various sections of the community. There was increasing hostility toward the continued emphasis on athletics to the detriment of any other form of recreational activity. Finally, the mayor brought his appointee in and told him that a deputy would be employed to perform all of the programming operations while he would serve as the city's official greeter and "glad-hander". Subsequently, a recreation-ist was appointed to fill the deputy's slot and the operation and administration of the agency were reorganized to meet the recreational needs of those who had previously expressed dissatisfaction with and disaffection to the current political administration. Although the ex-Olympic athlete remained on the city's payroll for many years, he was never really responsible for any of the programming enterprises. He joined all of the local civic and service organizations and was utilized as a front for the agency. In terms of professional capacity he proved to be a nonentity. Insofar as building good will for the department was concerned he did provide a sound public relations image. Of course, this person should have been employed in a public relations capacity right from the start.

To the public, the political appointee, as the "leader" of his agency, symbolizes leadership in the field of recreational service. Although professional recreationists are not taken in by this false image of leadership, they are nevertheless powerless to combat its negative effects so long as recreational services are subject to political pressures. Only when the state recognizes recreational service as part of the obligation which it owes its citizenry and requires professional preparation, entrance examinations, licensing, and registration within the field, will true leaders emerge to provide faithful and dedicated service to all.

SELECTED REFERENCES

Korman, A. K., "Experiences as Determinants of Performance," _Journal of Applied Psychology,_ Vol. 55 (1971), pp. 218-222.

Luttbeg, N. R., "The Structure of Beliefs Among Leaders and the Public," _Public Opinion Quarterly,_ Vol. 32 (1968), pp. 398-409.

Meyers, L. C., "Some Effects of Facilitator Training on the Attitudes and Performance of People in Leadership Positions," _Dissertation Abstracts International,_ Vol. 37, No. 5 (Nov. 1970), pp. 2962-2963-B.

Scontrino, M. P., "The Effects of Fulfilling and Violating Group Members'

Expectations About Leadership Style," *Organizational Behavior and Human Performance,* Vol. 8 (1972), pp. 118-138.

Smith, H.C., *Sensitivity to People* (New York: McGraw-Hill Book Company, 1966).

Smith, S. and W.W. Haythorn, "Effects of Compatibility, Crowding, Group Size, and Leadership Seniority on Stress, Anxiety, Hostility, and Annoyance in Isolated Groups," *Journal of Personality and Social Psychology,* Vol. 22 (1972), pp. 67-79.

Spruill, V.J., R.L. Frye, and J.R. Butler, "Differences in Leadership Stereotypes Between Deviants and Normals," *Journal of Social Psychology,* Vol. 79 (1969), pp. 255-256.

Stein, R.T., "Accuracy in Perceiving Emergent Leadership in Small Groups, " *Proceedings of the Annual Convention of the American Psychological Association,* Vol. 6, No. 1 (1971), pp. 295-296.

Stires, L.K. "Leadership Designation and Perceived Ability As Determinants of the Tactical Use of Modesty and Self-Enhancement," *Dissertation Abstracts International,* Vol. 30, No. 8 (Feb. 1970), p. 3551-A.

Swingle, P.G., *The Structure of Conflict* (New York: Academic Press, 1970).

Taub, R.P., *Bureaucrats Under Stress* (Berkeley, Cal.: University of California Press, 1969).

Toch, H. and H.C. Smith, *Social Perception* (Princeton, N.J.: Van Nostrand, 1968).

PART III

Leadership for Recreational Service

CHAPTER TEN

Characteristics of Recreational Service Leaders

I n view of our contention that personality traits of leaders cannot be generalized across different encounters or problems, it may seem contradictory to discuss characteristics of recreational service leaders. But researchers in personality theory and leadership are beginning to suggest that certain traits must be present for leadership to emerge and that other considerations must also be taken into account. F. E. Fiedler maintains that the leader's effectiveness in the group depends upon the group's makeup and the situation, incorporating interpersonal perceptions of both leader and followers.[1] He is convinced that the inclination of group members to be influenced by the leader is indeed conditioned by leader attributes, but that the nature and orientation of this influence is dependent on the group relations and task structure. Thus traits characteristic of leaders must be studied in their relationship to followers' perceptions of these traits.

Group members hold certain expectations regarding both the leader's performance and the personality traits they recognize as pertinent to the task at hand. Their expectations are therefore subject to change. A personality examination of any randomly selected group would probably reveal that nearly all individuals have acceptable traits for leadership. It would therefore seem that, instead of hard and fast leadership positions, there should be an assortment of leadership responsibilities as situations change. Whoever is capable of assuming the leader's role at a given time should be able to persuade the group to follow him.

THE IDENTIFICATION OF POTENTIAL LEADERS

What is the possibility of correctly estimating the potential leadership capacity of an individual? What clues might enable a vocational counselor to detect leadership abilities? As yet we have no firm answers to these questions, although the problem of predicting leadership ability remains a subject of continuing research.

In the specific case of identifying potential recreationists, we offer the

1. F.E. Fiedler, *A Theory of Leadership Effectiveness* (New York: McGraw-Hill Book Company, 1967), pp. 29-32.

hypothesis that the individual who interacts easily with his peer group is more likely to be chosen by them as a leader than one who attempts to dominate them. In the recreational situation, which is highly permissive as far as participants within activities are concerned, the recreationist who can meet the emotional needs of people will more than likely earn their confidence and have influence with them. Thus the individual who is concerned primarily with the needs of potential followers as opposed to meeting the demands imposed by a hierarchical organization is more apt to be accepted as a leader. In order for a recreationist appointed to a headship position to demonstrate true leadership, he must be as concerned with his followers as he is with his superiors. A recreationist, like any other leader, desires to lead but is also aware that his authority is limited to the agency situation; he is therefore unlikely to exhibit a compulsion for mastery and more likely to view his role as a responsibility to those dependent upon him. He will thus have minimal apprehension about his own status, be highly oriented toward the performance of his function, and be very adaptable to the requirements of whatever situation he finds himself in.

Of the many characteristics associated with leaders, only two are inherent and absolutely essential for a potential leader. First, the individual must have the *desire* to become a leader. This is a psychological necessity, but it does not follow that one who has the need will also achieve the aim. The individual's need to lead serves as the initial impetus which drives him toward a participation in group problems which may eventuate in leadership. How can we determine whether a person has the desire to lead? The most valid approach seems to lie in observation. The identification of the future leader may very well be made easier through observation of the individual in relation to his attempts at leadership. It must be kept in mind that even successful attempts at leadership do not necessarily indicate the presence of the drive. A potential leader's drive is so strong that neither failure nor success can stop it. If a person continually seeks new situations and opportunities to lead and succeeds in attaining leadership, it can be safely concluded that he has the basic drive necessary for leadership.

The second inherent quality the potential leader must possess is *intelligence*. The observations and empirical analyses of many researchers indicate that intelligence plays a vital role in the attainment of leadership. Indeed, at one time it was thought that high intelligence was the only requirement for leadership. But while recent research still shows a positive correlation between intelligence and ability to lead, many now support the thesis that a successful leader will be more intelligent than his followers, but not excessively so. In the words of Hollingworth: " . . . the leader is likely to be more intelligent, but not too much more intelligent, than the average of the group led."[2]

---

2. L. S. Hollingworth, *Gifted Children* (New York: The Macmillan Company, 1926), p. 131.

One aspect of intelligence to be sought in a potential leader is the ability to verbalize. A number of significant studies have determined that verbal skill is a necessity for a leader. Terman, in his early work on leadership, reported a positive relationship between verbal aptitude and leadership.[3] Bass and others have consistently found that verbal aptitude or the ability to take an active verbal part in an initially leaderless discussion group constituted some attempt at leadership.[4] There have been many studies concerning an individual's amount of verbal participation in a group and the effect that such participation has upon other group members in influencing their subsequent behaviors.

Another aspect of intelligence to be sought in potential leaders is the ability to empathize with others, or the possession of social intelligence. While no conclusive study shows absolute correlation between the ability to empathize and success as a leader, in the educated opinion of many experts this aspect of intelligence certainly rates a place. The best known study is by Gibb, who theorized that acceptance by others is due to a more accurate perception of others.[5]

Thus a person seeking to discover leadership potential will look for intelligence, bearing in mind the many aspects of intelligence. He will look for the social intelligence that will enable the would-be leader to understand group members, and also for the verbal intelligence that will open the door to communication with potential followers.

The ability to verbalize well is a traditional indication of overall intelligence. In addition, the ability to "think on one's feet," have the assurance to come up with ideas on the instant and express them well, is a form of verbal intelligence particularly marked in leaders. Since the leader is generally conceded to be a more highly energized and consistent participator than other members of a group, it is logical to assume that an individual who displays these characteristics may be a potential leader.

Measures of the various aspects of intelligence may be obtained from standardized intelligence tests. However, such a procedure can be costly and time-consuming. And even if the tests were to give completely reliable results, it would still remain to determine whether the individual has the requisite drive to lead. Therefore, the best method for initially identifying leaders for the field of public recreational service is by direct observation. If the individual's attempts at leadership have often met with success and if he continues to seek opportunities to lead, it can be assumed that he has both

3. L. M. Terman, "A Preliminary Study of the Psychology and Pedagogy of Leadership," *Pedagogical Seminar,* II (1904), pp. 413-451.

4. B. M. Bass and others, "Situational and Personality Factors in Leadership Among Sorority Women," *Psychological Monographs, Vol. 67, No. 366 (1953), p.10.*

5. C. A. Gibb, "An Interactional View of the Emergence of Leadership," *American Psychologist,* Vol. 9 (1954), p. 502.

the drive and the intelligence that characterize a potential leader.

The Intelligence Factor in Leadership

Intelligence is the power to know, an inherited capacity upon which environmental factors exert pressure. Unless an individual has the ability to understand and the capacity to perform, he cannot be a leader. Intelligence is, in fact, the key to leadership. As Fiedler indicates:

> It should, of course, not be surprising that the leader's intelligence affects his behavior. Intelligence may be seen as a resource which enables the individual to understand and structure tasks, which enables him to deal more effectively with his environment and thus remove the threat and anxiety which might be experienced by the relatively less well endowed person.[6]

Intellectual power, or the ability to apply learned experiences to the solution of immediate problems, is the capacity of the individual to behave effectively within his environment, to think in abstract or symbolic terms, and to function in such a way as to make the greatest use of his capacities. Through intellect and imagination the individual can shape the future. Not only can he conceive ideas; he can also formulate effective means for realizing them.

Let us examine three aspects of intelligence that underlie all interpersonal contact: social intelligence, moral intelligence, and communicative intelligence. These are the "open sesame" to leadership and thus of vital importance to every recreationist aspiring to a position of leadership.

Social Intelligence Social intelligence may be defined as sensitivity to others. It is the ability to understand and manage othe· and to act knowledgeably in human relations. Both sympathy and empathy are essential aspects of social intelligence. Empathy is a process by which the individual can completely identify with the object of his immediate experience because of a past event under similar or identical circumstances.[7] Empathy should not be confused with sympathy. Sympathy is concern for another person's trouble; that is, the one who sympathizes wishes that the misfortune had never occurred. The empathizer feels with the individual because he has actually experienced the sensation or is so sensitive to the needs of people that vicariously he can place himself in someone else's shoes. Empathy is a two-way street: the individual who identifies with

---

6. F. E. Fiedler, "Personality and Situational Determinants of Leader Behavior," in E. A. Fleishman and J. G. Hunt, eds., *Current Developments in the Study of Leadership* (Carbondale, Ill.: Southern Illinois University Press, 1973), p. 52
7. R. F. Bales, *Personality and Interpersonal Behavior* (New York: Holt, Rinehart & Winston, 1970), pp. 24-25.

another and responds to expressed needs also receives identification from those with whom he empathizes.[8] Because of his capacity for both empathy and sympathy, the leader is able to satisfy, to a great extent, even the most pressing needs of his followers. They in turn recognize the fact that the leader is aware of their needs and can help them to accomplish their aims. In general, the leader's sensitivity to others is perceived by the recipients, and they answer this tendency with recognition of his ability to do so.[9]

Cattell and Stice have stated, with a high degree of certainty, that the empathetic tendency, or what they call "adventurous cyclothymia," is one of the more significant factors in distinguishing leaders from non-leaders.[10] Bell and Hall succeeded in showing that the leader would have to be perceptive of group members' needs.[11] Greer, Galanter, and Nordlie, in an experiment with army infantry rifle squads, illustrated the relationship of empathy and leadership. They concluded that the ability to understand, or accurately determine, the needs of another would result in problem-solving for the individual. They further stated:

> Research indicates that such problem-solvers are often chosen as leaders; the more a leader is perceived as a problem-solver, the more the followers appear to be motivated to help the leader. A person possessing greater accuracy in social perceptions can act with more certainty and confidence in the consequences of his interpersonal behavior. He is in a position not only to achieve with more certainty the goals of others, but also the social goals that he has for himself.[12]

Illustrative of this concept is the following, taken from the record of a public recreational agency:

> Walter, a member of the steering committee of the Youth Center, was given the responsibility for making an address to members of the Youth Center. He took the assignment in the committee meeting, where he was gregarious and outspoken. When the moment for presenting the address was close, however, he withdrew his support and asked to be relieved of the assignment. He stated that he could not bring himself to speak in front of all those strangers and requested that the recreationist assume

---

8. E. Stolland, S. E. Sherman, and K. G. Shaver, *Empathy and Birth Order* (Lincoln, Neb.: University of Nebraska Press, 1971).

9. C. A. Gibb, "Leadership," pp. 225-226.

10. R. B. Cattell and G. F. Stice, *The Psychodynamics of Small Groups* (Champaign-Urbana, Ill.: Human Relations Branch, Office of Naval Research, University of Illinois, 1953).

11. G. B. Bell and H. E. Hall, Jr., "The Relationship Between Leadership and Empathy," *Journal of Abnormal and Social Psychology,* Vol. 49, No. 1 (Jan. 1954).

12. F. L. Greer, E. H. Galanter, and P. G. Nordlie, "Interpersonal Knowledge and Individual and Group Effectiveness," *Journal of Abnormal and Social Psychology,* Vol. 49, No. 3 (July 1954) pp. 411-414.

the responsibility for making the talk. The recreationist realized Walter's withdrawal was a direct result of "stage-fright." He was insecure in the face of many individuals, and it appeared that he was not prepared to deal with such a situation. The recreationist made him understand that nearly everybody, when faced with a large group of strangers, freezes or exhibits nervousness to the extent where he cannot perform. The recreationist cited several cases of famous actors and actresses whose fear of people had more than once caused them to faint or become nauseated before going on the stage. He pointed out the fact that the steering committee was depending upon Walter and that the responsibility for this job was Walter's. The recreationist showed Walter how to gain the attention of the crowd and how to gesticulate in order to emphasize points; he then reassured him by saying that he would be available should the situation require him. Although he faltered at first, Walter was able to secure the group's attention. He held their attention and ended on a rising note of confidence which earned him the plaudits of the assembly.

In this instance, the quality of sensitivity toward the needs of another enabled the recreationist to help Walter by sharing his confidence to achieve successfully. The ability to perceive or sense the needs of others and to satisfy those needs with a behavior pattern designed for the alleviation of whatever condition is out of balance marks the true leader.

Moral Intelligence. Moral intelligence may be defined as the ability to discern what is right or true, regardless of contrary social pressure or mass opinion. It is, perhaps, the one aspect of intelligence which can be taught and learned. Moral intelligence is, in fact, "good character."

Morality is developed during the formative years. Respect for truth and belief in the value of performing, not so much for the good of the individual as for the good of the greatest number of people, are sound principles on which to develop character. The earlier these principles are acquired, the greater the individual's opportunity for developing moral intelligence.

Simply to verbalize a convenient set of moral standards is no substitute for ingrained moral values. As long as decisions arise which entail alternative courses of action, the ability to discern the intrinsic value of each course will be vital in the decision-making process which is leadership. The morally intelligent person is quick to cut through pretense and to evaluate ideas, ideals, and patterns of conduct in the light of principle.

Communicative Intelligence. Communicative intelligence is the ability to interpret symbols and other abstractions and formulate them into logical concepts, and then transmit these concepts in terms which are easily assimilated and understood. Communicative intelligence enables the individual to reach others and, in turn, to be reached by others. It is this aspect of intelligence that allows a leader to persuade, to influence, and to establish good will. It is also the best way to instill his own goals in his followers. The latter requires skill because the leader must influence followers to accept his ideas as if they were their own. One approach which has been used by recreational personnel illustrates how leaders can instill goals in followers without dictating to them:

1. A supervisor of athletic personnel, in a short discussion on physical fitness, says, "With fellows of your age, enthusiasm for the game, and intelligence, it is unnecessary for me even to mention improper health habits, such as smoking, drinking, or staying out late. You are all aware, I am sure, of the harm such activities can do to your athletic fitness and personal health."

2. A group worker says, "This is one of the best groups with which I have worked; you really apply yourselves in meeting the goals which you have set."

3. A superintendent of recreational service says to one of his general supervisors, "You have the initiative and knowledge to produce a high quality and quantity of work for the betterment of this department and the community."

4. A camp counselor says, "This unit is the neatest in the entire camp."

This method of suggesting an idea in such a way that listeners interpret it as their own is just one example of using communicative intelligence. Other approaches will be more appropriate in other situations and at other times. Communicative intelligence involves a well-developed sense of timing with regard to social situations; that is, the individual must have the ability to do or say the right thing at the right time.

Character Traits

Although there is little evidence to support the trait theory as a selection mechanism to determine leaders, certain traits nevertheless crop up in almost every investigation relating to the leadership phenomenon. Courage, sincerity, stability, and other such qualities are generally admirable and looked to in times of stress. Such characteristics often manifest themselves in surprising situations and under trying conditions with achievement or influence the results. These character traits seem to be important and warrant some further explanation, particularly as they function in combination with intelligence.

Loyalty is the quality of constancy, illustrated by the act of remaining faithful to an individual, group, or cause. It involves steadfastness in the face of adversity and upholding principles against all odds. Loyalty is normally associated with strictly ethical concepts, but individuals may show just as much loyalty to a cause which is immoral or destructive. Thus the trait of loyalty must be tempered with intelligence.

Integrity is the quality of honor which leads an individual to seek truth and justice in any given situation. Integrity embodies a moral obligation to adhere to ethical principles of conduct. It implies honesty and consistency in thought, word, and deed. Integrity must be guided by intelligence if a person is to adhere to principles as he confronts choices and makes decisions.

Discretion is the quality of caution. It involves discernment and application of good judgment or tact to interpersonal situations. Where conflict is possible, careful appraisal and analysis are needed to alleviate tension or mediate pressure. Discretion is indispensable in those who would guide and teach others. Discretion also implies the quality of keeping someone else's confidence and can be used as a powerful weapon by unscrupulous persons seeking gain through threatening to reveal information given them in confidence. Discretion, when used in combination with intelligence, enables a leader to help people solve their personal problems and thus influence them toward socially acceptable and ethically correct behavior.

Reliability is the quality of stability and dependability, a measure of individual competence. Reliability, more than any other quality, reflects the level of the individual's achievement in any job. The reliable person who undertakes an assignment can be counted on to achieve it, through methods characterized by balance and proportion. Emotional balance is another characteristic of the reliable person. Sometimes reliability is used pejoratively, indicating that the person is "in a rut," or never varies his habitual patterns of behavior. But when found in combination with intelligence, reliability is a positive quality that attracts followers.

Responsibility is the quality of moral obligation. It implies steadfastness of purpose and faithfulness in the discharge of some duty, function, or trust. The knowledge that a responsible person is handling a problem provides those who have entrusted it to him with a sense of security. Sometimes responsibility has the negative connotation of answerability; it implies guilt. This sense of the term is particularly pertinent where the obligation involved is not of the person's own choosing but is, rather, assigned to him arbitrarily by some authority. Thus, his motivation for fulfilling it is not based on personal ethics but on fear of possible consequences. Fear impedes intelligence. The quality of responsibility is most likely to influence others and produce beneficial results when it is accepted on the basis of free choice.

Tolerance is the quality of understanding. It grows from respect for individual dignity and implies an intellectual rather than an emotional response to situations. It provides the individual with the power to endure the great variety of human failings. It is a disposition toward fair play and the exclusion of bigotry and prejudice. The ability to understand sympathetically the feelings of other people or to empathize with others is derived from prior experience and a great regard for human nature. The tolerant person accepts each individual as he is rather than stereotyping him. Sometimes a person who appears tolerant is merely refusing to face the responsibility of having an opinion. True tolerance is guided by intelligence.

Talent is the quality of creative potential or skill. It implies a native ability for some specific pursuit. A talent may be put to both good and evil use. For example, the talents of machinists, scientists, and administrators were used by Hitler for the subjugation of other nations, whereas western democracies have attempted to use the same talents to subdue tyranny for the good of society. When talent is guided by intelligence it can make significant and worthwhile contributions to people's lives.

Sociability is the quality of getting along well with others and enjoying their company. It involves adapting to social situations in which various types of personalities come together. By demonstrating his concern with the things which are of greatest significance to individuals with whom he works or with whom he finds himself, the sociable individual can gain insight into their needs. If he is of leadership caliber, he may also be able to help them translate such needs into satisfying outlets. Helen Hall Jennings has discussed this quality in relation to leadership:

> They [leaders] apparently earn the choice status of most wanted participants because they act in behalf of others with a sensitivity of response which does not characterize the average individual in a community.[13]

A leader's sociability requires more than hail-fellow-well-met exuberance. Identification with the needs of others and an understanding of how such needs can be satisfied may be accomplished only through the application of intelligence to the quality of sociability.

Perseverance is the quality of persistence. It entails continuing to do something in spite of difficulties, or pursuing a course of action until a stated objective is reached. Tenacity and courage are often requisite attributes. Perseverance can also be taken unfavorably to mean stubbornness or annoying obstinacy. It is apparent that the quality of perseverance must be guided by intelligence if positive aims are to be achieved.

Initiative is the quality of confident aggressiveness. It is the combination of sureness and self-activation. A person who has the ability to discern

13. H.H. Jennings, "Leadership — A Dynamic Redefinition," *Journal of Educational Sociology,* Vol. 17 (March 1944), p. 431.

advantageous conditions and act upon them, motivated by the will to succeed, has initiative. The person with initiative does not depend on "lucky breaks." He is driven by a sense of urgency that allows him to work hard to overcome obstacles; because this urgency is a form of anxiety, the person with initiative needs intelligence to moderate his drive and maintain mental balance.

Personal Attributes

Although personal attributes, like character traits, may not actually differentiate the leader from a non-leader, there are certain personal attributes a recreationist must strive for in order to advance his professional career.

Appearance. The recreationist may have no control over his facial structure, but he can do something about his clothes and the way he wears them. Appearance can be an asset for those who work with people. First impressions are difficult to overcome; if the recreationist is particularly careless about his appearance, people may regard it as a personal insult — he has so little respect for their opinion that he cannot be bothered even to present an agreeable appearance. On the other hand, if group members receive a positive first impression, he will more quickly and easily win their confidence and thus be more effective in fulfilling his professional obligations. The recreationist can only help his own cause by being suitably dressed for the occasion, whatever it may be. His taste in clothes should be moderate, not ostentatious. His physical cleanliness must be above reproach. A handsome face, a distinguished mien, or impeccable taste in clothes may have no actual effect on others in terms of leadership, but they are all assets that can help create a favorable attitude toward the person fortunate enough to possess them. But an individual need not have such exceptional attributes in order to present a pleasing appearance; personal neatness and good taste in dress are quite enough.

Speaking Ability. Speaking ability is important to a recreationist who aspires to leadership. It is essentially through his ability to verbalize that he captures and fires the imagination of others. Merely to express oneself well in writing is not enough. The leader needs speaking ability in order to transmit his ideas effectively to his followers. Public addresses or simple conversations can be meaningful and stimulating both in content and expression; they can be just parrotings of someone else's good ideas which lose their force through poor delivery; at worst, they can be banal in both content and expression. All the skills of public speaking are invaluable tools for the leader, especially the ability to project personal warmth and sincerity through the use of tone and gesture. Although speaking ability is a great advantage to the potential leader, it is not an absolute necessity — if he must, he can have someone else deliver his ideas. Nevertheless, recreationists are frequently sought as public speakers. It behooves the recreationist to cultivate whatever speaking talent he has.

Educational Preparation. Leaders who are uneducated are relatively rare in any field today. The vast increase in knowledge of all kinds prevents the educationally unprepared from actively participating in leadership situations where technical knowledge is important. Educational preparation does not produce leadership per se, but it can give the individual specialized knowledge and help him gain the insight he needs if he aspires to leadership.

Mental and Physical Health. The recreationist must have good mental health. Responsibility for the emotional, and often physical, lives of many people is entrusted to recreationists. Only individuals with sound mental health can assume such responsibility. Mental stability is a primary requisite for employment in recreational service, and is certainly a leadership quality. It promotes confidence among followers who need to feel that they can rely upon the leader's words and actions, and it ensures against mercurial shifts in temperament or in goals as the leader guides his group toward objectives.

Good physical fitness and stamina are also basic requirements for the recreationist. In a few situations, certain physical disabilities are not detrimental to the performance of functions, but in many cases physical capacity in the fullest sense is necessary for the effective production of work and the handling of responsibilities required of the recreationist.

A recreationist works with people in a wide variety of capacities. He may be required to work in athletic programs, to give speeches, to direct plays and group singing, to enter into community building projects, or to conduct surveys within the community. Whatever his responsibilities, he must have the vitality and the resources which will enable him to complete the task effectively. Optimum physical and mental health are extremely important for recreationists working in any leadership capacity.

CHAPTER ELEVEN

Leadership at the Functional Level

R ecreational leadership may be divided into three levels on the basis of specific activities performed by the recreationist: functional, supervisory, and managerial. This chapter deals with the functional — or program, operational, or basic — level of leadership in the field of recreational service.

Who Is the Recreationist? What Does He Do?

Ideally, the professional recreational worker, or recreationist, is a person who has earned a degree in recreational service education from an accredited institution. In addition, he may be certified, licensed, or professionally registered in the field. (A few states have such procedures, registration being the most common, but quite innocuous, practice.) This preparation has equipped him with a professional philosophy and a broad overview of the relationship between the field and other areas of applied social science, as well as a system of personal and professional ethics and conduct.

The recreationist's primary obligation is to serve the recreational needs of the community in which he works and to be ready at all times to deal with both individuals and groups.[1] His ability to perform such services is based on a thorough knowledge of individual needs, abilities, and experience. He leads people, at their own pace, toward satisfying recreational experiences which may take many forms. In addition to guidance, the recreationist may be called upon to provide the needed facilities or setting where people can find recreational activity for themselves.

What Activities Constitute a Recreational Program?

Among the activities termed recreational are those that have proven, on the basis of experience and evaluation, to have beneficial effect upon the participants. The basis of any recreational program should include such activities: sports and games, arts and crafts, music, dramatics, dance, verbal intercourse, and interest groups.

---

1. J. C. Charlesworth, "A Bold Program for Recreation," *The Annals,* Vol. 113 (September 1957), pp. 143-147.

Some activities are best suited to a particular group. By comparing activities which have worked well in similar settings, the recreationist is able to construct a value scale and suggest those activities he feels will have a wholly beneficial effect upon individual group members. This is not to imply that the recreationist cannot be inventive or that he should conform to established programs. Rather, his first duty is to see that basic recreational opportunities for all are made available. Then he must face the task of stimulating his membership toward these activities.

The recreationist who sets out to offer new and atypical recreational experiences must first understand the composition of his group and the needs and interests of the individuals who form it. Only then can he exercise his creative ability and ingenuity. Rather than overreliance on physical activities programming, the most widespread pattern, the recreationist at the functional level has the responsibility, as well as the opportunity, to bring the many other areas of experience to the attention of group members. He must persuade those with whom he works that satisfaction may be derived in an infinite number of ways, some of which may move out of the center and into the community-at-large for resources. All people, young or old, should be provided with opportunities for understanding that leisure activities of a recreational nature can be anything that is socially acceptable. The recreationist is faced with the fundamental problem of leading people to discover that their opportunities are not limited. Once a group is freed from false constraints, it can participate in developing the recreational program most suitable for itself, a program worthwhile, spontaneous, self-actualizing, and leading to significant consequences in the lives of the participants.

It is in this area of programming that the recreationist expresses true leadership. It must be borne in mind, however, that evolution of interests and appreciation is a prolonged process. The recreationist must, with patience, overcome preconceptions, misconceptions, and limited backgrounds. He must strive to increase awareness of potential, inquiry into specific activities, exposure to idea-provoking experiences. He must suggest projects designed to lead to subsequent investigation and exploration. In these ways he reveals to his group the wealth of possible recreational activities.

General Leadership Guidelines for the Recreationist

The professional recreational worker views objectively individuals who make up his agency's constituency; yet he shows by his behavior and methods of approach that he has recognized and understood their problems. Arousing interest, then, becomes a matter of understanding the individual and knowing his background so that new and unfamiliar activities can be related to prior experience. People's interest can also be stimulated through personal affection; an individual may be motivated because of an emotional attachment to the leader.

With these facts in mind, let us detail some of the responsibilities the recreationist undertakes in providing individuals and groups with satisfying recreational experiences:

1. Realizing that all people are unique in their interests, needs, and abilities.

2. Granting every individual a share of human dignity and respect for his own self-esteem.

3. Believing in the right of individuals to guide their own destinies and to belong to any social agency in which they feel a part.

4. Being aware that each individual brings a variety of thoughts and ideas into the social milieu and that such contributions, though they may be widely divergent from the established patterns, may have merit in their own right and are, therefore, worthy of time and consideration.

5. Achieving empathy with others.

6. Accepting others as they are without attempting to moralize to them, unless the standard of behavior is of such low character as to warrant an uplifting moral force, and not adapting or identifying oneself with such substandard behavior.

7. Accepting the wide range of behaviors, from affection to hate.

8. Using his knowledge of human behavior to understand the various patterns which are exhibited, even though such patterns may appear meaningless to the casual observer.

9. Realizing that all behavior is useful and important as an indicator of human needs although it may not always be socially acceptable.

10. Performing within the spectrum of leadership — from strong or direct roles to resource person, depending on the situation.

11. Directing those who need guidance without prejudging them.

12. Limiting group or individual behavior when necessary and being permissive with those who require help in making decisions or performing.

13. Enabling group members to reach decisions without dictating to them.

14. Clarifying problems and indicating possible courses of action.

15. Realizing that his professional position places him over a group and may therefore create hostility rather than the acceptance accorded an indigenous member.

16. Understanding the recreational needs and interests of those the agency will serve.

17. Providing active leadership to participants in the program.

18. Representing the agency for which he works by understanding its

policies, philosophy, purpose, and functions.

19. Coordinating, through scheduling and supervision, the use of recreational structures, facilities, and space.

20. Referring agency constituents to other agencies in default of specific facilities or aid.

21. Guiding volunteers toward optimum service in their specialization.

22. Keeping abreast of current techniques and practices by in-service education and attendance at clinics, workshops, conferences, institutes, and schools where theory and practical learning experiences are available.

23. Maintaining professional integrity toward clients, the agency, the community, and oneself.

The Functional Level

Recreationists on the functional level, working directly with their constituents, are typically concerned with carrying out a schedule of various activities which provide recreational experiences for both participants and spectators. Such work will generally take the form of organizing, promoting, or directing group games, sports, and aesthetic activities, or providing services related to maintaining good public relations, such as answering questions posed by individuals who come to the recreational agency or any of its facilities. Instructing individuals in various skills is also an aspect of leadership at the functional level: guiding, coaching, assisting, or enabling those who participate within the agency-operated programs to achieve a certain measure of satisfaction and, perhaps, competence in an activity of their choice. Usually, these duties are performed within the confines of a recreational center, park, playground, or other specialized facility that provides recreational opportunities. Responsibilities may range from assisting in the direction of a seasonal operation on the playground to assuming complete responsibility for a center.

Initially, the recreationist performs simple activities, often working in a leadership capacity with groups of young children or assisting a more experienced leader directing other types of groups. Usually the beginning recreationist works under supervision until he is thoroughly acquainted with the operating techniques of the agency. Most agencies offer specific guidelines of methods and procedures to be followed, and a beginning worker is subject to periodic observation and appraisal as he learns on the job. His performance is evaluated and must meet agency-established standards.

The variety of duties a beginning recreationist at the functional level performs may be seen from the following list of typical activities:

1. Assists in issuing and collecting supplies, materials, and equipment necessary for specific activities within the recreational program, particularly playground and arts and crafts materials.

2. Helps to organize various activities, for example, games, groups, dramatics, singing, dancing, athletics, arts, crafts, and nature-oriented activities.

3. Gives instructions, guidance, or coaching in several activities, which may include explaining the rules of playing certain games or the techniques useful in various athletic endeavors.

4. Assists in establishing league play, tournaments, or other competitive activities.

5. Sees that necessary precautions are observed to insure the health, safety, and welfare of participants and spectators.

6. Provides preliminary first aid in the event of minor injury to participants.

7. Performs routine inspections of equipment in order to maintain optimum efficiency and safety to users.

8. Performs minor custodial functions of a routine nature.

As a functional recreationist gains on-the-job experience, he is assigned more difficult and complex responsiblities. He may perform skilled and technical tasks requiring direction of a great many recreational activities at a designated facility. He may be responsible for the planning, coordination, and direction of activities in a specific program area, or he may assist in directing and coordinating the entire spectrum of activities offered by the center. Usually, he is under the supervision of an immediate superior, generally an area supervisor. He, in turn, may supervise the activities of a subordinate recreationist or volunteer workers.

Characteristic of the duties which a more experienced recreationist performs at the functional level are the following:

1. Helps to administer the recreational program at a center or directs a recreational program at an assigned facility.

2. Performs such public relations work as is necessary to stimulate and maintain the interest of potential and actual participants in the recreational activities of the facility in which he works.

3. Organizes, guides, conducts, and directs many recreational activities, including competitive and non-competitive sports, games, contests, hobbies, special interest groups, youth groups, children's groups, and older adult groups.

4. Has custody of and issues supplies, materials, and equipment necessary for conducting a variety of activities, or supervises a subordinate in the performance of this function.

5. Examines equipment and recommends needed repairs or replacements.

6. Keeps records and reports on the operation of the facility.

7. Assists in formulating recommendations or makes recommendations concerning the place his facility has in the overall community recreational system.

8. Helps analyze citizen interest in and support of the recreational service system.

Large agencies often have a third step at the functional level (in smaller agencies, a recreationist may move directly to the supervisory level). This third step requires definite managerial ability on the part of the recreationist, as distinct from positions which require particular skills or technical proficiencies. Such a recreationist may direct a multitude of recreational activities at a large playground or center or assist in the direction of a regional recreational center. He is responsible for initiating ideas, planning, coordinating, and providing some supervision to subordinate employees as well as to the activities themselves. He works with all age groups. His unique position allows him some latitude in exploring new programming experiences and broadening the scope of agency-sponsored activities. Most of his work is performed on his own initiative.

Some examples of service performed by such a recreationist are the following:

1. Initiates, plans, organizes, and coordinates a great variety of recreational activities in a center or on a playground.

2. Analyzes the recreational needs of people living in the neighborhood or using his facility and formulates immediate and future recreational programs on the basis of his findings.

3. Provides recreational services for community organizations.

4. Provides, upon request, individual guidance as well as group guidance on civic, social, or recreational matters within the area served by his facility.

5. Supervises issuing and collecting of recreational supplies, materials, and equipment.

6. Sees to the maintenance and proper use of such items.

7. Is authorized to give general supervision to subordinate professionals and volunteers to ensure proper performance of their assigned tasks.

8. Organizes in-service educational activities.

9. Assists in development studies of the facility and neighborhood which it serves.

10. Attends staff conferences, clinics, professional meetings, and other educational workshops or institutes required for his professional growth and development.

Specialists

Specialists are agency employees who have excellent technical proficiency in activity areas such as have been mentioned. Such workers may be recreationists, but usually they are part-time employees hired because of some talent or skill integral to the agency program. Often specialists hold full-time jobs or have professional careers outside the recreational service field. Specialists are assigned the responsibility for developing a comprehensive program in their particular area of specialization. Part of their job may be to offer instruction in their particular skill to recreationists within the agency so that the agency can broaden the scope of its program and reach more members of the community. Specialists may be employed expressly to influence entire groups residing in a target neighborhood or community which the agency serves.

The Detached-Worker Specialist

An especially useful person is the detached-worker specialist, who is assigned the responsibility of contacting and working with hard-to-reach groups within the community. In metropolitan communities, for example, such a worker may be hired because he has a particular ethnic, racial, or neighborhood identity that uniquely enables him to communicate with and influence members' behavior.

As an example of how such a worker might qualify for the job of working with a street gang, we offer the following. He should have expert knowledge about the area, people, mores, traditions, ethnicity, jargon, and habits of those who are part of the neighborhood. He should be young enough to join a neighborhood street gang, but old enough to display the maturity that will enable him to become one of the central figures around whom a gang might gather for information or ideas. One approach to gaining entrance might be to infiltrate the infrastructure of the gang by residing in the neighborhood and casually seeking out gang leaders and their cohorts. Such an assignment could be dangerous for a recreationist, unless he also happened to be comfortable with and capable of making and retaining close association with the particular group.

The detached worker, as the term implies, is not assigned to a center or other recreational facility. He roves the streets and is employed by the department in neighborhoods or communities requiring his particular skills. He has no permanent base or office, but reports to a department official from the central office of the agency, to the general supervisor of the district in whose jurisdiction he works, or to the executive in charge of special services for the department. When an agency program calls for a significant attempt to modify behavior of antisocial groups or to provide a modicum of information for people who are ordinarily outside the communications network used for providing information about recreational activities and opportunities, the detached worker is employed.

The above descriptions of recreationists and specialists at work at the functional level of leadership within recreational agencies are typical of day-to-day operations in the field. Terminology differs from department to department and from municipality to municipality; in the main, the functions, duties, and responsibilities described are those which normally occupy personnel working at this level.

Our discussion so far has been concerned primarily with recreationists working within public or community departments of recreational service. In recent years, however, a new area of specialization has arisen to meet the needs of those citizens who are confined to medical institutions for emergency, chronic, long-term, or custodial care and treatment. The ill, home-bound, or disabled person requires as many or more recreational opportunities than do unafflicted members of the community, but they cannot come to a center for help. Hence, therapeutic and adapted recreational service is a rapidly growing area of specialization. With greater integration into the community of persons who are atypical, public recreational service departments will be employing more therapeutic recreationists to work out adapted recreational activities to meet the limitations imposed by disability.

The Need for Recreationists at the Program Level

A recreational service department's most direct contact with its constituent public is at the program level. It is here above all that full-time professionals are needed to fulfill the year-round recreational responsibility of the agency. Yet, many departments consistently employ seasonal workers, part-time specialists, or fill-in assistants to operate their full-fledged programs.

The excuses, sometimes legitimate, for this lapse are lack of money, the pressures of tradition, and political coercion. In many communities, the recreational service department is expected to provide jobs for a portion of the community population or summer work for the youngsters. The immediate outcome of such a practice — overreliance on nonprofessionally prepared and special-skill employees — is poor leadership and poor programming. The long-range effect will be the loss of respect, understanding, and financial support of the community.

A recreational service department can be no better than its professional staff. The recreational leader requires educational preparation, but this must be a springboard from which to learn and grow. That is the foundation of a dynamic recreational program. Recreationists should be well-rounded, take an active part in community affairs, and have private recreational interests that can contribute to their identity as interesting, socially sensitive, and responsive personalities. The study of human development, motivation, and group dynamics, the reading of professional literature and attendance at professional meetings contribute more specifically to the recreationist's professional competence.

Paradoxically, the recreationist at the program level, where true leadership is most vital, is the lowest paid, least respected, and most expendable employee. Perhaps departments will finally realize that program level personnel should be professional in every respect and possess those personality and intellectual strengths which enable them to provide the highest quality service to their clients.

CHAPTER TWELVE

Leadership at the Supervisory Level

S upervision in any field is an attempt to improve worker competencies to optimum levels. The supervisor in any organization holds the unique position of mediator between those who manage it and those who carry out its functions at the program level. He translates administrative policy into action and serves as the channel through which employee suggestions and grievances become known to management. Among the supervisor's many responsibilities is facilitating the production of those services for which the organization is established. In the field of recreational service, this means obtaining the cooperation of all subordinate workers and enhancing their work performance in every way to ensure the finest recreational activities for those people who comprise the agency's constituency.

THE NATURE OF SUPERVISION

The supervisory process is inextricably bound to all the concepts and functions which define the leadership process. Too often, supervision is taken to mean simply the overseeing of subordinate workers or the imparting of technical knowledge to obtain more competent performance on the part of subordinates. Supervision, as we define it in the context of recreational leadership, includes responsibility for participant satisfaction, employee competence in direction and instruction of activities and in program organization and development, and growth in individual and group work performance. It includes a commitment to seek new and more effective methods for providing recreational services to an ever greater number of people. Supervision, then, may be defined in terms of the objectives for which it is used, aims which give meaning to the methods applied, and as a positive force for the development of interpersonal relations designed to free the talents and intellect of all those who come within its purview.

If we consider supervision a leadership process, it is clearly not the exclusive property of recreationists employed at the supervisory level. As a process through which expert technique is applied to provide the best possible arrangement of facilities and experiences for public benefit, supervision may occur at any leadership level. The program worker supervises the recreational activities of participants and, on occasion, co-workers, just as the executive or administrators exercises supervision in carrying out his many responsibilities. Indeed, self-supervision is an attribute of successful recreationists whatever their position within the organization.

The Supervisory Level Within the Agency

In the field of recreational service, the supervisory level can be thought of as the heart of the organization, whereas the program and administrative levels may be described as the extremities and the head, respectively. Supervisors perform the vital work without which the agency cannot begin to operate effectively. A competent supervisor pumps the life blood of expertise and encouragement from management to the program level and back again. He executes decisions made by administrative personnel, interprets agency philosophy, policy, practices, and scope to subordinates in functional positions, and acts as the spokesman and buffer between the program worker and the administration. One of the supervisor's functions is to bring to program personnel a better understanding of administrative practice. The supervisor allies himself with neither the administrative nor the program level workers, but serves as counselor to both. It is the function of the supervisor to offer such expert technical assistance to the administrator and to the program level workers that success in the various spheres of work assigned to them is more likely to be reached.[1]

A supervisor in the field of recreational service performs the following functions:

1. Exercises leadership and is quick to ascertain leadership ability in others and to stimulate this capacity whenever it is discovered.
2. Studies and works to improve the activities presented in the recreational program as well as the materials, supplies, and equipment, the leadership methods used, and the group processes developed as a result of agency initiation.
3. Interprets recreational and agency objectives to workers within the agency as well as to the community-at-large, Internally, this may be considered as the guidance and instruction of recreational personnel and volunteers. Externally, it is part of the public relations function designed to explain the purpose and operation of the agency.
4. Evaluates each worker's ability and inclination for learning new

---

1. W. H. Burton and L. J. Bruechner, *Supervision: A Social Process*, 3d ed. (New York: Appleton-Century-Crofts, 1955), p. 11.

methods of activity presentation and for accepting work suggestions or advice.

5. Assists workers in their professional development, encouraging them to develop objectivity toward their work and the problems which may confront them, instructing them in professional objectives, and stimulating their dedication to the field.

6. Seeks to provide the best possible in-service education for workers so that they may improve their personal work habits. This may be done through individual or staff conferences, constructing situations in which workers can observe better-prepared recreationists in action, maintaining a professional library, or requiring attendance at clinics, workshops, conferences, or other learning situations.

7. Observes workers on the job and conducts personal interviews of personnel for the purpose of aiding in the improvement of worker technique and recommending desirable changes in the program. This function is carried out through the analysis of records and reports as well as inspection and examination of the leadership methods in use by workers.

8. Seeks to improve competence at the supervisory level through education and evalution of the technical proficiency of supervision with recommendations for necessary modifications. This aspect of supervision is urgently required if the supervisor is to be current in his knowledge and techniques. Self-supervision is thus implied, as well as consistent objective appraisal of supervisory tasks and methods.

Effective supervision must take into account changing conditions within the community or agency as well as the basic aims and policies of the department or system. Methods and techniques used will vary according to situation; the effective supervisor must have an exceptional ability to evaluate situations and adapt techniques to suit.

Types of Supervision

Supervision can be classified into four distinct types: critical, custodial, instructional, and creative. With the possible exception of critical supervision, each type can be employed successfully, depending upon the situation and the personality of the supervisor.

Critical. The danger in using criticism as a supervisory technique is the fine line between constructive and destructive criticism. Destructive criticism rarely obtains more effective work, but contributes to the breakdown of personnel morale, undermines employee loyalty to the agency, and may finally be the major factor causing good employees to leave the agency. Fault-finding is never difficult, particularly if the fault-finder feels no obligation to suggest ways to remedy the fault. And even when the criticism offered is constructive, the way in which it is offered may arouse such hostility as to render it useless. It is a rare supervisor who can use the technique of criticism successfully.

Custodial (Prescriptive). The philosophy behind custodial or prescriptive supervision is "an ounce of prevention is worth a pound of cure" — it is better to see that a worker avoids difficulty in the first place than to let him get into an inextricable position. Thus a supervisor anticipates difficulties of which the worker may not be aware. These may be the nature of the assignment, facts about the local environment, citizenry, and customs, or any of a number of circumstances with which the supervisor is already familiar. Although this type of supervision is self-explanatory, one point should be made clear: as the supervisor assists and guides subordinates in avoiding difficulties, he must be careful not to usurp completely their functions and take on their responsibilities. A worker learns through experience, especially experience in solving problems. The supervisor must direct his effort to seeing that workers understand where and why problems may arise so that they are better able to confront and handle a given situation. To be helpful, the supervisor need not have direct personal experience of all the difficulties which may confront a recreationist. His business is to consult, analyze, explain, and offer a rational plan of action which the worker might take to resolve whatever problem he faces. One difficulty inherent in the prescriptive technique is that, unless the supervisor is skillful in its use, workers may receive the impression that the supervisor is so lacking in confidence about their ability to handle responsibility that he tries to second-guess them or anticipates problems where none exist. This creates an atmosphere of mistrust and impedes the functioning of the system.

Instructional. Instructional supervision is akin to teaching. The supervisor who uses this technique is cognizant of weaknesses and aids workers to recognize and understand the reasons for such failings; at the same time demonstrating, in a constructive manner, how they may be remedied. This technique involves establishing an atmosphere of cooperation in which logical advice can be both freely offered and freely taken. One who uses it successfully usually has had a considerable amount of education and experience which enables him to expose subordinates to entirely new areas of knowledge. The emphasis is on suggestion rather than command.

Creative. Creative supervision focuses on increasing the worker's effectiveness and productivity. The supervisor acts as a resource person, giving advice and assistance where needed, but encouraging the worker in his own ideas, fostering a spirit of cooperation, and stimulating self-evaluation. The purpose of creative supervision is to instill within the worker a desire to discover or produce an idea which may be utilized for more effective and enjoyable recreational service. Creative supervision flourishes where the atmosphere is conducive to innovation.

The Supervisor's Authority

Given the hierarchical organization exhibited by most recreational service agencies, the role of supervisor carries with it a built-in confusion about what constitutes the supervisor's authority. In order to lead most effectively, a supervisor must adhere to democratic principles and procedures. But some, interpreting democracy to mean the absence of authority, are unwilling to use democratic procedures for fear of losing their ability to direct subordinates and obtain their cooperation. This dilemma, while common, is a false one.

Authority has a significant and definite place in the supervisory process. Indeed, a basic tenet of democracy is recognition of the need for some kind of authority in those who are responsible for a group. This authority should be understood to be synonymous with official appointment and the execution of specific duties and responsibilities. For any joint enterprise there is always a need for authority, whether it is legal in nature, based upon knowledge or expertise, assigned by some institution, or given official designation. Whatever the source, authority is a genuine component of democratic cooperation.

Perhaps the most fundamental question a supervisor faces is how to determine the proper measure of authority he should exercise in any situation. No matter how competent a leader a supervisor may be, at some time he will have to deal with subordinates who either cannot function within a democratic framework or who exploit the democratic situation for their personal benefit. Usually, organizations have a set of disciplinary actions to which the supervisor can resort in order to bring recalcitrant employees into line, for example, demotion, suspension, or even discharge. Thus, the temptation to use the authority of his position to obtain cooperation from subordinates through threat may be very strong. Yet threats have no place in the leadership process. Rather, the effective supervisor will find ways to make disciplinary action unnecessary, choosing from an array of creative techniques and routine instructional procedures as befits the particular case.

A newly appointed supervisor will find the problem of exercising authority particularly delicate. By virtue of his position in the organization, the supervisor has the power not only to discipline subordinates but even to deny them economic security. Thus, any supervisor, particularly an unknown, offers a potential threat to workers' livelihood; as long as workers feel threatened, they will not be able to perform effectively. The work atmosphere will be characterized by anxiety, mistrust, and conformity.

A supervisor's first task is to dispel subordinates' anxiety and establish rapport with them. When subordinates realize that the supervisor plays no favorites, has high expectations of work performance, respects his fellow professionals, and sees to it that they have a chance to participate in the decision-making processes which shape agency operation, they will reciprocate in kind. The trust and confidence that ensure cooperation have to be earned by the supervisor; he cannot demand these qualities from subordinates simply by virtue of his position within the organization. Once rapport is established, disciplinary problems and petty rule infringements — tardiness, slovenly appearance, poor preparation, or discourtesy — tend to disappear. Naturally, such an environment cannot be created overnight. It requires patience, understanding, insight, and an appreciation for the other person's point of view.

Of course there will be occasions when, despite a supervisor's every effort, an employee will continue to infringe upon the established policies or rules of the agency, displaying conduct that is detrimental to the service or that causes friction among other employees. In such cases, the supervisor has no choice but to exercise disciplinary authority. Although the supervisor's relationship with subordinates is characterized by consideration and personal warmth, this does not mean that he should be a pushover. The rapport established between him and his subordinates does not make him less objective. It probably increases his objectivity as it increases his insight into both the immediate and the long-term needs of those who work for him and makes his perception of their strengths and weaknesses keener. Because the supervisor's first obligation is to the agency and to the working group as a whole, he must take whatever steps are necessary to eliminate disruption, regardless of his personal feelings. A supervisor is not devoid of emotion, but he cannot allow it to cloud his judgment. When a supervisor notices minor infractions, he can discuss them privately with the employee. Often, if he can ascertain the reason for the behavior, he can help the employee to correct it without having to take disciplinary action. But no infraction can be tolerated for very long because other employees will become dissatisfied, feeling that the supervisor is showing favoritism.

The relationship between the extent of supervision and its effects upon employee attitudes and productivity is well researched. Broader spans of control and few levels of authority seem to result in a more effective organizational structure and produce greater numbers of highly competent employees, with coincidentally, heightened morale and output. Conversely, where workers are under close supervision, there is a drop in morale and productivity. (Close supervision is defined here as the absence of delegation of authority, an excessive control of what workers do on the job and how they do it.) In a study conducted by Day and others, it was shown that close supervision adversely affects worker desire and capacity to perform.[2] Thus a supervisor's goal is to delegate to each individual the maximum authority he is able to use wisely. As the subordinate proves himself able to handle the authority and concomitant responsibility, the supervisor diplomatically withdraws until the subordinate is autonomous. In this way, the supervisor makes a significant contribution not only to the agency but also to the entire field of recreational service, by increasing the number of competent recreationists.

DEMOCRACY AND SUPERVISION

Supervision is most effective when it fulfills the program demands of the organization while equally satisfying the needs of the workers. Both facets of organizational life — agency demands and employee needs — are quite consistent and complementary.

As a supervisor channels his efforts toward maintaining employee morale and establishing the rapport that fosters an atmosphere of democratic cooperation, he does so not only with the goal of increasing employees' technical competence but also of stimulating their desire to remain with the agency. The more competent recreationists an agency has, the better able it will be to offer the highest quality service to the community. Therefore, the supervisor best fulfills his obligations to both the agency and his subordinates when he encourages employees to participate in agency policy-forming as well as in program execution. Only when workers feel they are integral and valued members of an organization will they remain loyal to it. The supervisor's role is central to democratic environment and a relationship between employee and agency that is mutually supportive and satisfying. To this end, there are a number of guidelines a supervisor may follow:

1. All decision-making functions should grow out of group needs that are directly related to organizational problems, programming, clientele satisfaction, or working conditions.

2. The physical environment should be conducive to maximum group productivity. For example, conferences should be held in a room that is adequate in size, well lighted and ventilated, furnished comfortably, and without distractions. People should be able to see and hear one another without straining.

2. R. C. Day and R. L. Hamblin, "Some Effects of Close and Punitive Styles of Supervision," *American Journal of Sociology*, Vol. 69, No. 5 (March 1964), pp. 499-510.

3. Responsibility for task completion should be shared equally among group members and assigned on the basis of individual interests, capacity to perform, and experience.

4. At planning sessions, sufficient time should be allotted to ensure that current problems as well as future plans receive adequate attention.

5. The supervisor's consideration for subordinates should be evident at all times. When workers recognize that their supervisor is genuinely concerned with their welfare as well as with job performance, they are more likely to trust his guidance.

6. The supervisor should be judicious in selecting workers to fill particular jobs. He should do all he can to see that they are placed in situations designed to promote their functional effectiveness.

7. The supervisor should be sure that outstanding service by subordinates is recognized.

8. The supervisor should inaugurate a program for encouraging creativity and see to it that the working situation is conducive to free expression. There must be continuous experimentation with new ideas and activities, and attempts at innovation should never be dismissed out of hand. With supervisory assistance (preferably without), each recreationist should be invited to submit any new suggestions for overall agency and program improvement. In such circumstances, program recreationists will gain self-confidence as well as the ability to evaluate their own proposals.

9. The supervisor must be able to adapt to individual differences in education, experience, ability, and interest. He will have to give as much attention as necessary to those who require it, without making them overly dependent upon his assistance. To some employees he will act as a resource, to others he will give guidance, and to still others he will give instruction. He should allot his time in accordance with the needs of those who comprise his staff, and when he makes appointments he should always keep them.

The Role of Communication in Supervision

Good communication is vital in obtaining the kind of cooperation necessary for optimum work performance. Although good communication is one of the fundamental aspects of leadership, it is also one of the techniques most often neglected by supervisors. The communicative process makes possible the transmission and execution of instructions and enables a supervisor to influence employees' attitudes and beliefs as well as their work. Thus, the supervisor's ability to gain cooperation and effective performance from his subordinate staff depends in large measure on the quality of his communication.[3]

---

3. "To Do Their Best Work, Everyone Must Communicate," *Industrial Research* (July 1970), p. 77.

Some guidelines to good communications are the following:

1. Recreationists must receive complete and honest supervisory appraisals on all matters which pertain to their work.

2. Recreationists must receive justification for policy statements issued by administrators.

3. Recreationists must receive clear explanations relating to any problems that affect the ability of the agency to conduct its operations.

4. Supervisors must develop a system for the free flow of communication throughout the agency.

5. Supervisors must elicit subordinate recreationists' ideas, suggestions, comments, and opinions in developing improvements in operations, policies, plans, programs, and general services.

6. Whenever possible, supervisors should be able to provide prompt answers to inquiries and render appropriate decisions on matters of immediate concern to employees in carrying out their functions within the agency.

7. Supervisors must strive for the greatest clarity before committing ideas to the communication channels.

8. Supervisors must examine the real objectives of each communication.

9. Supervisors must take into consideration the possible impact of a message upon its receiver.

10. Unless it is unfeasible or for some reason inappropriate, supervisors should consult with others concerned in a situation before preparing a communication regarding it.

11. Supervisors should always be aware that messages frequently carry overtones and meanings which may not be desirable, and so should be examined to eliminate unintentional nuances.

12. Supervisors should always make sure that communications sent are useful to those who receive them.

13. Supervisors must follow up communications to be sure that recipients have understood the message, even when the supervisor is sure that he has communicated clearly.

14. Supervisors must regard the communications process as vital to developing and maintaining good personal relations as well as to imparting information.

The Role of Counseling in Supervision

Individual counseling is an effective technique for assisting subordinates to improve their performance and for providing them with an accurate appraisal of their status in the organization. It also offers both the supervisor and the subordinate a chance to develop a personal relationship, and thus build rapport. Such a one-to-one relationship is most effective in clearing up misunderstandings and eliminating confusion.

Often a supervisor in the counseling situation is able to detect unsuspected qualities or latent talents which may be potentially valuable to the agency's program and to the worker's professional career. With encouragement, the individual may be able to develop these abilities for both his own and the agency's benefit. Counseling is also a way to get at the root of negative behavior on the part of the subordinate without embarrassing him in front of his peers.

The counseling procedure promotes personal growth reciprocally. The worker matures as he begins to perceive his strengths and weaknesses and is able to profit by such insight. The supervisor widens his experience in personal relations and is able to use the counseling technique with increased self-confidence.

The Role of Incentives in Supervision

Incentives are rewards that motivate a worker toward achievement. A supervisor can stimulate workers to greater effort and productivity by offering them certain incentives which he has determined on the basis of his understanding of their needs and desires. Of all incentives, the ones with the greatest potential are the nonmaterial appeals to ego-satisfaction or self-actualization needs. Promotion, for example, is an effective incentive because it represents fulfillment of an ego need. A raise in salary is a material incentive, but often the concomitant increase in status and prestige is the stronger incentive. Public acknowledgement of outstanding work is another proven incentive based on appeal to the ego.

A key incentive at the supervisor's disposal is the delegation of authority. Fundamentally, delegation is a process of job enrichment. When the supervisor feels a subordinate is ready to take on greater responsibility, he can delegate to the worker some challenging task. Successful completion will leave the worker with a sense of achievement and increased self-confidence, and at the same time free the supervisor for other duties. Delegation constitutes a public display of confidence which provides a subordinate with the opportunity to earn a more significant place within the organizational hierarchy, permits him to express himself through his skills and knowledge, and offers valuable experience for future tasks. The subordinate realizes that he will be held accountable for the assigned task and that his contributions will be duly noted in terms of the authority which he handled.

In order to delegate appropriate assignments, the supervisor must know his subordinates well, understand their strengths and weaknesses, and be able to predict their attitude toward the work to be performed. Of great importance will be the subordinate's interest in advancement as well as his ability to act autonomously. When using delegation as an incentive, the supervisor must be quite certain that accomplishment of the task is within the capability of the worker.

SELECTED REFERENCES

Bass, B.M, "Some Effects on a Group of Whether and When the Head Reveals His Opinion," *Organizational Behavior and Human Performance,* Vol. 2 (1967), pp. 375-382.

Boyd, B.B. and J.M. Jensen, "Perceptions of the First-Line Supervisor's Authority: A Study in Superior-Subordinate Communication," *Academy of Management Journal,* Vol. 15 (1972), pp. 331-342.

Day, D.R. and R.M. Stogdill, "Leader Behavior of Male and Female Supervisors: A Comparative Study," *Personnel Psychology,* Vol. 25 (1972), pp. 353-360.

Denhardt, R.B., "Leadership Style, Worker Involvement, and Deference to Authority," *Sociology and Social Research,* Vol. 54 (1970), pp. 172-180.

Evans, M.G., "The Effects of Supervisory Behavior on the Path–Goal Relationship," *Organizational Behavior and Human Performance,* Vol. 5 (1970), pp. 277-298.

House, R.J. and A.C. Filley, "Leadership Style, Hierarchical Influence, and the Satisfaction of Subordinate Role Expectations: A Test of Likert's Influence Proposition," *Journal of Applied Psychology,* Vol. 55 (1971), pp. 422-432.

CHAPTER THIRTEEN

Leadership at the Managerial Level

T he purpose of management is to determine and obtain an organization's goals. By effective coordination of the organization's human and material resources, the best possible good or service at the least possible cost is provided. In a recreational service agency, the quality of managerial personnel — both those who determine policy and those who are responsible for administering it — is a major influence on the quality of service the agency provides.

Administering At the Managerial Level

Administrative positions are concerned with the management of some specific function and the personnel assigned to that activity. An administrator executes policy and is responsible for selecting the best methods to accomplish the day-to-day assignments for which his department is responsible. To this end, administrators are concerned not only with personnel resources but also with all items of a material nature which are necessary to provide a worthwhile program of recreational services.

Administrative personnel may be called by many titles, among which are director, manager, general or area supervisor, and administrative assistant. Whatever the title, their function is basically the same. Some may be charged with staff responsibility as personnel or office managers; others may be responsible for providing technical assistance to line personnel so that the latter can perform more effectively.[1] Still others — for example, administrative assistants — shoulder some of the agency's more routine and time-consuming daily operations, including translating policy statements into action. In some instances, they may be called upon to act in the absence of the agency's chief executive, but in the main they assist him with technical and special aid.

Administrative personnel function under the direction of the agency's chief executive, as assistants to him or as administrators of one complete

---

1. A line employee is one who is directly responsible for the execution of recreational program functions; a staff employee is one who provides line personnel with technical advice and guidance.

phase of the agency's operations. As such, they have broad latitude in making decisions and recommendations and in implementing policy, subject to review and approval of the chief executive. In addition, administrative personnel participate in the formulation of policies which govern the administration and operation of their particular department.

Some typical administrative duties are:

1. Establishing methods to govern the control, collection, and distribution of donations, gifts, bequests, grants, endowments, and awards for recreational purposes.

2. Assembling, studying, and analyzing statistics and other information in order to prepare comprehensive reports and draw up recommendations.

3. Assisting in the preparation of the annual report.

4. Helping in the negotiation, preparation, and administration of regular, periodic, and special forms of agreements the department makes with others.

5. Assisting in the management of complex and delicate public relations situations.

6. Preparing, after collection and examination of technical and advisory narrative data, numerous state, local, or regional requests.

7. Assisting the chief executive in whatever capacity he requires.

8. Fulfilling the chief executive's commitments when he is unavailable.

9. Advising with the chief executive on most matters in preparing the preliminary and full agenda of the local authority.

In addition to the duties listed above, an administrator may also be called upon for some of the following services, depending on his position within the organization:

1. Speaking before various community and professional groups.

2. Dealing with sensitive issues concerning employee relations within the agency.

3. Handling public relations, and especially answering queries or complaints about the area he administers.

4. Recommending types of recreational facilities, structures, spaces, and equipment to be provided for such public institutions as schools, parks, municipal buildings, and hospitals.

5. Representing his agency in the activities and programs of various local, regional, state, and national recreational organizations.

6. Directing the pre-service orientation of new staff members and the in-service educational program of others.

7. Managing the budget for a particular phase of agency operation.

In summary, administrative personnel see to it that all those activities are carried out which are necessary to maintain a high degree of efficiency and effectiveness in providing the service for which the agency was created. It should be understood, however, that no one individual would be expected to have such an expanse of knowledge or technical skill that he could function in every capacity listed above. The various segments of agency operation, each headed by a separate administrator, include office management, personnel management, fiscal administration, maintenance, supervision of all phases of the recreational services within a particular geographic area, planning administration, or management of specific personnel throughout the system who are in charge of recreational facilities.

The relationship between chief executive and administrators must be characterized by close cooperation and coordination. More often than not, the executive selects his administrative subordinates. If the agency operates under a civil service or merit system, the executive chooses his administrators from a list of qualified persons, and he can decide whether to fill a position or leave it vacant. Where the agency operates at the behest of local governmental authority, the executive recommends the employment of individuals he feels will qualify for the position and who will be most likely to support him, his policies, and his practices without creating undue friction. Hence, a compatible relationship will usually exist between the administrative and the executive levels in the hierarchy of the organization.

The administrative worker is a specialist in some aspect of recreational service. He therefore has a professional obligation as well as a positional responsibility to assist in keeping the executive informed, not only of the problems and needs of his own division, but also of developments and achievements in the entire field which have a bearing on the area of his technical expertise. If the administrator feels that he is doing his best to fulfill the demands of his position but that his efforts are being frustrated because of deficient equipment or facilities or incompetent personnel, it is his duty to bring these problems to the attention of the executive with definite recommendations for their solution.

Policy-Making at the Managerial Level

Responsibility for policy-making lies with the chief executive of the agency. Within the field of recreational service, this position usually carries the title "Superintendent" or "Commissioner." The term "executive" implies a greater range of responsibility than manager, director, supervisor, or coordinator. The executive is the individual solely responsible for the operational effectiveness and efficiency of agency employees. He directs and controls all aspects of agency projects, programs, and operations. He alone has the final responsibility for the quality of service provided by his agency.

Not only must the executive have the necessary education, technical proficiency, and prior experience in order to be effective in his position, he must also have considerable administrative skill and a great capacity for hard work. In order to keep all agency operations running smoothly, the executive must understand and be able to apply the basic principles of organization and direction. He must give close attention to fair employment practices and see that everything possible is done to establish an atmosphere in which good personal relationships among agency employees can flourish. He must bring all the principles of leadership to his work, formulating his objectives clearly, planning with his subordinates the procedures to follow for the execution of these aims, and setting up a reporting system to ensure that his directives are being followed. A primary attribute of a good executive is the ability to separate issues of major significance from those of minor significance and to delegate responsibility to subordinates for implementing all but the most important. It is this ability to view the entire scope of agency operations and focus the requisite amount of atttention on the changing areas of crisis that marks the executive who is truly a leader.

Typical Duties of the Superintendent

Whether ultimate responsibility for the provision of recreational services to the community lies with a board, council, or commission or with a single official such as a mayor or city manager, the superintendent of a recreational services agency has certain powers and duties that do not vary with organizational structure.

As chief executive, he has direct and unshared responsibility for the effective and efficient functioning of his operation. He is responsible for the general organization, administration, management, and supervision of his agency and its employees and exercises all necessary powers incident to it. The superintendent is always associated with the management and control of personnel practices, fiscal administration, methodology, and the plans and operation of the overall recreational program in all the facilities, areas, and centers of the system.

When a board of directors oversees agency operation, the superintendent occupies a seat on the board and shares equally with other members in discussing and deciding on all matters before the board. He attends all meetings of the board and its committees. He compiles, collates, and prepares for board examination the minutes of all meetings, the annual report of the system, the annual budget message and financial statement, and all estimates for appropriations. He prepares annual, periodic, and special reports of recreational services provided throughout the community and distributes them to other agencies within and outside the community. He analyzes, collects, and assembles information that may be useful, required, or desired by the board and recommends any actions that promote recreational services to the community.

The superintendent is responsible for the progressive development of recreational service throughout the community, in accordance with approved principles, methods, and practices in the field. He keeps abreast of new developments and improvements and applies whatever is advantageous. The superintendent's duties may be divided into eight parts: 1) personnel management; 2) the service function; 3) space and facility management; 4) finance administration; 5) data keeping; 6) public interpretation and relations; 7) planning, research, development, and analysis; and 8) education and negotiation. While most of these duties are specifically delegated to subordinate specialists for execution, the ultimate responsibility resides with the superintendent. The following activities are normally associated with the executive of the recreational system.[2]

Personnel Management. The superintendent has the responsibility for the recruitment, in-service education, and supervision of all personnel (professional, ancillary, and volunteer); development of equitable personnel practices, standards, and levels of compensation; a position classification procedure; adoption of a merit as well as seniority system for workers; periodic appraisal and evaluation of workers; and maintenance of proper working conditions for personnel of the agency. He is authorized to:

1. Employ for a three-month period at established rates of compensation such part-time and special employees as may be needed in the recreational service function to fulfill the provisions of this responsibility.

2. Suspend for cause, pending investigation of the merits of the case, any employee for a period not to exceed thirty days.

3. Accept the resignation of any employees, grant leaves of absence, make all assignments or reassignments of personnel to various regions, districts, or areas within the community of his jurisdiction, sign or countersign payrolls, and perform other such managerial duties which may be required of him.

4. Provide administrative and technical supervision to the assistant superintendent and through him to all other employees of the system. He exercises this direction by generally planning the work of his subordinate, setting the objectives to be achieved, interpreting and applying the broadest policies, providing solutions to the most difficult problems, advice on in-service educational programs, and any needed information.

---

2. G. D. Butler, *Municipal Recreation Administration,* 4th ed. (New York: McGraw-Hill Book Company, 1967), p. 506.

5. Be generally responsible for the character and performance of all employees.

The superintendent also promotes morale and group spirit of lay and professional groups in the community by working on recreational problems which have interest for them and by stimulating cooperation among group members in the solution of common problems. He will assist individuals in developing the skills and attitudes that enable them to contribute to the group effort. He is interested in increasing group solidarity toward recreational objectives and in creating additional groups when needed to solve community recreational problems. He will attempt to discover the causes for the development or lack of development of group cohesiveness and morale. He will continue to seek out groups which have recreational interests or potential recreational problems.

Service Function. The rationale and justification for the local recreational agency is the provision of recreational services for the people of the community. The superintendent's objective is to facilitate effective recreational services through a program of activities which will actually satisfy the recreational needs of people. To this end, he exercises three spheres of authority in establishing this service:

1. *Program planning* is the interpretation of philosophy and policy into concrete experiences of a recreational nature. Such practice will be initiated from community interests and demands as well as selective criteria necessary for the provision of the program.

2. *Program direction* is the management of personnel and materials in a coordinated manner so that specific duties will be executed with a minimum of friction and a maximum of service. This phase of work is carried on through a system-wide utilization of records, periodic inspection and observation, reports of supervisors, staff conferences, and the analysis of studies relating to the departmental program.

3. *Program balance* is the maintenance of a well rounded, full-range, year-round program offering a variety of activities in which all may participate if not restricted by physical or mental limitations. Thus, each age, sex, and racial, ethnic, social, and economic group is served without discrimination or inequality as to the types and variety of experiences.

Space and Facility Management. The superintendent is responsible for the planning, design, construction, and maintenance of all recreational spaces, places, areas, facilities, and structures which constitute the physical property or plant of the system.[3] At all times, he must bear in mind the

3. These terms are differentiated as follows: *space* is a three-dimensional expanse, a non-specified area; *place* is a designated location or particular site; *area* is a level surface or piece of ground, i.e., playground; *facility* is a particular piece of equipment, building, or portion thereof designed for specific recreational activities, i.e., a gymnasium; *structure* is any construction.

health, welfare, and safety of the users. A master recreational plan will permit him to acquire advantageous sites in optimum locations before they are priced beyond departmental means. In the construction of new facilities, the superintendent must be aware of and use the latest materials, designs, and methods; conform to local building codes; and ensure against inferior workmanship and materials. He is also charged with the responsibility for improving existing property and acquiring additional equipment and supplies for which a need has been expressed. He must always be alert for expanding the recreational system's holdings through gifts, donations, or bequests. His is also a custodial function, delegated by him to subordinate personnel, for the upkeep and maintenance of spaces and facilities.

Finance Administration. The superintendent is responsible for all fiscal control and management. It is upon his estimate of services to be provided, the program needed, and the personnel to operate the program that appropriations will be made. For this reason he has recourse to past records and reports of the agency's operations. He must be prepared to study them in detail in order to arrive at a figure which will be utilized for operating the agency. He must look at past performance, expenditures, and accomplishments and relate these to the departmental program for the year ahead. He must:

1. Be prepared to explain and justify each item which he calls for in the budget.

2. Countersign all checks issued to the department or board, if any, and no person may incur expenditures against departmental funds without prior approval of the superintendent.

3. Establish methods to govern, collect, and distribute donations, gifts, bequests, and endowments presented to the agency.

4. Supervise accounting and fiscal procedures in the department, which includes estimating adequate budget controls and developing accurate records, procedures, and reports of expenditures, investments, and collections.

5. Be responsible for the preparation of periodic and annual financial reports, determine the cost of operating units within the system, and supervise the collections of fees, charges, and income from concessions or other services rendered.

Data Keeping. All of the written information relating to the daily operation of the recreational system is submitted to the superintendent by program personnel. They include in their summaries an objective statistical accounting of the day-to-day activities carried on by the agency. Their subjective narrative records deal with behavior patterns of individuals participating in the program. The superintendent then:

1. Uses the written material collected in records and reports for

making periodic studies and surveys for the continuous improvement and guidance of personnel.

2. Develops or designs and approves forms for records and reports in relation to the handling of departmental business, to ensure continuity by personnel and to facilitate the process whereby information may be readily obtained.

3. Sets up inventory procedures for control of office, program, maintenance, and administrative supplies, materials, and equipment.

4. Maintains records, central and field file controls, and adequate filing systems for the preservation of correspondence, studies, and legal papers of all kinds.

Public Interpretation and Public Relations. Public interpretation is the dissemination of information to the public on matters of interest to it. Where questions of policy statements, activity offerings, or agency priority schedules exist, these must be clarified for the public. Public relations is usually concerned with the reduction of conflict situations between the agency and its constituents. Since the executive is the chief public relations officer in the department, it is up to him to establish a procedure by which the agency is interpreted to the public. He is, in effect, the administrator of complex and delicate relations with all public and private agencies, the clientele which they serve, and all of the citizens of the community involved with requests for improvements, leadership, facilities, program, land acquisition, and numerous correlated matters.

Planning, Research, Development, and Analysis. As the executive officer for the public recreational service agency, the superintendent must necessarily be involved in the study, survey, and analysis of the condition of recreational needs, both personal and physical, of the community, and must compile and report on such information. He will provide or prepare technical and advisory data and materials for numerous requests made by community, county, regional, or state departments offering services of a recreational nature. He is also required to furnish specific data on standard civil service prerequisites, efficiency or merit rating systems, retirement, budget, fiscal procedures, departmental organization, rules, regulations, plans, designs, and construction standards for indoor and outdoor recreational spaces, structures, and equipment.

Upon request, he will cooperate, guide, and advise in the development, organization, and structuring of local recreational agencies, departments, or systems for local legal subdivisions; give technical assistance in the design, layout, and development of recreational areas, facilities, and structures; and will offer competent aid in the planning, financing, and administration of public recreational services. Using his judgment and discretion, he will authorize the collection, analysis, and reporting of material facts and statistical studies on recreational services in specific areas. He searches source literature — publications, manuals, abstracts, periodicals, and other published materials — on the trends and developments in the field of recreational service, studies this material, and makes recommendations on its use and application.

He makes studies, in existing programs or agencies, of attendance, population, metropolitan and community trends and characteristics, and economic, physical, geopolitical, topological, age, and sex makeup of population for use in determining expansion and renewal of capital improvements. He prepares maps, charts, graphs, or exhibits in connection with these studies. He composes and sends questionnaires to other recreational service systems throughout the United States to discover the most widely accepted principles and practices for recreational service, specifically in public service administration and community organization. He correlates and analyzes data upon receipt of answered questionnaires and reports his findings. The superintendent is also responsible for the preparation of replies to queries which his agency receives. He studies, analyzes, and has prepared general and specific professional materials from which references or reproductions can be made for use by departmental staff or the departmental library.

Education and Negotiation. As chief executive the superintendent may be required to negotiate, prepare, and administer regular and periodic agreements between the agency and public, quasi-public, and private agencies or individuals for the purposes of enhancing the recreational services within the community. By virtue of his position, the superintendent attempts to educate the public to the need for recreational activity and the benefit that each individual will derive from participating in some phase of the agency's program. He further has the responsibility for providing activities of an educational nature (for example, adult classes) for the purpose of finding an interest suited to everyone in the community. As an educator and negotiator, the superintendent has the following duties:

1. Although he delegates the actual work, the superintendent is responsible for the external information program carried on by the department. To this end, he collects, compiles, and prepares for regular dissemination interpretive data to be used by the communications media and also collects for departmental use all material obtainable on cultural, aesthetic, creative, social, group, physical, educational, or other recreational experiences within the community.

2. After having conducted a general information-gathering service on recreational functions both by phone and correspondence, the superin-

tendent may act as consultant to other agencies on these matters.

3. He is responsible for initiating the selection and purchase of professional books, other pertinent literature, and audio-visual material for use in the departmental library. He is responsible for all other details, by delegation of authority, of the establishment and maintenance of public good will.

From the above compilation of duties, functions, and responsibilities, it can be seen that demands upon the superintendent are manifold. If these were all his position required of him, the work would be more than sufficient to keep him busy. But beyond the required execution of executive assignments and the shaping or initiation of policy by which the agency operates, there is also the need to provide leadership. Many executives neglect this concept. They believe that once they have achieved the superintendency, they are automatically leaders. This, as we have discussed at length, is fallacious. A superintendent must first earn his leadership status and then maintain it with those in the community and with the staff of the agency in order to run the most effective operation and provide the highest quality recreational service. The superintendent's concepts of human relations and interpersonal development will become the pervasive influence within his agency. If he is democratic in outlook and practices organizational democracy, this will be reflected at all levels of the hierarchy. And if, in addition, he has the flexibility and imagination to seek new approaches to the multitude of problems confronting his agency, he will be able to provide leadership in the best sense.

Essentially, then, a recreationist at the managerial level — whether executive or administrator — is all of the following:

1. He is a planner. As a conceptualizer of the organization, he is responsible for the philosphy which will permeate the agency and guide its personnel. He must project his plans and ideas in such a way that agency employees will be able to maximize their time, talent, and knowledge. Managerial personnel anticipate the future, coming to grips with the potential problems posed by given sets of circumstances, selecting solutions and alternatives, and taking advantage of trends.

2. He is an organizer. Personnel at the managerial level mobilize all of the resources of the agency — human, material, economic, or technical — and weld them into a smoothly integrated, cohesive unit so that primary objectives can be reached with optimum efficiency, maximum effectiveness, and a minimum of friction, duplication, and waste.

3. He is human relations specialist. He selects personnel not only with an eye to filling an agency need but also to the individual's potential for professional growth.

4. He is an allocator. He determines what functions must be executed,

assigns personnel the authority and responsibility for carrying out particular tasks, formulates standards by which performance may be measured, and holds workers accountable for meeting these standards.

5. He is an evaluator. He directs the efforts of subordinates by maintaining a feedback system that provides him with sufficiently early warning that he can take corrective measures if necessary. This system also provides him material for initiating incentive plans and apprises him of outstanding performances on the part of subordinates. Through evaluation, he contributes to increasing worker proficiency.

6. He is a leader. He sets up open lines of communication throughout the organization so that information about working conditions, job satisfaction, and organizational objectives can flow freely. He is concerned with the development of interpersonal relationships among those who work for the agency. He attempts to develop rapport with subordinates so that an atmosphere of democratic cooperation is created. Finally, his leadership style inspires members of his organization to undertake their respective functions willingly and in a way that reflects professional esteem, zeal, and technical competence. In all of his behavior, he exemplifies those characteristics which make others want to emulate him.

PART IV

Leadership Practices

CHAPTER FOURTEEN

Leadership Methods and Techniques

The leadership process involves several general methods with which every leader must be familiar. None of these methods is, by itself, sufficient to cope with every circumstance. However, in the overall actions of the leader, each lends itself to the construction of a base of operations from which leadership can be effectively exercised:

1. *Challenging the accepted.* A leader must not automatically accept the status quo, but continually seek new and better ways of performing.

2. *Inquiring mind.* A leader constantly searches, questions, and is vigilant not only for his safety, but to keep progressive and current in his thinking.

3. *Common touch.* Sensitivity to others, the ability to perceive the general need of people and incorporate it into programming, is the basis of the common touch which a leader cultivates in order to estimate correctly the force and trend of social conduct.

4. *Unity.* By finding a common denominator which can appeal to all, a leader combines many diverse elements into an effective force.

5. *Promoting cohesiveness.* It is a leader's responsibility to create the atmosphere conducive to cohesiveness or solidarity through which group aims are best achieved.

THE DISCERNMENT OF OBJECTIVES

Unless the leader has a goal to which he directs all his efforts, he will fail. The leader cannot gain popular support without representing some concept which can elicit public attention. His well-defined aim assures that his actions are always purposeful. The leader also has to be able to evaluate goals. He must be able to select a project the achievement of which will satisfy the greatest number of people. In the process of satisfying those who support him, he will also attain the leadership position which he seeks.

How can the leader establish a meaningful and stimulating environment? How can he keep his followers? How can he arouse interest in his plans and provide incentive to those who support him? All of these questions relate to the performance of the leader, and there are certain methods which the leader uses to establish and maintain his position. Leadership is considered effective when situations are so arranged that followers want to act on a leader's idea, when they have a chance to act, and when they achieve success.

The end which the leader visualizes is the direction or channeling of the energies of his group into constructive paths which will accomplish a common objective. He needs to sustain the interest of those whose energies he taps and controls. Therefore, it is essential that the leader make his goals coincide with those of his potential followers and make them seem worth the effort which it takes to achieve them. Enthusiasm from the leader helps to transmit the desirability of the goals. When the leader can make every question and each effort seem exciting, when he can transfer some of his dynamic belief to his followers so that they will be stimulated to try and maintain their direction, he is using an effective leadership method.

Ends: Paths To Follow or Objectives To Reach?

One way to view goals is as directions for human growth and development, paths to follow rather than ends to reach. For instance, a leader may demand concerted action, and this is his aim. Some other leader may have group productivity as his aim. The major consideration in these cases is not what is acted upon or what is produced, but that the people concerned unite in their efforts, thereby achieving mutual satisfaction.

There are two critical aspects of goals as paths to follow: the situation in which each individual finds himself and from which he must develop; and the way or the step-by-step process by which he may continue to progress. Goals as directions are methods for movement, and guiding performance is furthered by providing plans on the ways to continue to the next stage of development.

Another view of goals is as objectives to be achieved or targets to be attained. Focus here is upon the destination rather than the path. Leadership aims conceived in this manner are not dependent upon the present environment of the follower nor upon the methods by which the end is to be attained. The ultimate goal is of primary importance; how it is arrived at is purely secondary.

In the philosophical and sociological literature of this century, so much argument has been put forth concerning "ends" and "means" that the two are often considered mutually exclusive. However, ends and means can be entirely compatible, the means supplying appropriate tools for attaining the ends, and the ends providing the frame of reference and the stimulus for discovering and utilizing the most effective means. Ends without methods for reaching them are dreams and are often obstacles to accomplishment. Methods without aims have no substance or appeal because they lack intent or design. All means may be viewed as immediate objectives; every objective, regardless of how remote from the immediate situation, does indicate some eventual path to follow from the original circumstance.

Ends and means are also inextricably associated by reason of the process in which they are inherent; the dynamics of leadership situations require that any goal or end be viewed as a means to some additional end. Hence an end is not, in fact, a finish because it always carries with it the germ of a new beginning. Methods can be seen as relatively urgent or immediate ends, and ends can be regarded as relatively more remote methods. The distinction between means and ends is better thought of as the difference between immediate and remote ends.

Immediate, Intermediate, and Final Ends

Some leadership goals are immediate. They deal with what must be done at once to relieve some crisis and preserve the atmosphere necessary for the furtherance of the leader's plans. Resumption of order is unlikely to be the final goal of leadership, for example; it is only meant to serve other ends. If every successive aim is regarded as aiding the completion of some future objective, there is little doubt that objectives, no matter how small, contribute to some final goal. Where the succession terminates may be called the final end, and steps which are found between the immediate and the final end may be termed intermediate ends.

Few are willing to dispute the existence of immediate and intermediate objectives, but there is no such reticence concerning final goals. Vigorous advocates champion the idea that the unceasing movement of the life process and human thought makes it impossible for any transitory aim to encompass the satisfaction of all human needs. Thus, they maintain, theories that purpose a final destination block progress and halt continuous exploration.

Others define a goal as any achievable aim on which one may concentrate regardless of its importance in leading to new goals. Some take the view, in partial accord with the idea that every aim leads successively to some final end, that an ultimate goal is vital to defining immediate and intermediate objectives. But the real goal is to discipline oneself in an effort to attain some ideal end to which all other ends are subordinate but which is, in the last analysis, unobtainable. An illustration of an unreachable final end is the satisfaction of all human needs. Each victory over deprivation can be regarded as a step toward this end, but although the goal can be approached infinitely, it can never be reached.

Achievable Ends

An example of an achievable end is the settling of differences between a group's mores and members' conformity to some social requirement. The aim of leadership in this instance would be to channel the conduct and behavior of followers into patterns acceptable by the community in order to maintain the cohesiveness of the group. Unless this adjustment was made, the possibility exists that the society would destroy the group. Group maintenance within a social context would be looked upon as an ultimate end, not necessarily to be approached by systematically achieving other aims.

Improving Conditions. One of the ends which the leader serves is achievement of better conditions for his followers. This end is also the means whereby the leader gains continued influence with others. Betterment of conditions embodies gaining political patronage, or raising the economic, housing, social, or cultural standards and status of those who are part of the group. A true leader never forgets those who assisted him in his rise to the position which he holds. He continually forages to determine how he can materially or spiritually aid those who have given him support during his formative years as an aspiring leader. He constantly seeks to raise his followers from their present level of existence to a higher level. Depending upon the background, experience, material goods, and services at the command of his group, the leader attempts to better the environment in which his followers live and the situation in which they find themselves. If the group has economic, educational, and cultural security, the leader can bestow rewards in the form of additional prestige and recognition upon those who support him.

Mutual Satisfactions. Another leadership method is to discern what it is that others lack and adopt those needs as an aim. By championing the cause of potential followers and satisfying their needs, the would-be leader attains his own goal of recognition and influence with others while he fulfills his obligations to his supporters. Again, we can see the utilization of ends as means and means as ends. The leader's end is to gain influence with others. His proximate end is to satisfy the needs or desires of others. By carrying out one, he succeeds in the other, thus creating mutual satisfaction.

The method of promoting mutual satisfaction is derived from the leader's abilities to discover others' needs. Through tireless study of these needs, he is able to gain insight into the eccentricities of human personalities and human motives. With this as his anchor, he is in the best circumstance to make his aims coincidental with those whom he wishes as followers. The leader may truly adopt the aims of constituents, but he is more likely to use this as a device to capture their attention, assure their loyalty, and certify their support; if he follows their cause, they will return the favor by granting him the position and status which he desires.

MOVEMENT TOWARD OBJECTIVES

Once an aim has been identified, immediate movement in that direction is vital. The leader must utilize the method of forward motion to allay any fears which his followers may have concerning the possibility and the speed of goal achievement. The ability to move ahead is one of the more effective techniques the leader uses to preserve the loyalty of those who support him.

Thought to Action

Basically, leadership begins with an idea. It is the thought which gives rise to the deed. The leader views his goals in terms of overcoming obstacles or resolving conflicts of interest. He visualizes a specific end as the object of his desire and plans accordingly. Unless there is some original concept which can be developed over time, there is no goal and therefore no method.

The method here begins with exploring possibilities, selecting standard procedures, and visualizing potential outcomes; the end product is practical action. The leader recognizes that the demands of the environment are modified as his group gains momentum. Some of his followers are partially aware of this modification. The leader has to explain the limitations which are imposed upon his group as each objective is reached and becomes a means for the attainment of a more remote goal. He clarifies and defines the criteria by which members will proceed.

The end in view is spawned by some thought which becomes the motivation for a particular program. All activity begins with an awareness of a need. The leader cannot rely upon hit-or-miss propositions to carry him along. He can never leave to fortuitous circumstance the probability that a set of conditions will evolve which will favor the situation. He must have a basic concept upon which to base subsequent activity. Hence, he must do as much preplanning for his campaign as possible. He must have an idea of the end which he seeks and the means to achievement, which is activity.

Alternate Planning

Planning is the development of program material of both a physical and conceptual nature. It is the establishment of one distinct course of action after many possibilities have been evaluated. The plan, therefore, is a documentation of logical steps which must occur in the achievement of certain aims. But one plan is never enough when dealing with the vagaries of human personality. Alternate planning is essential if the various needs of individuals are to be met, and should not be construed as vacillation or willful change of direction.

While it is logical and consistent for the leader to have some preconceived idea as to the methods by which to achieve goals, it is poor practice to be inflexible. He must always be open-minded and astute enough to listen to and weigh the various possibilities contributed by others to his cause. The leader should never attempt to force the membership into accepting something which seems alien to them. Being in the leadership position, the leader may very well influence members to accept his proposal even though they have misgivings about it. However, when group members are unable to formulate or to verbalize their ideas, and it is necessary for the leader to fill that void with fruitful suggestions of his own, either of two positive results may follow: the group will utilize one of the suggestions, or their inarticulateness will disappear under the stimulation of the leader's suggestions. In either case the group will profit. The product of alternative planning is achievement of objectives.

Usually, group members, diverse in their interests, have their own ideas about what should constitute the program of activities they want to undertake. If the leader has had experience with any of the types of activities which group members nominate, he will be able to evaluate these in the light of individual attitudes, abilities, and needs, as well as needs of the group as a whole. If he finds the suggested experiences potentially valuable or beneficial to both individuals and the entire group, he will reinforce the plan. If he feels that the results will be of doubtful benefit in the present situation or that their attempt is likely to end in failure, he will undoubtedly reject and seek to discourage any suggestions of that kind.

Continuous Progress

Vitally important in keeping the leader in a position of influence is continuous progress toward an objective. Through sheer force of forward momentum, the leader is perpetuated even as his ideas gain credence and acceptance. The most difficult thing to fight is an idea, and once an idea is carried into action, it is indeed a formidable task to halt the process and dampen the enthusiasm.

Leaders realize that they must press onward if they are to retain status and wield influence with others. A moving target is hard to hit, and concrete accomplishments are hard to refute. But a leader's policies and activities become easy marks when movement forward is obstructed. The leader who allows his projects to become bogged down through indifference, apathy, or antagonistic interference is vulnerable. As long as followers are aware that some advancement is taking place, they will be restimulated to work toward aims. Nothing causes flagging interest or hope more than immobility.

It is necessary for the leader to plan his movements with care, seeing that possible interference with his activities is checked before it can take hold. By following up his plans with consistent action, he will leave no time for doubt and dissension to arise.

DEVELOPING SECONDARY LEADERS

Empires have been built by men of iron constitution and unbending will only to fade or vanish after the demise of the builder because he failed to develop a new leader who could carry on after his death. History is replete with illustrations. Groups, like empires, have also come to ruin because a leader has not prepared subordinates to succeed him and to hold the group together.

In order to maintain and reinforce continuity of policy, objectives, standards, and aims after the departure of an original leader, it is necessary to have on hand individuals who believe in the ideas and methods of the former leader and who are prepared to assume leadership responsibilities. Preparing such individuals is one of the basic methods used by a leader for the preservation of his group and the ideals for which he stands. Secondary leaders, if they are properly prepared by the leader, are ready to assume full leadership responsibility and generally are well received by group members as the logical successors to their leader. Such a procedure is especially possible when the leader organizes and specifies the succession of leadership for the welfare of the group. In most cases, the leader prepares every follower for leadership; only certain ones will have the necessary combination of desire, drive, insight, attractiveness, and other attributes that can make them acceptable as leaders.

One method the leader uses to develop successors is delegation of responsibility and concomitant authority. Another is the teaching of skills, knowledge, and practices to members of the group so that they can participate in leadership situations and exercise their potential for group influence.

Delegation of Responsibility and Authority

As the leader attempts to initiate secondary leadership within the group, he must work to develop a proper sense of responsibility among those who are potentially capable of assuming the reins of leadership. One purpose of delegating authority for carrying out responsibility is to build confidence in the person to whom this trust is given. In order to live up to what is expected of him, the person is motivated to increase his productivity and competence. Proper use of the technique is vital to developing leadership potential within a group. No leader can ever hope to prepare future leaders as anything except puppets unless authority and responsibility are delegated. Reluctance to do so is an indication of lack of confidence in the selectee and a sign of ineffective leadership.

In order to delegate the responsibility and the authority necessary for achieving any assignment, the leader must take the following steps:

1. The hierarchy of the organization must be used; that is, communications must proceed from level to level so that no one's authority is bypassed.

2. The developing leaders must be clearly advised on the nature of their assignment, but not be instructed in the method for fulfilling the obligation placed upon them. They alone should be held responsible for whatever results they achieve, and the leader should avoid intervening in the responsibilities which have been delegated.

3. Recognition should be given for displays of resourcefulness and competence. Such recognition should closely follow the activity.

4. Every effort to allow potential leaders to perform the functions of the next higher level in the organizational hierarchy should be made. Practical involvement in the problems encountered by superiors will develop an appreciation for the complexity of the position and the stability necessary to complete appointed assignments.

5. Provision must be made to ensure that a person is assigned to duties in keeping with his limitations and capacities.

6. Complete objectivitiy must be maintained in evaluating the performance of potential leaders. Alleged mistakes or failures must be investigated thoroughly and impartially, and support should always be tendered until conclusive and unbiased proof indicates that support should be withdrawn.

These methods are useful in the development of secondary leaders during the tenure of the leader, without whose continual support and justifiable confidence, secondary leaders cannot be prepared. To obviate the negation or destruction of his work, the leader must take time to prepare those who will come after him.

Teaching

The significance of the teaching aspect of leadership must not be underestimated. The leader imparts knowledge, creates an atmosphere conducive to the transmission of ideas, and contributes to the learning process of followers as he encourages them to ever higher levels of aspiration and achievement. Regardless of community sanction or social acceptance or rejection, it is the leader who daily sets the assignments, helps individuals in his group develop at their own particular rates of speed, and shapes and molds their behavior patterns in conformity with his own concepts of what such patterns should be. It is the leader, in his teaching capacity, who stimulates, accepts, or rejects habits, attitudes, productivity, or personality traits. It is he who shapes group character and enables followers to approximate their potential in a social context. It is his philosophy of life, applied to the group situation, which is of the utmost importance. It is the leader's obligation to teach leadership behavior to his followers. No one else is in a position to do so.

SELECTED REFERENCES

Kavanagh, M.J., "Leadership Behavior As a Function of Subordinate Competence and Task Complexity," *Administrative Science Quarterly,* Vol. 17 (1972), pp. 591-600.

Lowry, R.P., *Who's Running This Town? Community Leadership and Social Change* (New York: Harper & Row, 1968.)

Luecke, D.S., "The Professional As Organizational Leader," *Administrative Science Quarterly,* Vol. 18 (1973), pp. 86-94.

McGinnies, E. and C.B. Ferster, *The Reinforcement of Social Behavior* (Boston: Houghton Mifflin, 1971).

Mehrabian, A., *Tactics of Social Influence* (Englewood Cliffs, N.J.: Prentice-Hall, 1970).

CHAPTER FIFTEEN

Leadership Evaluation

T he process of leadership evaluation concerns the outcome of leadership, the success of on-going leadership, and the prediction of
attempts at potential leadership. Leadership evaluation, then, is the
process of formulating judgments that are to be utilized for subsequent
action. It comprises the establishment of objectives, collecting evidence
dealing with progressive movement toward objectives or, conversely, lack
of progress, making appraisals of the evidence, and revising methods and
objectives accordingly. It chiefly covers three things: 1) the subjective
actions which occur as a result of leadership; 2) the quality of leadership,
i.e., its effectiveness; and 3) the personal contributions of the leaders
insofar as influence and other attributes are perceived by followers. What
factors are defined as essential for the evaluation of leadership? What is it
that the leader must be or do in order to be recognized as having influence
with others? How is successful leadership determined? The answers to
these questions will serve as guides for the development of criteria which
can be used to evaluate leadership. Therefore, a preliminary analysis of
existing values and objectives is of major concern; secondly, some
interpretation of values and objectives into behavioral terms; and finally,
development of an evaluation instrument by which evidence can be
appraised.

WHAT SHOULD BE EVALUATED?

The following types of information are needed by evaluators of
leadership: 1) attitudes toward group activities; 2) attitudes toward the
agency of concern; 3) attitudes toward self; 4) attitudes toward existence; 5)
interests; 6) identifications; 7) feelings toward other group members; 8)
immediate objectives; 9) long-range goals; 10) anxieties; 11) preferences;
12) modifications in self-concept; 13) modification in role perception in
relation to significant groups within the social milieu; 14) needs and
emotional patterns which have developed from influences derived from
group membership and significant others; 15) emotional disturbances or
problems which accrue in consequence of social impacts.

Evaluation should be a process that is essentially self-correcting. It should be designed to identify errors and modify procedures before negative effects are felt. The objective of examining the results of leadership is to determine whether goals have been accomplished; the objective of examining techniques is to determine whether certain methods are being followed. The reason for comparing outcome with technique is to determine whether the techniques should be changed in some way.

The evaluation of leadership is primarily pragmatic and subjective, although some objective criteria may be applied. Any basic understanding of leadership is concerned with the ability to measure it accurately. However, the relativity of evaluative attempts to measure leadership is well-known. In spite of all attempts to be objective, there are so many variables which may be inculcated into an evaluating instrument that its practical use may be relegated merely to the individual who uses it at any given time. Each person who evaluates leadership does it from a different point of view. Because it depends upon the source of individual orientation, leadership evaluation has never been developed to the point of applying a constant set of standards.

Perhaps the best indicator of leadership is the pragmatic approach, i.e., does it succeed? If leadership is adequate, it is successful. But this brings up the question of defining adequacy and success. What appears as success to an observer may be conceded as failure by the participant and vice versa. Previous studies attempted to evaluate leadership by using case histories, ratings, classifications, and other related methods. However, these have been highly subjective, imprecise at best, and heavily biased where opinions are the only criterion.

The evaluation of leadership may best be made from several selected variables based upon distinct categories or points of view. Thus, leadership may be considered from four characterized orientations: participant membership, agency, leader, and evaluator.

Participant Membership. The group member or individual participating within a given activity views the leader's adequacy in terms which are dependent upon specific needs or desires. Presumably, if the participating individual can achieve his goals, he will classify the leadership as "good." Leadership adequacy can actually be based on whether or not, in the follower's judgment, the leader is functioning in a competent manner. Personal liking for the individual who performs the leadership role may have an effect on an appraisal of adequacy, but this is discounted in stress or problem situations, where the leader must be able to activate others. In less critical situations, personal friendship may influence judgment to favor the leader, but in emergency cases, competence becomes the criterion.

The participant's confidence in the leader's ability will be indicated by leadership emulation — imitation of dress, speech, mannerisms, walk, attitude, opinions, stance, method of problem-solving, etc. — and the intensity or quality of participation undertaken by the group at the instigation of the leader. This personalization continues to develop as long as the leader is able to maintain follower confidence. The same aspect is noted in individual participation. When the follower believes in the plans and objectives of the leader or in the leader's adequacy, he is more willing to engage in activities, suggestions, or projects which the leader devises. While intensity and quality of participation are not interchangeable, the presence of either indicates some sort of tacit leadership acceptance. Where both of these factors are present, the likelihood that the individual wholeheartedly accepts the leader is apparent. Intensity of participation refers to consistency or continued presence within the group. Quality of participation refers to actual involvement and absorption in any given enterprise or experience which the group undertakes.

Agency. The orientation from the agency's point of view is interesting to observe. Here, agency appraisal is based on examination of group processes and outcomes as they are effected by the leader. The object of this approach is to compare the experiences of group membership with proposed or desired agency policies, principles, or standards. To the extent that group members are influenced by the leader, the agency will be examining the following set of outcomes:

1. Group membership involving formation, size, adhesion, hedonic tone, and group direction toward ethical and achievable goals.

2. Group conformity to established agency standards of conduct, philosophy, or policy.

3. Membership retention through personal interaction, degree of need satisfaction or frustration, decision-making, and desireable attitude change or development.

4. Technical knowledge and skill assimilated as a result of leadership effectiveness.

From the agency point of view, the most essential form of leadership evaluation is the direct measurement of what has been produced. The agency is concerned with the degree of approximation group members have achieved to conform to specific objectives. Depending upon the agency, this achievement may be in terms of personal development, knowledge achieved, skill, health, profit, satisfaction, or some measureable goal. Ultimately, the test of leadership adequacy will be evaluated by individual followers' achievements.

Leader. From the leader's standpoint, his degree of influence with individuals, his ability to initiate and carry out concepts, and the ultimate success of his plans will be the best measure of his adequacy. The leader really has only one criterion — achievement. If he is successful in formulating ideas, organizing a followership, and ethically implementing his program until attainment of specific objectives is reached, then leadership has occurred, and he has performed in a manner consistent with his aims. If he has used methods which are socially acceptable, moral, and just, the product may be considered as the surest form of achievement.

The leader will be satisfied with his performance standards if he gains the confidence of those from whom he must obtain action in the pursuit of objectives. As the group moves in the direction suggested or emphasized by the leader, he will note improvement in his technique. Whether it is through rapport-building, increasing sensitivity to the needs of the group membership, or the ability to enhance the group's perception of him as having a higher degree of concern for their well-being, the leader's self-evaluation should be able to focus on gains or losses made as influence is achieved.

The leader will have certain expectations of objectives, agency directives, or group ambitions. The leader should understand how he is performing in relation to such expectations and develop strategies to attain the goals which incorporate group and agency desires. Because of the complexity in separating personal inability from superimposed intrusions, it is difficult to treat shortcomings as problems to be overcome rather than as personal failures. In the final analysis, only the leader can know if he has improved his effectiveness.

One of the chief functions of the leader is to create a situation in which individuals find group life so attractive, by virtue of its activities or its leader, that they resist other lures and remain steadfast to the group. The leader's own evaluation should detect the interactions and interpersonal responses which develop as coelescence and adherence to the group. It is on these bases that leadership may be pronounced most effective and real.

Evaluator. No matter who evaluates a leader, his interpretation will vary according to his perception. When leadership is evaluated from a superior, subordinate, or peer viewpoint the outcome depends upon what it is that is required of the leader. Thus, superiors in an organization may come to view the leader's behavior from the standpoint of group goal achievement or productivity. The emphasis will be upon task accomplishment. Subordinates will have other needs to be satisfied, with task accomplishment being only one factor in determining their appraisal. In all probability, subordinates or followers will perceive the most effective leader as one who shows the most consideration for them — consideration being a dimension of behavior that is characterized by impartiality, reliability, communicativeness, and a concern for the welfare of the membership. Superiors will rate the leader as being effective if he accepts the norms and values of the superior authority, thereby carrying out the role assigned to him by the organization. Simultaneously, the leader must win the voluntary followership of those who are subordinate to him. If he can do this, he will be able to exercise authority and influence which has been freely accorded to him. Under such circumstances, he will be rated highly by group members who utilize him as a buffer against the impersonalilty of the organization or of society-at-large, depending upon the situation of the group in question.

Whether evaluation is carried on by those who are directly affected by the leader, the leader himself, by extra-group observers, or by those within an organization in which the leader is a subordinate, the outcomes will be considerably influenced by either predisposed expectations or perceived behaviors and the consequences of such actions upon objectives gained, group members satisfied, problems solved, membership maintained, or other criteria used as measures.

Evaluation should not be confused with research.[1] Although it utilizes the devices and products of research and may develop leads for research, evaluation is neither technically capable nor sufficiently precise to perform as research. Evaluation is a dynamic process with intrinsic values that can be executed by anyone who wants to improve performance and has the determination to submit to the rigorous analysis, scrupulous observation, and those instrumentalities which are available and applicable. For practical purposes, the fundamental measurement-appraisal factors in evaluation must be discretely applied in a general pattern of leadership planning that involves an initial consideration of basic objectives and a subsequent use of remedial devices.

CRITERIA DEVELOPMENT

In evaluation, one criterion is the behavior, and its outcomes, of members achieved by a recreationist in practice. Since the recreationist (leader) performs in a highly complex situation, where his or her efforts are influenced by the interaction of personality, personal skills, and various situational variables, criteria concerning leadership effectiveness will vary over time and change with the job situation. Among the personal variables comprising one aspect of interacting factors are intellectual and affective structures, perceptions, previous experiences, and habits of decision-making. Situational variables will probably include personal characteristics of group members, needs as perceived by group members, the objectives of the recreational agency involved, the immediate objectives of the group

---

1. M. Provus, "Evaluation or Research, Research or Evaluation," *The Educational Technology Review Series,* No. 11 (Jan. 1973), pp. 48-52.

and the leader, the physical setting, social pressures, and other external forces tending to influence the group and/or the leader.

The interaction of leader behavior and situational variables is dynamic and interrelated. It must be understood that the situational variables provide the basis for leadership performance. When there is dynamic interaction between leader and social milieu, there is a leveling effect on leadership performance. It is suggested, therefore, that criteria designed for evaluating leadership performance should recognize both the personality factors and characteristics which the leader brings to the working situation and the conditioning influences tending to delimit activity which his or her position in the agency places upon the individual.

Formulating Evaluative Criteria

Although often omitted, or given short shrift, an important step in evaluation is the selection of determining standards. These standards are objective statements of particular values to be sought and measured. Whatever the paramount objectives of recreationists, they should be included in the leadership evaluation process. A satisfactory set of valid objectives will probably be identified if an attempt is made to classify all of the possible contributions which a leader must make if he is to be successful and those personality factors which seem to be consistently reported as meeting the needs of the various groups in which recreationists serve. Once identified, they may then be translated into behaviors that can be observed or measured objectively.

The first step in recreational leadership evaluation at the departmental level is determining what is important in leadership. This procedure is essential to the evaluation process because it serves as the foundation for identifying the particular leader behaviors and consequences of behavior that are desired (criteria), producing means to measure these behaviors and outcomes (measurement), and comparing measurement and desired results (evaluation). In attempting to define those factors which are considered important to leadership, several questions must be answered:

1. Who will determine the criteria and their relative significance?
2. What procedure will be utilized to gather the data necessary for making such decisions?
3. How will the data be analyzed?

Criteria decisions are effectively improved if they are developed from the pooled judgments of experts rather than the intuition of any single individual. The convention of authorities could be accomplished by involving the entire known group of experts dealing with the subject matter of leadership, if it is relatively small, or by drawing from a random sample of known authorities in the field. The panel method may include any combination of individuals to make a group of experts who can develop criteria which are unbiased.

Procedures

Any number of procedures may be used to gather information, including free responses, statements, and impressions; responses to checklists; position description and analysis; description of critical incidents or detailed descriptions of actual occurrences and behavior that have been observed by experts; time studies or detailed samplings of leader behaviors based on systematic observation and recording over a period of time; psychosocial methods or the determination of factors and their importance by panel members, using such procedures as ranking and paired comparisons.

Analysis of Responses

After experts reflect on the aspects of criteria they feel are important, a final choice must be made of the criteria and their respective procedural requirements. A systematic and comprehensive approach needs to be instituted to choose pertinent criteria, which should involve descriptions of each criterion and statistical techniques to reveal the important operational behaviors associated with the attainment of the leadership objectives. Leadership evaluations will be effective only if criteria are founded on reliable information about the essential characteristics and behaviors required for leaders in the field of recreational service. Such information is obtained from close study and controlled investigation.

Particular Leadership Behaviors

Although behaviors for leadership effectiveness cannot be generalized because the behaviors and outcomes of such behaviors are peculiar to each situation, nevertheless, certain behaviors have been identified in the research literature dealing with leadership. They are stated here for those responsible for criteria selection and development:

1. The leader expresses ideas, objectives, and goals which closely approximate the unarticulated needs and preferences of those who make up the group membership.

2. The leader's style reflects the needs of those who follow and the social milieu in which he finds himself. The leader is capable of dealing with several kinds of followers differently, in order to meet specific needs, and has the ability to adjust his tactics from one situation to the next. He is flexible.

3. The leader utilizes a complex conceptual frame of reference. This seems to be associated with the idea that analysis and diagnosis of any situation is required for leadership, i.e., that judgments must be made in

relation to goals and group needs, and that selection of correct alternatives for group success must be made.

4. The leader initiates structure. Group members appear to handle information more effectively when patterns for group operation are provided. Structure offers the security of knowing which member is responsible for what function, thereby permitting interpersonal reactions, group activities, and relations with other groups, individuals, or collectives.

5. The leader facilitates communication. Effective leadership is based upon the leader's ability to maintain a central position within the communications network of the group.

6. The leader initiates action. This behavior is viewed as suggesting prominence and persuasive ability on the part of the individual. The behavior associated with initiative appears to have an element of recognition-seeking and achieving by the leader through the group's acceptance of the projects and standards determined by the leader.

7. The leader promotes adhesion. The degree to which group members function as a cooperative body having little or no internal dissension may be one of the most significant elements of leadership effectiveness.

8. Hedonic tone is closely related to leadership effectiveness. If, through his behavior, the leader is enabled to promote hedonic tone, then the group is more likely to exhibit adhesion, goal achievement, intimacy, participation, potency, and stability.

Techniques for developing criteria for leadership evaluation seem to be moving toward a descriptive base and away from that which is by nature inferential. In fact, some of the newer procedures tend to emphasize description rather than evaluation and value judgments on the part of the observer.

DATA COLLECTION AND ANALYSIS

In practice, the activities of identifying leader performance criteria and identifying data-collection and interpretation techniques run parallel. The dual functions are defined more by interaction than by a consecutive relationship. The criteria supply the central issue of the evaluation by signaling the evaluator, and the individual who is being evaluated, what behavior, objects, or conditions relate to performance success; the techniques of data collection denote how information will be acquired and the measuring devices that will be used; and the methods of data analysis systematize the collected data so that explication may be made and conclusion reached.

Planning for Data Collection

Planning for data collection is a vital step that is frequently overlooked or skimped in the evaluation process. Many evaluation efforts are found to be faulty because of a lack of planning. Plans for the acquisition of data should be accomplished concomitantly or immediately following criteria designation. The planning effort should supply answers to the following questions: What is the source of the data? In what form will it be assembled? What will be the sampling procedures used? Who will collect the data? What preparation will the collector require?

Sources of Data. Initially, identification of data sources is required. Usually, sources are known at the time the criteria for evaluation are defined. However, it is necessary for the evaluator to investigate possible sources that may have been neglected during earlier stages. He needs comprehensive information about the kinds of data that may be collected and the types of measuring devices that may be applied. Typically, the sources of information include those persons who might be expected to have observed the leader's behavior and its results. Because most of the data develop from some human experience, evaluators must recognize ethical standards concerned with its acquisition and application in evaluation. Access to data may be made easier if the evaluator first explains the objectives of the evaluation.

Kinds of Data. The form in which the data will be collected will have implications for any analysis that can be made. Whether data is gathered in "raw" or "refined" form will be a significant factor. Generally, the objective of the evaluation determines the form desired, and the form of the data materially changes the techniques used to collect and analyze it. However, if the data are not readily available in the form deemed most appropriate, adjustments in the collection and interpretation procedure will occur.

Sampling Procedures. The sampling procedures to be used in evaluating leaders must be planned for data acquisition. Sampling procedures are designed to gather only components of the entire sum of available data from previously determined sources. In leadership evaluation, sampling techniques are applied for two basic reasons: it is not possible to acquire and interpret all the available information; they permit the evaluator to allot the information needs over the available time and data sources in order not to impose unduly upon any one individual.

In applying observational techniques, sampling has its drawbacks. It has been found that when interaction analysis techniques are used, multiple observations need to be arrayed carefully over a given period to sample a leader's behavior adequately. Even when the extraneous presence of the sampler is discounted, data from observational techniques has to be interpreted with caution.

Choosing Measuring Devices

In the evaluation of leadership, measurement techniques are funda-mental for the collection of data. They sometimes exert direct influence on the type of information to be gathered. They benefit collection by ordering the data, thereby reducing probable errors which can accompany informal human observation. Leadership evaluation is dependent upon measure-ment as a determinant of quality and quantity.

In making choices of measuring instruments, the evaluator should select the techniques and tactics that can provide the required data. The features that indicate the adequacy of any evaluative instrument should be considered before final selection is made. The adequacy of instruments will best be determined by the characteristics of validity, reliability, stability, pertinency, and facility.

1. *Validity* is concerned with whether the instrument actually measures the behavior, situation, or thing it was intended to measure.

2. *Reliability* is concerned with the accuracy of the instrument to measure from one application to the next.

3. *Stability* is concerned with the consistency of the instrument over time.

4. *Pertinency* is concerned with whether the instrument actually measures a factor that is considered important.

5. *Facility* is concerned with the practical application of the instrument in the evaluation process, i.e., its ease of administration, cost, time, and resistance factors.

Who Will Collect the Data. It is typical for the employing agency to determine who will evaluate its personnel. This may sometimes be performed by the immediate superior of the individual in question, or it may be assigned to some outside party (perhaps a consultant) who is brought in specifically to assess leadership accomplishment. Frequently, evaluation of personnel is performed by an administrator who has discretionary authority not only to make the evaluation, but to translate its outcome into substantive action: praise, promotion, or other emoluments; admonishment, criticism, or punishment. If the evaluation process is to serve its most important function, i.e., the improvement of performance, the evaluator must be an individual who is prepared to maintain complete objectivity regardless of information generated and to act purely on the basis of what is best for all concerned. Whoever the evaluator, he must be a professional in terms of education, experience, and disinterested performance.

Evaluator Preparation. In order to collect pertinent information on which to carry out the evaluation process, the collector must understand why evaluation is necessary and what its major contributions may be to the agency and its personnel. Therefore, the evaluator must have some formalized education in the processes and techniques of evaluation. The evaluator must have developed skills which will permit the coordination of methods and capabilities to function most effectively in his technical role. If the evaluator is well prepared, he will have assimilated the concept which will affect the agency's ability to operate. The evaluator must retain the idea that information collected in the course of the process will be readily available, valild, and useful within the decision-making milieu.

Whoever performs an evaluation will probably refer to the various standardized instruments which are currently available. However, it may be necessary to modify old or develop new measuring devices as the situation demands. It is vital that a variety of instruments be selected so that a more complete picture may be obtained. Among the variety of measuring devices useful in evaluation and which should be given careful attention are:

Ability tests	Anecdotal records
Performance tests	Leadership tests
Personality tests	Attitudinal modification
Rating scales	Group direction
Checklists	Skill and knowledge achievement
Achievement tests	Membership retention
Intelligence tests	Observation
Sociometric instruments	Interviews
	Questionnaires

Ability tests concern maximum performance. These tests have been utilized to predict performance in actual field situations. Tests are designed to determine the ability of the person being tested to respond instantly to various stimuli, to determine the degree of expertness in handling on-the-job demands, and the ease with which the potential leader permits himself to be distracted from pertinent objectives in a group dynamics circumstance.

Performance tests require the subject to demonstrate his skill in reaching some objective. Performance tests are also used to study general mental functioning, usually in conjunction with verbal tests. Verbal ability and the conveyance of ideas seem to correlate with leadership capacity as well as affording a well-differentiated opportunity for clinical observation. The great variety of tasks and the interest which they normally evoke are extremely helpful in determining interpersonal comparisons.

Personality tests place emphasis on scores which lay claim to empirical validity. Such tests seem to have the ability to discriminate against individuals who might not have the personal qualities necessary for leadership performance. In nearly every field, personality and mental health are critical. Workers with inadequate personal adjustment are unsatisfactory, particularly when a part of the role they may be required to play is interpersonal relationships. Personality tests have varying uses, but are most useful in eliciting information about home, health, social, and emotional adjustment.

Rating scales are used to summarize observations and to obtain descriptions of the subject from evaluators who are familiar with the subject's past behavior. Ratings are used as standards and as fundamental sources of information for many kinds of research. Furthermore, such scales have a practical application in selecting group workers and those who are to be placed in leadership situations. Rating scales are typically employed to reduce perceptions to an easily processed form, and normally consist of a list of traits to be judged, the appraiser being requested to indicate the degree to which each behavior is characteristic of the subject. All rating scales are subject to rater bias. Thus, a halo effect is created when the observer forms a general impression of the individual being rated and the ratings which are given tend to reflect the general impression of favorableness or unfavorableness.

Checklists aid objectivity in scoring. Evaluation of performance is assisted when an objective record is made of what the subject does. Checklists are particularly helpful for showing how the individual performs, his style, and work procedures, as well as errors made. Such a record focuses on weaknesses so that they may be reduced or eliminated by better educational methods. Checklists also systematize observation records, for example, an ability checklist typically lists the correct behaviors and the weaknesses to be acted upon. For such work it may provide a series of sections for categorizing activities. With this instrument, highly differentiated particular acts may be recorded quickly with extensive objectivity.

Achievement tests try to ascertain how much an individual has learned from an educational experience. Motivation can be improved by developing competitiveness based on equitable criteria. Showing a person the particular ways in which he needs further skill is a superior method for motivating study. Tests aid in standardizing the instruction provided for the assimilation of leadership skills. Thus, any deviation from standardized objectives would be noted in scores and thereby force instructors to offer the kinds of information necessary to effect positive leadership outcomes.

Intelligence tests, as now widely applied, are the most objective methods for determining the general mental capacity of an individual. Through successively difficult items an individual can display the tendency to select and sustain a particular direction; the capability to make personal adjustments in order to achieve a desired objective; and the ability to undergo self-examination. All of these tendencies display general intelligence which appears to be a significant endowment in the makeup of a leader.

Sociometric instruments are designed to show how others view an individual. These techniques are neither observations nor self-reports although they closely approximate rating techniques, with the reports made by the subject's peers rather than his superiors. Sociometric instruments are tests which consist of descriptions of roles played by actual or potential leaders and other members of a group. Each group member responds to each description by indicating the individual he believes that description suits. Such instruments may be used for studying the social structure of groups and are also valuable for providing insight into developed cliques, leadership hierarchies, and other interpersonal dynamics.

Anecdotal records are an attempt to obtain a complete and realistic picture of the subject. The observer is permitted to note any behavior which appears important, rather than concentrating on the same characteristic for all subjects. Frequently, the anecdotes are reports of behaviors which are manifested by group members (if performed by the leader) or specific actions observed by the actual or perceived leader (if performed by an outside evaluator)— in daily contacts. The anecdotal record should be divorced from any interpretation and describe only and precisely what has been observed. The record is made immediately after the observation to avoid errors of recollection. Gathered over a period of time, the descriptions offer a much clearer picture of behavior than do other techniques of equivalent simplicity.

Leadership tests evaluate emotion and reactions to frustrating situations. Most such tests are very practical since they are generally employed for filling positions of responsibility. It is to the agency's benefit to determine as accurately as possible, before the candidate is appointed to an authoritative position, how well or whether he can cope with stress, criticism, and thwarting. If the agency, which desires individuals to fill leadership positions, had data about the intellectual processes, emotional reactions, and social responses of candidates, it would be in the enviable situation of being able to choose an elite for staffing purposes. Leadership tests, though not able to provide the entire picture, do have the function of supplying information about the individual's penchant for cooperation, reaction to authority, interpersonal behavior, and so on. Such tests have become increasingly important in selecting leaders in all fields.

Attitudes may be subjected to study and measurement. Discriminatory practices, for example, of a racial, ethnic, religious, political, social, or economic orientation, may be quickly discerned. Attitudes toward self, agency, other group members, morals, health, and a large variety of personal beliefs are directly testable. Since one major objective of the agency may be to change individual attitudes on certain subjects, this may be an objective method to diagnose the influence of the leader. Since the leader ideally reflects the objectives of the agency toward particular values, the degree of modification of attitudes on the part of group members may well mirror actual leadership adequacy.

Group direction of several varieties can be measured. One of these deals with group movement toward desirable goals and the other with individual conduct or behavior. Observation of group members after the leader has made his presence felt should indicate whether or not his influence is real. Other techniques may be used to determine individual modifications of morals, integrity, esprit de corps, emotional stability, and social development. Sociometry can determine peer status in terms of acceptance, rejection, or isolation which affects the degree of group participation, satisfaction, and security. Value changes concerning acceptance or rejection of agency standards and objectives, or in a broader sense, society's standards illustrate group direction.

Behavior modifications in individual members may be validly tested by the use of standarized measuring devices which can, if properly administered, appraise the degree and kind of modification over a period of time. Behavior scales may reveal the nature of behavior which will probably undergo change determined by particular situations, and the variation in observed behavioral modifications in relation to the age of the individual, the adequacy of the leader, and other pertinent facts. Analysis of the written records of recreationists acting as group leaders will also provide a basis for leadership evaluation.

Skill and knowledge achievement are highly susceptible to testing devices and accurately reflect any individual changes. If the agency is interested in measuring leadership on the basis of skill or specific knowledge achievement, there are many evaluative instruments which have proven reliable in practice for such purposes. Where agency objectives coincide with the production of individuals skilled in motor activities or knowledgeable about manners, social conduct, morals, ethnic tolerances, and a wide variety of other assimilated facts, these may readily be discerned. Insofar as the recreationist responsible for the development of group members is able to instill the required knowledge or skill so that individuals in his charge are able to perform well, this may be taken as a measure of his adequacy as a leader.

Retention of membership over a period of time or for the life of the group will surely indicate leadership. The ability of the recreationist to hold a group of individuals together or to provide some ideas, projects, or goals which stimulate and interest members so that they remain within the group is a mark of effectiveness on his part. This is only true for the voluntary situation where no external pressures, i.e., forced attendance, assessment of fees which are not returned for drop-outs, etc., are employed. When the recreationist can collect and stabilize a group, it is an outcome of his influence with them. Conversely, where a large number of individuals leave the group or where group cohesion is not attained, leadership adequacy is questionable.

Observation is probably the most common method of determining whether or not leadership performance is adequate. It is a fairly routine and recurrent procedure enacted to ensure that particular standards are met and maintained. By actually inspecting the performance of employees, nature of activities conducted, or behavior shown, some evaluation can be made as to the proximity of achieving the standard required by the employing agency. Observation is performed in order to ascertain if preconceived standards set forth by department policy are receiving compliance.

In the unlikely event that recreationists are negligent in their duties, specific measures are then undertaken to alleviate those conditions. Observation reveals instances of incompetence, repeated tardiness, inefficiency, or substandard behavior or performance. Of course, it also indicates highly effective leadership performance as well.

Observation, like bank audits, must be carried on without the fore-knowledge of persons or employees who are to be observed. It is a method which allows the observer to appraise leadership performance at close range without injecting any artificial conditions of apprehension or falsity of action because the subject knows that he is being observed. The success of observation hinges upon relieving worker anxiety and allowing him to perform, for better or worse, as he does habitually and naturally. In this way, a factual representation of leadership adequacy may be partially gathered. Observation is merely one method which can be used. Other methods should supplement his technique to gather a composite picture of the worker in several situations and under varying conditions.

Interview, unlike observation, is conducted because there is a desire on the part of the superior to maintain personal relations with employees on the job. It is a procedure in which current information about leadership problems may be obtained for further study and use. Interviews are usually conducted in order to assist in the solution of a particularly pressing problem, to clear up personnel policy misunderstandings, or to explain new policies or procedures. The interview may be carried on informally, which is perhaps the best method, so that the interviewee is placed at ease and may more freely express his ideas.

Interviewing is an effective means of acquainting the recreationist with specific problems or by which pertinent information concerning group or individual needs may be obtained and then satisfied. It is a ready tool for those who must learn about personal needs and practices. By personally interviewing a random sampling of people in any neighborhood and then checking whatever findings are elicited, compliance with standards of effective leadership performance may be ascertained. Questions concerning manners, appearance, personal enthusiasm, skill, and leadership adequacy are brought up by interview.

Questionnaires are desirable when information is needed from subordinate personnel concerning a superior or from a closely-knit group concerning a member of that group. As a questionnaire allows the respondent to remain anonymous if he so desires, he is more likely to reply with what he conceives to be the truth. The questionnaire is also important as an instrument for measuring leadership in terms of prepared statements so that the respondent does not have to formulate preconceived notions about the topic, with the corresponding biases which might also be included. Of course, the questionnaire itself must be developed so as to omit leading questions, "loaded" sentences, and prejudicial concepts. Objectivity is of greatest benefit in the use of the questionnaire.

LEADERSHIP BEHAVIOR

Personality and Performance

Because leadership requires both personality inputs and a changing pattern of functional roles, the entire process of personality evaluation is one of enormous complexity and inconsistency. There is always the chance that relationships between personality and role performance may not be reflected in an investigation. As conditions change for a particular group there may be specific personality traits which will be absolutely essential for achieving leadership of that group. Because situational demands vary from group to group, it becomes impossible to identify those personality traits which will always accompany an installation of leadership. Under such circumstances, it would be wise to adhere to Bavelas' advice:

> Instead we must try to define the leadership functions that must be performed in these situations and regard as leadership those acts which perform them.[2]

A review of psychological literature shows a number of studies which have investigated leadership performance. Among these analyses have

2. A. Bavelas, "Leadership: Man and Function," *Administration Science Quarterly*, Vol. 4 (1960), p. 494.

been suggestions that leaders exercise authority, make decisions, behave in ways that imply a sound knowledge of human nature, have empathy, and so on. Several studies have revealed important distinctions between outstanding and poor leaders, while others have attempted to analyze the behavior of leaders and other group members by direct observation. Among exhibited behavior by leaders, two were consistently revealed as being significantly different from those of followers. Leaders typically analyzed the situation in which they found themselves, interpreted possibilities, and then provided information as to how the group should proceed. Carter and others found that behaviors which characterized leadership in one situation did not necessarily carry over to another:

> There seem to be interesting differences in behavior depending on whether the group was working under emergent or appointed leader conditions. It appears that in the appointed situation the leader may perceive his role as that of a coordinator of activity or as an agent through which the group can accomplish its goal. In the emergent group, on the other hand, the person who becomes the leader may take over the leadership by energetic action and by trying to get the other members to accept his leadership.[3]

Perhaps the best method of evaluating leadership is to determine the major factors of personality and performance, which characterize those who lead, and develop an evaluative instrument which can assess the presence or absence of these qualities. It is obvious that the kind of person the leader is relies heavily upon a number of factors. The behavior of any leader is closely associated with the needs of those who constitute his followers, the aims or purposes of the group at any given time, and the type of individuals who compose the group and their relations with one another.

Due to the variety of personality types which leaders exhibit and the different roles each leader must play, there are actually few generalizations which can be made about leadership behavior. It now seems apparent that leaders bring vastly different attributes to their diverse tasks, and changing tasks may require them to modify their behaviors or produce different qualities if they are to achieve success. It is very likely that all leaders have specific salient personal attributes. Currently, no measuring instrument is yet available that can appraise these attributes qualitatively. One can only surmise that such qualities exist and that they may be observable. To this extent, some investigation should be imposed to determine whether quantitative patterns are measurable. It is not possible at this time to indicate in what amounts or to what degree such attributes would have to

3. L. Carter, W. Haythorn, B. Shriver, and J. Lanzetta, "The Behavior of Leaders and other Group Members," *Journal of Abnormal and Social Psychology,* Vol. 46 (1951), p. 591.

appear in order to accomplish a given task or to solve a particular problem in a given situation. Moreover, it is not known in what combination such qualities would be needed as situations varied. It is also logical to state that in the case of leadership, the sum of the parts does not always equal the whole. Even if the qualities of personality could be reproduced at will, it would still require something more to produce a leader. This "something" more is the force which characterizes the leader and is beyond the total of personality components.

Having provided precautionary guides, some of the factors which contemporary research distinguishes as being characteristic of leaders and leadership behaviors are offered here. Many of these factors have been reported in diverse studies for the past twenty years. For the most part, these reported behaviors are not discrete units, existing in isolation from all others. Rather, they are closely associated and, in fact, impinge on one another as demand requires. Currently, these qualities of personality reflect the best of what the leader is and may be quantified empirically:

1. *Sensitivity* or *empathy* is a personality trait that suggests the individual's ability to respond to emotional needs of others. Such social awareness as is implied by the term empathy permits the individual to perceive the needs of others, and fulfill them in such a way as to gain a reciprocal perception. More significantly, empathy permits insight and the ability to interact favorably with others who make up a potential following.

2. *Consideration* may actually grow out of empathy, but it also connotes a concern for those who constitute the followers. This really means practical assistance, explanation, willingness to communicate, and deference paid to the input of other members of the group. Additionally, it denotes a tendency to provide emotional support to those who require it in the advancement of tasks or the achievement of goals.

3. *Emotional stability* is a factor of vital importance to the individual's capacity to function calmly, objectively, and rationally despite the passions of those who surround him and the fluctuations of the circumstances which prevail. This behavior factor indicates an absence of suspicion, anxiety, and lack of trust. It shows a well integrated personality with ego-strength and the capacity to accept and deal with negative actions or behaviors directed against him or found within the group which he leads.

4. *Fairness* is an attribute marked by objectivity toward others, weighing facts before reaching conclusions. It implies consistency and reliability on the part of the leader. Of course, this may also be perceived in the dimension of emotional stability. Fairness assures group members

that the leader deals justly with all individuals, does not show partiality, and can be depended to follow an agreed-upon decision.

There may be many other behavioral dimensions which can be reported and evaluated, but these four personality qualities seem to be essential for the leader. Without these attributes, the leader's ability to lead becomes untenable. He will be looked upon with fear, hatred, suspicion, and uncertainty. The composite picture of a leader is much more complex than any mere cataloguing of personality characteristics. Those traits which seem absolutely vital, if an individual is to be selected or emerge as a leader, are nullified if the desire to lead is not present.

Evaluation can be based on those leadership behaviors which contribute to group adhesion, harmony, task definition, problem resolution, secure adherence to group structure, the facilitation of communication, or assisting the group to move along those vectors which will end in individual member satisfaction and final attainment of the ends for which they originally joined with others.

There have been a variety of studies which have employed a number of variables closely related to the leadership contributions. These studies may be utilized as the basis for an evaluative instrument capable of serving as a measurement of leadership actuality and effectiveness. For example, task-centered behaviors have been a primary focus of Likert and his collaborators,[4] who differentiated between job-centered and employee-centered supervision. Subsequently, other investigators have reinforced the idea that "consideration" and "initiating structure" could be viewed as having major significance for the behavior of leaders.[5] More recent studies have concluded that task orientation and social-emotional differentiations of leadership are the chief factors of leader behavior.[6] In fact, it may be shown that one of these factors operating to the exclusion of the other can be detrimental insofar as leadership effectiveness is concerned.[7] Leader effectiveness is supported on the grounds of equity in social interaction, with the leader obtaining status and wielding influence while assisting the group to accomplish desired mutal expectations as well as such individual social emoluments as recognition. Task accomplishment by itself is not a sufficient basis for effective leadership, however. Both high consideration

---

4. R. Likert, *New Patterns of Management* (New York: McGraw-Hill Book Company, 1961).
5. E. A. Fleishman and D. R. Peters, "Interpersonal Values and Leadership Attitudes and Managerial Success," *Personnel Psychology,* Vol. 15 (1962), pp. 127-143.
6. F. E. Fiedler, " A Contingency Model of Leadership Effectiveness," in L. Berkowitz, ed., *Advances in Experimental Social Psychology* (New York Academic Press, 1964), pp. 149-190.
7. J. Misumi and T. A. Tasaki, "A Study on the Effectiveness of Supervisory Patterns in a Japanese Hierarchical Organization," *Japanese Psychological Research,* Vol. 7 (1965), pp. 151-162.

and structure were most successful.[8]

Consideration is the leader's concern for followers, manifested in practical assistance, improved conditions, or personal welfare associated with group activity. High consideration will probably be readily perceived and appreciated by followers. Structure is the relationships and responsibilities which group members mutually share, as well as membership functions and performance. Follower perception of these relationships is clarified by leadership and the result is group structure.

Description

This device is based upon the previously stated premise that individuals who make up the group in association with a leader are in the best possible position to provide descriptions of the leader's behavior. Such a hypothesis implies that leadership is basically interaction between the leader and the led. In devising the descriptive instrument, a method has been provided which can effectively evaluate leadership in any group situation. It is also usable in many research designs where the problem of personal interaction between various leadership levels as well as within individual groups might be under investigation.

Based upon an operational definition of leadership, the description of leadership behavior is then classified in terms of specific functions or behaviors which the leader has consistently exhibited in expressing his influence with group members. A most important development of this technique came when John Hemphill and others created the *Leader Behavior Description Questionnaire.*[9] This method for obtaining descriptions of the leader's actual behavior and of what would be ideal leadership behavior for any given situation gave a precise measure to leader adequacy. Thus, leadership adequacy may be evaluated by computing the discrepancy between actual leader behavior and the behavior which is standardized as the criteria for ideal leadership. When the discrepancy score between actual and ideal leader behavior is small or negligible, the leader is adequate; as the discrepancy score increases, less adequate leader behavior is noted. This measure may be used as a self-reporting device, by a subordinate reporting actual leader behavior, or by a subordinate recording his concept of ideal leader behavior. As an evaluative technique, the descriptive method has proved fairly reliable and practical.

Evaluation is a day-in, day-out process. Each person functioning in a leadership capacity must have some model concepts upon which to base his

---

8. E. A. Fleishman and J. Simmons, "Relationship Between Leadership Patterns and Effectiveness Ratings Among Israeli Foreman," *Personnel Psychology,* Vol. 23 (1970), pp. 169-172.

9. J. K. Hemphill, *Leader Behavior Description Questionnaire* (Columbus, Ohio: Personnel Research Board, The Ohio State University, 1949).

actions. Only by formulating standard leadership principles can the individual compare himself or be compared to an ideal. Objective ratings of leadership are completely dominated by so many variables and individual orientations as to be almost impossible. As Helen Jennings stated: "It is necessary to ask, leadership in what respect? For whom? In what sort of group?[10] For this reason, evaluation scales can merely be theoretical. The theory must be validated in experimental programs. The aim here, then, is to produce understandable concepts so that anyone can devise his own scale in accordance with the established principles provided.

The basic problem, therefore, is to list and define the objectives of leadership which may vary with the leader, the situation, the group, or other pressures impinging upon the prevailing conditions. For example, objective measurement could be concerned with discrete items produced, field goals kicked, speed records broken, retention of personnel, bull's-eyes scored, art awards won, paperwork processed, bond issues passed, team captains chosen, dramatic leads cast, etc. Each goal depends upon the objective, and there are an infinite variety of goals. In spite of this, leadership may be operationally defined, its component parts listed and defined, and an instrument constructed to determine adequacy.

An example of one leadership objective which could be applicable to the practice of recreational service is presented in scale form with pertinent questions. This illustration may then be extrapolated for any leadership objectives in all their various forms. The scale deals with one leadership objective—the development of physical fitness or the degree of effectiveness and efficiency of organic processes, i.e., strength, tone, physique, stamina, agility, etc. For simplification, the scale is divided into five equal points ranging from one to five, with each number corresponding to a reply which can be measured or observed:

One equals *no*
Two equals *qualified no*   1   2   3   4   5
Three equals *undecided*
Four equals *qualified yes*
Five equals *yes*

1. Does the individual recognize the need to become physically fit?
2. Does the individual understand the methods and practices required for achieving physical fitness?
3. Does the individual agree to perform and practice the routines necessary for achieving physical fitness?

10. H. H. Jennings, "Leadership and Sociometric Choice," in T. M. Newcomb and E. L. Hartley, eds., *Readings in Social Psychology* (New York: Holt, 1947), p. 408. Reprinted by permission of Harcourt, Brace & World, Inc.

4. Does the individual actually perform the scheduled motor movement necessary for achieving physical fitness?

5. Is the objective ethical and measurable by observation or standardized testing devices?

Evaluation

The preceeding paragraphs have described aspects of leader behavior and vital characteristics without which the likelihood of leadership attainment would be unthinkable. Such descriptions have been useful in generalizing at least two behavioral products: consideration and structural establishment. The first obviously refers to task orientation and the latter to socio-emotional support, with all of the ramifications which these terms imply. It is probable that there are optimal degrees to be reached for both of these behaviors. Thus, after a certain point, consideration is no longer an effective behavior in obtaining group goals. The same is also true for initiation of structure. It would appear from previous investigations that a critical point is reached above or below which no advancement toward objectives is discernable. According to Fleishman and Harris, a study of foremen indicates that consideration is the more essential of the two behavioral modes. More particularly, the study suggests that low-consideration foremen are always ineffective, while high-consideration foremen can exercise high degrees of task orientation without endangering efficiency.[11]

The question remaining here is one of perception. When leadership is evaluated from a superior, subordinate, or peer viewpoint, the outcomes depend upon what it is that is required of the leader. Thus, superiors in an organization may come to view the leader's behavior from the standpoint of group goal achievement or productivity. The emphasis will be upon task accomplishment. Subordinates will have other needs to be satisfied, with task accomplishment being only one facet in determining their appraisal. In all probability, subordinates or followers will perceive the most effective leader as one who shows the most consideration for them, consideration being a dimension of behavior that is characterized by impartiality, reliability, communicativeness, and concern for the welfare of the membership. Superiors will rate the leader as being effective if he accepts the norms and values of superior authority, thereby carrying out the role assigned to him by the organization. Simultaneously, the leader must win the voluntary followership of those who are subordinate to him. If he can do this, he will be able to exercise authority and influence which has been freely accorded to him. Under such circumstances, he will be rated highly

---

11. E. A. Fleishman and E. F. Harris, "Patterns of Leadership Behavior Related to Employee Grievances and Turnover," *Personnel Psychology,* Vol. 15 (1962), pp. 43-56.

by group members who utilize him as a buffer against the impersonality of the organization or of society-at-large, depending upon the situation of the group in question.

An evaluation of leadership will be biased by the orientation of the evaluator. Whether evaluation is carried on by those who are directly affected by the leader, the leader himself, by extra-group observers, or by those within an organization in which the leader is a subordinate, the outcomes will be considerably influenced by either predisposed expectations or perceived behaviors and the consequences of such actions upon objectives gained, group members satisfied, problems solved, membership maintained, or other criteria used as measures.

TYPES OF LEADERSHIP TO BE EVALUATED

Two kinds of attributes may be utilized to evaluate leadership: 1) those which describe the behavior of the leader; and 2) those which focus on the outcomes which occur to the group in consequence of leadership. In the former instance, evaluations can be made by utilizing instruments which measure frequency of selection of a leader as the most sought-after, most popular, most relied upon, most revered, most idealized, or the one to and through whom communications pass or are initiated. In the latter instance — such group oriented factors as cohesiveness, hedonic tone, goal achievement, and membership satisfaction — leadership may be considered for effect along one, some, or all of these dimensional lines. In fact, as early as 1951, Cattell suggested that leadership could be evaluated by measuring group performance along lines of syntality change.[12] Syntality is to a group what personality is to the individual. To the degree that a leader can effect group syntality and produce positive changes, leadership can be measured.

If leadership is looked upon as a means to some end, rather than an end in itself, then leadership can only be evaluated in terms of its effects upon a given group in relation to norms, goals, and membership satisfaction. Since multiple goals occur in any group at any given time, there must be numerous ways for evaluating leadership. Almost any variable can be employed as a criterion on which to measure leadership technique or effectiveness. As previously indicated, the criterion used will undoubtedly reflect the bias of the evaluator. Whether evaluation is made from a democratic or authoritarian orientation will certainly color the results of any evaluation. The status of the evaluator will also impose some value judgments on an interpretation of measured outcomes.

---

12. R. B. Cattell, "New Concepts for Measuring Leadership in Terms of Group Syntality," *Human Relations,* Vol. 4 (1951), pp. 161-184.

INSTRUMENTS FOR EVALUATING LEADERSHIP

1. Leadership Opinion Questionnaire (Stogdill and Coons: 1957)
2. The SRA Supervisory Index (Schwartz: 1956)
3. Leadership Practices Inventory (Nelson: 1955)
4. How Supervise? (File and Remmers: 1948-1971)
5. Ideal Leader Behavior Description Questionnaire (Hemphill and others: 1957)
6. Superior-Subordinate Scale (Chapman and Campbell: 1957)
7. Leader Behavior Description Questionnaire (Hemphill and others: 1957)
8. Leader Behavior Description Questionnaire, Form 12 (Hemphill and others: 1971)
9. Leadership Evaluation and Development Scale (Mowry: 1964)
10. Leadership Opinion Questionnaire (Fleischman: 1960-1969)
11. Leadership Practices Inventory (Nelson: 1955-1967)
12. Leadership Q-Sort Test (Cassel: 1964)

All of these devices may be found in J. P. Robinson, R. Athanasiou, and K. B. Head, *Measures of Occupational Attitudes and Occupational Characteristics,* (Ann Arbor, Mich.: Institute for Social Research, 1969); and O. K. Buros, ed., *Tests In Print* (Highland Park, N. J.: The Gryphon Press, 1974).

Glossary

Adapted recreational activity. Modified recreational activities — changes of rule, time, or equipment — to accommodate whatever physical or mental limitations prevail so that handicapped persons may participate.

Adequacy. The ability to cope with one's problems.

Administrative leadership. See Managerial leadership.

Affiliation. A desire to establish relations with others. A fundamental social motive.

Aggression. The tendency to attack rather than to withdraw or compromise when faced with stressful situations. Hostility may or may not be involved.

Alienation. A general feeling of loneliness and meaninglessness.

Anxiety. A state of emotional tension characterized by apprehension of vague fearfulness.

Asch's theory of interpersonal perception. The theory that people use individual pieces of information to form a complete picture of someone else. Each trait influences the way in which others are identified, but the total impression is not one that could be predicted from the indivdual traits alone.

Attitude. Mental predisposition or "set" related to referential patterns which are developed in consequence of previous training or experience.

Authoritarian. A personality pattern characterized by unquestioning obedience to authority rather than individual freedom of judgment and action.

Authority. The right to give commands, take action, or make final decisions in consequence of delegation or usurpation of power, or position within an organization.

Autocratic personality. One who, upon assuming a position of leadership, makes all group decisions, is aloof from group members, and treats group members in a negative, condescending manner.

Autonomy.

In group dynamics, the degree of independence from other groups or organizations in making decisions, functioning, and goal achieving.

Bales' theory of leadership roles.

The theory that there are two distinct leadership roles: a task specialist devoted to overcoming or resolving particular problems; a socio-emotional specialist concerned with overcoming interpersonal problems and maintaining group cohesiveness.

Behavior.

The way in which an organism reacts to stimulation or stress.

Bias.

An error or inaccurate estimation.

Body language.

Physical movements or gestures which may be interpreted to convey symbolic or specific meanings.

Catharsis.

Discharge of emotional tension usually associated with repressed traumatic material.

Central figure.

An individual who serves as a dynamic focus around whom group formative processes occur.

Charisma.

An individual who is thought to be devinely inspired and therefore infallible. Recently, the term has been narrowly construed to mean having magnetic personality to which others are drawn. In its most popular sense, it is thought to be possessed by certain political or religious leaders.

Clique.

Any subgroup within a group or an exclusive small group which tends to be highly cohesive, impermeable, and relatively active insofar as its own objectives are concerned. It may be the locus of disaffection and the nucleus which persaudes others to oppose whatever current leadership the group has.

Coacting group.

A group in which two or more people are working on simultaneous tasks without any interaction between them.

Coalition.	A subgroup acting jointly to enhance the results of their activities at the expense of others within the group. It may also mean the banding together of individuals with dissimilar interests or skills in the hope of producing a synergistic effect, thereby achieving some stated aim.
Coercion.	Utilization of force to compel adherence to some policy or action. There is the implication of some threat in order to exact obedience or behavioral compliance.
Cognitive dissonance.	The idea that simultaneous belief in two opinions that are psychologically opposite arouses cognitive dissonance. Since dissonance is unpleasant, its attempted removal necessitates changing one of the beliefs to make it logically consistent, or the addition of other beliefs.
Cohesiveness.	In group dynamics, the ability of a group to maintain itself in the face of disruptive forces. It is the degree of total attractiveness of all the individuals within the group to the group.
Communication.	A process in which information is transmitted from a sender to a receiver in order that influence may be attained or to effect behavioral changes.
Communication network.	The pattern of communication opportunities available to the leader and, to a certain extent, to the group membership.
Comparative function of a reference group.	The process by which a group provides information about reality to its membership.
Conformity.	The tendency of a group member to change what he says and how he acts in order to correspond with group expectations. Conformity may also be explained in terms of the extent or degree to which individuals adhere to a norm. Leaders may not have to conform as much as do other members of the group.
Consideration.	A dimension of leadership behavior that refers to the extent to which a leader is characterized by warmth and trust in his interpersonal relation-

ships. Additionally, it means the degree to which the leader is concerned about and takes care of the condition in which his followers exist.

Contingency theory of leadership.   As developed by F. Fiedler, the theory is concerned with whether task-centered or person-centered leadership is more effective according to a given situation. According to Fiedler, in situatins that are either very favorable or very unfavorable to leadership, the task-centered leader is more effective than the person-centered leader. If, however, the situation is moderately favorable, the person-centered leader is more effective than the task-centered leader.

Control.   In group dynamics, the degree to which group members' behavior is regulated by the group. This occurs because the group has great significance for the individual member. Therefore, the member is willing to conform to group expectation about behavior.

Cyclothemia.   In leadership theory, a personality facet characterized by high energy output, extroversion, volubility, and warm emotional response to others.

Defense mechanisms.   Those behavioral responses to untenable personal or environmental conditions which tend to protect the ego.

Dehumanization.   Thinking of other people as not being human. This tends to permit heightened aggressiveness against such people, thereby producing behavior which is at best brutal.

Democratic leadership.   Valid leadership. The leader allows all group members to participate fully in the decision-making process.

Dictator.   One who rules without recourse to law. An individual in a leadership "position" whose influence rests upon coercive rather than democratic means.

DNA.   Deoxyribonucleic acid. The molecule which is the carrier of genetic information. The molecule is formed by paired strands in the shape of a double helix. The basis for all characteristics of living matter appears to be contained in the arrangement of the nucleotides in the DNA molecule.

Domination.

Subjugation of another by whatever means are available. In group dynamics, the ability to compel another to conform to preconceived objectives or behaviors publicly although such individuals may disagree privately or covertly.

Dynamic.

Pattern of interactive factors resulting in a specific event or condition.

Dyad.

A two-person group. A situation where personal interaction occurs between two people only.

Empathy.

A dimension of leadership wherein the individual who leads has the ability to satisfy deficiencies or problems of others due to his sensitivity to their needs. It may be defined as the ability to vicariously experience the thoughts, feelings, and motives of others. The empathetic tendency has been more generously noted in leaders than in followers.

Expectancy.

Refers to another's perception of some object or person. In group dynamics, it is typical behavior usually associated with group norms and applicable to many persons.

Extrovert.

A personality type often associated with a leader. Characterized by interests directed toward the external environment of people and things rather than toward inner experiences and oneself.

Facilitator.

In group dynamics, one who is capable of assisting others to achieve satisfaction, resolution of problems, or attainment of objectives.

Festinger's theory of communication and social influence.

The theory that all social groups implement some pressure toward uniformity and that the extent to which the members of the group attempt to reach concensus is determined by initial differences, cohesiveness, and issue relevance for the group.

Group.

Two or more individuals in psychic interaction behaving in ways designed to achieve desired goals.

Group dynamics.

The functions of any group and the behavioral reactions of the membership in response to group functioning.

Group effectiveness.

The extent to which a group accomplishes its objectives and satisfies the needs of its membership. A measurement of leadership effectiveness.

Group formation.

The transformation of a collection of individuals into a group. Among the conditions necessary for group formation are commonly held needs, stressful situations which cannot be resolved by individual action, and physical proximity.

Group function theory of leadership.

A theory which states that leadership is not vested in individuals, but is derived from group structure. Any member of the group may undertake leadership functions as group needs or goals change.

Group identification.

A feeling of commitment by an individual to a particular group. This has generally been taken as a "we" feeling which occurs as involvement and affiliational bonds are strengthened.

Headship.

The degree of authority obtained as a result of position achieved or held within the hierarchy of any organization.

Hedonic tone.

A dimension of group syntality and one means whereby leadership effectiveness may be measured. It is defined as that degree of pleasantness, enjoyment, or satisfaction which is derived from being associated with or having membership in some group or organization.

Homeostasis

The physiological and psychological processes which contribute to maintenance of organic equilibrium.

Imitation.

Copying the behavior of another. In group dynamics, it is the method utilized by followers to become more like the central figure or leader.

Influence.

The single factor which determines whether leadership is present and occurring. It is the ability to persaude others to modify their behavior in order to achieve one or more preconceived goals. Used in a leadership context, it is persuasion by ideas without the use of manipulation or coercive means.

Initiating structure.

A dimension of leadership behavior that refers to the extent to which a leader organizes the work performed by the group, defines standards of performance, establishes routines, and identifies the relationship between himself and his followers.

Interacting group.

A group in which the members are free to interact with each other as they set about working out common problems.

Interaction.

A situation in a factorial design in which the effect of one of the independent variables changes with respect to the level of the others. In group dynamics, it is the change in behavior that occurs as individuals meet, react, and attempt to cope with their problems or reach specific objectives.

Interaction approach to leadership.

The theory that to predict who will assume leadership in a particular group, one must take into account the characteristics of group members, group structure, environment, problems confronting the group, and personal characteristics which may thrust one person into the leadership position.

Interpersonal behavior.

Behavioral relations on the part of one or more persons in response to intimate associations by those in whom rapport has been developed.

Intimacy.

In group dynamics, the degree to which group members are mutually possessed of the personal details of one another's lives. The greater the degree of intimacy, the more control the group has for the member and the higher will be the significance of the group in the member's life.

Isolate.
In group dynamics, an individual who, although a member of the group, is usually alone or functions on the fringe of the group. The individual who is least chosen by other group members.

Laissez-faire situation.
In group dynamics, where the nominal leader is extremely permissive and passive, primarily acting only when directly requested to do so. In such situations, the group members are permitted complete freedom to do whatever they wish — an anarchical condition prevails.

Leader.
One who intentionally gains influence with others without employing manipulative or coercive means.

Leaderlike behavior.
Behavior that facilitates or contributes to group goals or problem resolution.

Leadership.
A process whereby one individual exerts influence on others by utilizing communication, structure, and positive dimensions of group syntality. Leadership occurs when someone exerts more influence than the other members of the group.

Leadership need.
A motivational force which impels certain individuals to seek positions of leadership. Any anxiety factor which can only be assuaged when the individual is actually leading.

Leisure.
Free time. That discretionary time remaining to the individual after obligatory functions have been completed. Leisure has also been construed as a state of being, not-time oriented, or in terms of values to be gained from utilizing leisure. In the context of this book, leisure is defined as free time.

Line personnel.
Those individuals employed in any organization whose primary function it is to carry out duties and responsibilities designed to achieve the reasons for which the agency was established.

LPC.

Least Preferred Co-worker test. A test created by F. Fielder to measure whether a leader is person-centered or task-centered. Leaders are requested to rate the most incompetent person they have ever had to work with in terms of personal traits. Low LPC leaders are task-oriented, while high LPC leaders are person-oriented, i.e., socio-emotionally supportive. The low LPC leader may be unable to differentiate between personal traits and performance. The high LPC leader presumably does differentiate between personal traits and work performance.

Mach scale.

A test that measures the extent to which persons endorse Machiavellian views, i.e., the employment of impersonally opportunistic tactics in controlling others, a cynical view of most people, and the idea that there are no absolute moral standards.

Machiavellian factor.

The ability to manipulate others for personal gain while appearing to present mutually beneficial advantages.

Managerial leadership.

A process whereby policy is translated into practice through the establishment of rapport. A communicative process which elicits cooperative effort so that coordination of men, materials, and money may be combined to produce optimum benefit to all concerned. (See also Supervision.)

Manipulation.

The practice of cynically managing the behavior of others through the shrewd use of persuasion based upon fraudulent or reprehensible means. Such practices are utilized by those in headship positions or those autocratic personalities who cannot tolerate opposition.

Morale.

In group dynamics, the mental condition of group members insofar as determination to achieve cohesiveness and unity for the successful resolution of problems or the attainment of a common goal. It is closely related to the syntality factor of adhesion.

Norms.

Accepted and expected patterns of behavior and belief that are established by a group. There is a reciprocal pattern of behavior wherein each member of the group takes the judgments of the others into account so that the final behavior is a concession to the expected norm. While group members as followers may have to conform to norms, the leader does not. One result is that in time the leader's non-conforming behavior may become internalized by group members as the norm.

Opinion leader.

Any intermediary within the group communications process who screens and interprets information which is then passed on to the receiver.

Organizational leadership.

See Headship.

Person-centered leader.

One who focuses on the people within the group rather than on the mission or task to be accomplished. Such a person is also called a socio-emotional leader.

Phenomenology.

The study of the psychology of existence. An attempt to explain human behavior in terms of ego maintenance.

Potency.

In group dynamics, the degree to which a group has primary meaning for its membership insofar as personal needs are satisfied through group association. If the group was disbanded, it would be reflected on the kinds of behavioral changes which the individual would have to make in order to satisfy what the group's existence now fulfills. To the extent that the individual relies upon the leadership of the group for problem-solving, the group becomes extremely important to that person.

Power principle.

Whatever works is good. Wrongly attributed to the philosophy of pragmatism to which ethics are attached. Individuals in headship positions sometimes justify their behaviors on the basis that if something works it should not be modified, or "why tamper with success." In unscrupulous persons, this may lead to the ultimate power statement: "The ends justify the means." This concept has long been associated with Machiavellian types and dictators.

Rapport.

In group dynamics, an interpersonal relationship characterized by the development of mutual trust and confidence. This is a necessary technique which all leaders must utilize if they are to gain influence.

Recreation.

A state of being characterized by complete intellectual absorption in any non-debilitating experience. Any consummatory, non-debilitating experience. This concept has no relation to time, place, or activity engaged in except as indicated.

Recreational activity.

Those activities which are performed voluntarily during leisure, for enjoyment, and which are socially acceptable.

Recreational service.

An applied social science field designed to provide recreational opportunities to a clientele. Based upon its sector of establishment, i.e., public, quasi-public, or private, the field serves its respective constituencies by offering physical resources, organized activities, more or less professional leadership, and recreational experiences with all of the supporting aspects which such endeavors require.

Recreationist.

A professionally educated and experienced person employed in a professional capacity within the field of recreational service.

Recreator.

One who participates in recreational activities.

Reference group.

The individual identifies with the standards and beliefs of specific groups and uses these as criteria against which he defines and identifies himself.

Role playing.

A leadership technique utilized to change attitudes among group members. It is a procedure whereby group members or others are required to act the part of another person or place themselves in someone else's situation. It is often effective against stereotyping.

Scapegoating.	The displacement of aggression to less powerful individuals or groups when the original source of frustration is not susceptible to attack. A technique often employed by demagogues and dictators to gain influence with a particular segment of the population.
Scientific approach.	A method utilized by leaders to minimize risks. It is the collection of raw data dealing with a problem, the refinement of that data to a relevant minimum, and the selection of feasible courses of action based upon the data. Inputs may be from the group, from the environment external to the group, or both. This is the leader's entrepreneurial function.
Self.	That part of our experience which we perceive as the essential us. Leaders must have an understanding of the self in order to gain better insight into the behaviors of others. This becomes part of the interpersonal life.
Self-actualization.	Defined either as the individual's attempt to achieve his ideal self or an attempt to achieve optimal psychological functioning. Leadership is a process designed to assist self-actualization of followers.
Situational leadership.	A condition of crisis or some unresolved problem which acts as a catalyst to propel an individual into a leadership position. A theoretical orientation which asserts that situations create leaders.
Stability.	In group dynamics, the degree to which a group has continuity over time while enjoying the same characteristics as when it was originally formed. A syntality factor which measures the leader's effectiveness in maintaining the group despite situational pressures.
Staff personnel.	Employees within any organization who, through technical or special proficiency, are utilized to assist line personnel in becoming more effective and efficient in carrying out their respective duties.

Stereotype.

Frequently defined as an inaccurate, irrational overgeneralization which persists in the face of contradictory evidence. A technique utilized by demagogues and dictators to castigate a group in order to be identified against them, thereby gaining influence or support from their nominal detractors.

Structure.

A function of leadership. It is the determination or arrangement of essential functions and responsibilities which must be performed if a group is to reach its desired goals. (See also Initiating structure.)

Subgroup.

A small group formed within an existing larger group in order to facilitate communication or, in some instances, to serve as a cadre of the discontented. Subgroups may be both positive or negative insofar as leaders are concerned. Positive subgroups may be active in disseminating information and supporting the leader. Negative subgroups may be instrumental in dividing the group or thwarting group goals. (See also Clique.)

Submission.

In a superior-subordinate relationship, it is generally thought of as the acquiescence of one to the persuasion or power of another. In submission, there may or may not be covert resistance or rejection. There is a reciprocal relationship between the dominator and the one who submits. Each is necessary to the other. It is possible that some followers require domination and eagerly modify their behavior or goals in accepting the influence of a leader.

Supervision.

A process of leadership wherein an individual in a supervisory role attempts to enhance the capacity or technical proficiency of a subordinate through the establishment of democratic procedures, rapport building, and the implementation of group syntality factors. The immediate objective of supervision is obtaining cooperative behavior in the achievement of some common goal.

Surgency.

In leadership theory, a personality factor characterized by congeniality, extroversion, sociability, a desire to catch and hold the spotlight. It is frequently attributable to the political aspirant or office-holder. (See also Cyclothemia.)

Syntality.

In group dynamics, those characteristics of any group along which the group may move or be moved in response to environmental conditions and membership needs. First attributed to Raymond Cattell. Such dimensions may be thought of as group personality factors. Syntality factors may be utilized to evaluate leadership effectiveness.

T-group.

A touch, encounter, or sensitivity training group where inhibitions are broken down and interpersonal relations are established through physical contact and/or revelation of personal details of life. Unblemished truth is also requested of participants in terms of their response to other group members.

Target group.

Any collection of people, whether group, neighborhood, or community whose social, economic, or resource deprivation makes it important to the political or influential forces of the local government to improve. This may result in sending in change agents, i.e., detached recreationists or social workers to attempt to influence behavioral modification; or it may mean provision of jobs, educational opportunities, or the development of physical facilities for the people residing in such a designated area.

Task leader.

One who focuses on the work to be performed by the group rather than upon the individuals who make up the group. (See also Person-centered leader.)

Therapeutic recreational service.

A specialized branch of the field of recreational service wherein clientele in treatment centers of various types are provided with medically prescribed activities designed to enhance the rehabilitation process. Such activities serve as modalities so that patients or clients are enabled

to recuperate more quickly or to habilitate those
for whom rehabilitation is impossible.

Trait approach   The theory that the main determinant of leader-
to leadership.   ship is the possession of unique leadership
                        personality characteristics.

Index